DELIA'S
HOW TO COOK

BOOK THREE

Photographs by Miki Duisterhof

Production Editor and Series Co-Ordinator: Sarah Randell
Sub-editor: Gill Wing
Props Stylist: Jane Molloy

May I say a big thank you to all those who have helped me produce *How To Cook Book Three*. Thank you to Flo Bayley, Miki Duisterhof and Karen Hatch for designing and photographing it, and to Sarah Randell and Gill Wing for getting it ready for press.

My thanks also to Lucy Crabb, Lindsey Greensted-Benech and Vicky Musselman for their help with recipes, photography and the series, to Jane Molloy for the wonderful props and elegant styling, and to Pauline Curran for recipe testing. Also, thank you to *Sainsbury's Magazine* cookery department and all the chefs at Norwich City Football Club.

I am, as always, indebted to my brilliant television crew: David Willcock, Philip Bonham Carter, Harry Banks, Annie South, Keith and Vivien Broome, Simon Wilson, Andy Bates, Steve Savage, David Scott, Katy Savage, Linda Flanigan, Emma Pollock, Bruce Law and Mandy Manning. Thanks also to Lesley Drummond, Sara Raeburn and Jeanette Farrier for hair, make-up and clothes, and to Paula Pryke for beautiful flowers.

And to my back-room team of Melanie Grocott, Liz Marris and Lorraine Street, a huge thank you.

Conversion tables

All these are approximate conversions, which have either been rounded up or down. In a few recipes it has been necessary to modify them very slightly. Never mix metric and imperial measures in one recipe; stick to one system or the other. All spoon measurements used throughout this book are level unless specified otherwise; all butter is salted unless specified otherwise.

Weights

½ oz	10 g
¾	20
1	25
1½	40
2	50
2½	60
3	75
4	110
4½	125
5	150
6	175
7	200
8	225
9	250
10	275
12	350
1 lb	450
1 lb 8 oz	700
2	900
3	1.35 kg

Volume

2 fl oz	55 ml
3	75
5 (¼ pint)	150
10 (½ pint)	275
1 pint	570
1¼	725
1¾	1 litre
2	1.2
2½	1.5
4	2.25

Dimensions

⅛ inch	3 mm
¼	5 mm
½	1 cm
¾	2
1	2.5
1¼	3
1½	4
1¾	4.5
2	5
2½	6
3	7.5
3½	9
4	10
5	13
5¼	13.5
6	15
6½	16
7	18
7½	19
8	20
9	23
9½	24
10	25.5
11	28
12	30

Oven temperatures

Gas mark 1	275°F	140°C
2	300	150
3	325	170
4	350	180
5	375	190
6	400	200
7	425	220
8	450	230
9	475	240

Contents

Chapter 1 *Equipment for cooks* 10
How to equip your kitchen from scratch and
invest in the right kind of tools for the job

Chapter 2 *Gadgets that work* 36
Ice-cream, espresso and bread machines, food
processors, blenders, and the chef's blowtorch

Chapter 3 *How to cook pulses* 70
The wonderful world of pulses – beans, peas
and lentils – and how to prepare them

Chapter 4 *First steps in preserving* 94
Mastering the essential techniques of
preserves, chutneys, jellies and pickles

Chapter 5 *Waist watchers* 116
An array of recipes that proves it's possible to
feast – not fast -- while counting the calories

Chapter 6 *Pâtés and starters* 150
From terrines to tarts, dishes to arouse the
appetite throughout the year

Chapter 7 *Hot puddings* 170
Steamed sponges, suet puddings and soufflés.
Traditional desserts for special occasions

Chapter 8 *Parties and gatherings* 186
Seasonal cooking for family and friends –
planning ahead for stress-free entertaining

The author's tree house (previous page), the harvests of Suffolk, a new generation of cats and Delia's team of chefs at Norwich City.

CENTRE PHOTOGRAPH BY J.P. MASCLET

Introduction

The third and final part of *How To Cook* has something no other book I've ever written has had. Normally, a cookery writer has to act on instinct and try to get a feel for where people are and what they want, the kind of instructions and techniques they need to know about, and what sort of recipes they are interested in.

Now things have taken a mighty leap forward and today we are living in an exciting age where communications have gone way beyond anything we could have dreamed of when I first started writing recipes. Thanks to the amazing technology of the internet, I have been able to directly ask you – my faithful followers – what you would like to see covered in this book and television series.

There is an ever-growing number of TV cooks, and never before has the whole subject of cooking been so well served, so it is even harder than ever to gauge what, if anything, is needed. As a result, it was an enormous help to be able – through the live chat line and Talking Point on our website – to be able to hear directly what was most wanted in this, the final volume and series. In addition, since I've taken up running the catering operation at Norwich City Football Club (with five restaurants and eleven chefs in tow), I've been introduced to lots of new recipe ideas – and have included some of them here.

This book is the result of all that feedback, together with some of the things I personally believe should be included, like some traditional – and forgotten – recipes that need to be revived. What I sincerely hope for now is that, collectively, the three volumes of *How To Cook* will provide a sound basis for any young person (or, indeed, older person) who wants to begin to cook well but lacks the knowledge. Equally, I hope that each of them will provide a collection of recipes that even those with more experience will enjoy and take inspiration from.

Thank you for all your e-mails, your letters and, above all, your enthusiasm, which has encouraged me through the years.

Delia
August 2001

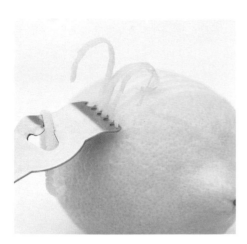

1
Equipment for cooks

As in Book Two, we're kicking off on a 'let's get serious' note. If you want to be a good cook and enjoy pleasurable, trouble-free cooking, then you're simply going to have to think about investing in the right kind of tools for the job. It's amazing that, when it comes to cooking equipment, there is so often a kind of make-do, 'I'll get around to it one day' mentality.

What so often lurks behind the doors of the very smartest designer kitchen cupboards is a whole battery of blunt or bent, cheap impulse purchases that, instead of serving you, will in the end just make life more difficult. So, if you are going to attempt to cook well, why not make it as easy as possible and begin by carefully selecting, bit by bit, the right kind of quality equipment that will serve you a lifetime?

How to survive the commercial jungle

My aim here is to try and steer you through the commercial jungle out there and help you focus on what's really useful. You have two problems to overcome: one is the dazzle of design and good looks – buying an item because it's aesthetically pleasing and not for how it performs; the other is being beguiled by price – why pay a lot when you can get away with paying less?

Both these attitudes need to be addressed. Number one is easier to come to terms with – it's a decision. I simply want only quality and performance, not dazzling design. Number two is more tricky. There are hordes of manufacturers out there trying to undercut each other on price, which means that any time A undercuts B, the quality suffers. It gets cheaper and flimsier and nastier.

Think carefully about price

Well, it's obvious if you think about it: twenty-four buckled cake tins bought over a period of years are actually going to cost you far more than one solid cake tin that lasts. How many scratched and peeling non-stick frying pans have you got through so far? If you're concerned about cost, then quality will actually be cheaper in the long run.

Where do I begin?

Right here. After a lifetime of cooking and experiencing all the pitfalls, I have compiled the following, hopefully comprehensive, beginners' guide to what is useful, helpful and performs well – and also what is superfluous to everyday requirements.

Knives and cutting edges

Ever since the Stone Age we have used cutting implements for our food, and number one on the list of equipment for any kitchen must always be knives. But what kind? Good news here, because you *don't* need a long list of hugely expensive and heavy chef's knives, as you probably won't be doing much skinning, filleting or boning. But you do need *good* knives. The best for home cooking are light to hold, with flexible blades. (The flexibility makes sharpening easier.) Here is what I would call my ideal set in order to make every task a simple one, though it is possible to start with just one or two.

Serrated palette knife: This is a beautifully versatile knife. It cuts bread and cakes, spreads icing and cream, loosens sticky edges around tins and slides under and lifts biscuits from baking trays. It is also useful to have a smaller one for spreading over and sliding round smaller dishes, such as ramekins.

Cook's knives: A 7 inch (18 cm) long cook's knife is essential for chopping herbs and slicing and chopping up meat and vegetables. I would also choose two smaller cook's knives with serrated edges and in different sizes, plus a rounded-end serrated knife, which is excellent for slicing tomatoes swiftly and easily.

Kitchen scissors: Got to have them – they have so many uses, from snipping chives to cutting air vents in pies. My great-grandmother's were called bacon scissors, but sadly, it's hard to find any bacon with rind nowadays!

Potato peeler: So often, much of the flavour and nutrients in vegetables is near the skin and with a good peeler, you really are removing only the peel.

Curved paring knife: I like my curved paring knife for paring and peeling thicker skins when a potato peeler won't do the job.

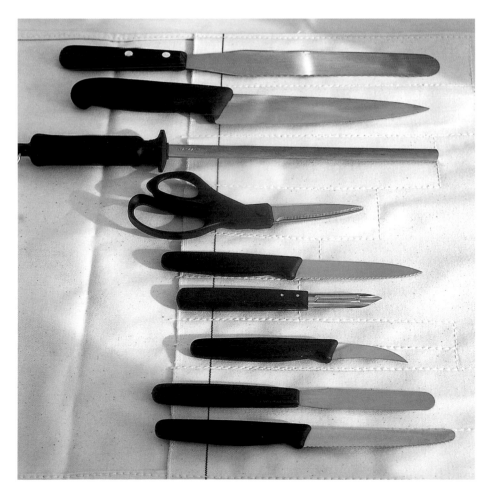

From top to bottom:
Serrated palette knife
7 inch (18 cm) cook's knife
Sharpening steel
Kitchen scissors
Small serrated knife
Potato peeler
Curved paring knife
Smaller palette knife
Rounded-end serrated knife

Taking care of knives

It's important to keep your knives sharp, and practice makes perfect when using a sharpening steel *(see photograph on page 13)*. Hold the steel horizontally in front of you and the knife vertically, then slide the blade of the knife down, allowing the tip to touch the steel, first on one side of the steel and then on the other. Start slowly and then speed up. Sharpen little and often is the best advice I was given by a butcher.

If possible, store your knives in a wooden block or on a magnetic rack, so they're not crashing around in drawers against other instruments, which can damage the blades.

Never chop on a laminated, marble or any other hard surface, as this can blunt blades. Instead, use wooden or polypropylene chopping boards, as these have a certain amount of give that will ensure that the blades don't get damaged.

Clockwise, from left: four-sided grater, Microplane® Grater, nutmeg grater, zester

Graters and zesters

Four-sided grater: A handy tool for grating small amounts of cheese or vegetables. Each side grates to a different fineness. I tend to use two of the sides: the coarse grater for, say, Cheddar, and the slightly finer side for Parmesan. The very prickly-looking side tends to grate too finely and gets very clogged up.

Microplane®Grater: This flat version is relatively new, and super-efficient at grating fresh ginger. There are three kinds: very fine, coarse and coarser again. Be careful when grating citrus zests, though, as I find it can remove some of the bitter pith as well.

Nutmeg grater: Worth mentioning here because nutmeg is a spice that quickly loses its edge if bought ready-ground. The small one pictured here incorporates a little box to hold one or two nutmegs, which makes it very handy and time-saving.

Zester: When you want only the outer zest of a lemon (or lime or orange) and none of the bitter pith, a zester does the job perfectly. The outer zest of the fruit contains all the fragrance and oils that give maximum flavour.

Grinding, crushing and squeezing

If flavour is the prime concern of the cook, then 'whole' is a very important word. Ingredients that come ready-ground lose much of their fragrance, character and flavour, so the ideal here is always to buy an ingredient whole and grind it yourself.

Pestle and mortar: (*see right*) The best investment you can make for grinding and crushing is a heavy, unglazed porcelain bowl (the mortar) with a rounded tool (the pestle) that pounds anything and everything. It will last a lifetime and serve you in countless ways: with it you can bruise rosemary leaves to release their fragrant oils, crush whole roasted spices, pound the leaves of basil and other herbs, and reduce a clove of garlic and some flakes of salt into a creamy mass in seconds – and there is absolutely no better way to combine ingredients for a salad dressing (see Book Two).

Salt and pepper mills: The virtues of whole peppercorns and flakes of sea salt are described in Book Two, but clearly they need mills to grind them. Not an easy one this, as about 80 per cent of what's on offer either doesn't work ever, or works for a while, then packs up on you. Avoid gadgets and hideous novelties that don't do the job. Stick with it, though; there isn't really any alternative but to go to a quality kitchen supplier and get ones that will last. I have had mine since I first started cooking and they are still serving me well.

Citrus reamer: (*see right*) Such a simple but fine invention. Push it into a lemon half (or other citrus fruit), twist it and out flows the juice.

Lemon squeezer: (*see right*) If you don't want to spend time fishing out pips, then a classic lemon squeezer will catch them for you.

Sieving, sifting and straining

Sieves: (*see left*) If you have been faithfully following *How To Cook* and have read all my notes on sauces, it could be said you'll never have to sieve out any lumps – and I would put money on that! However, you *will* need to sift flour and icing sugar, extract the pips from soft fruit and use a sieve for puréeing small quantities. I have two sizes of metal sieve and one nylon – the latter is best for soft fruit as the metal can sometimes discolour it. I also keep a tiny sieve, like a tea strainer, in my spoon drawer – perfect for sprinkling a small amount of cocoa or icing sugar.

Dredgers: (*see left*) I think two of these would be ideal: one for sprinkling flour lightly and evenly all over pastry when you are rolling it out; the other one for icing sugar – great at Christmas when you are baking batches of mince pies that call for a hefty dredging.

Colander: (*see left*) Can't live without this one. Straining liquid from a pan with the lid slightly off is not a good idea – either too much water is left behind or some of your, say, spaghetti escapes along with it. A colander guarantees no hassle and if you want to squeeze the juice out of spinach, chop cooked cabbage, soak and drain aubergines or strain anything at all, it will do the job perfectly.

Spoons, forks and whisks

Spoons: (*see left*) A selection of wooden spoons in varying sizes would be ideal, plus a large and a small one with a pointed end, which is useful when you need to get into the corners of pans. A long-handled, large-bowled metal spoon is useful for basting without burning your arm, and a shorter-handled version is what's needed for folding mixtures quickly and efficiently. Two draining spoons (a long-handled and a short-handled one) are indispensable for skimming and separating – or even lifting baked beans on to toast without too much juice.

Forks: (*see left*) I love wooden forks for scrambling eggs or fluffing rice, and a large metal fork has one-hundred-and-one uses, such as beating eggs for an omelette instead of whisking.

Whisks: (*see left*) A balloon whisk is for spontaneous whisking when you don't want to drag out the electric version. The Wonder Whisk does the same for very small quantities – it will bring a salad dressing together in a trice, for instance.

Spatulas, slices and tongs

Spatulas: (*see left*) There are now dozens of versions of the famous Rubber Maid® spatula, but it is still an absolute whiz, as it can miraculously clean up every last bit of mixture from any shape of bowl.

Slices: (*see left*) Every kitchen needs a good flexible fish slice, but beware, though – there are lots of good-lookers around that don't do the job. Flexibility is the key here – if it's too heavy or rigid it will be awkward and difficult to use, so try to find one with lots of bendy give in it. You'll also need a good triangular cake slice, similarly flexible, which will double up for lifting out wedges of pie or prising biscuits off baking trays.

Kitchen tongs: (*see photograph, opposite*) Not least for turning sausages effectively and efficiently. There are lots of awkward duds around but I've discovered some professional chef's catering tongs that are the best ever.

Weighing and measuring

I fervently believe that, for the most part, cooks should always weigh everything. If you are someone who has cooked every day, all day, for a lifetime and have a fairly modest repertoire, then perhaps your instincts and judgements are so well developed you don't need to use scales. If so, lucky you. For the rest of us, living in the fast lane, trying to juggle our commitments, careers and families, this is absolutely not so. What scales do is remove the fear and the worry when you don't have time to think what day it is, let alone what 4 oz (110 g) of pasta actually looks like. Weighing leaves you be, leaves you free and yet guarantees perfection every time. There are, of course, occasions when it's impossible to be precise. How sharp is a lemon? How much juice does one lemon have compared with another? Weighing or measuring does not prevent you from tasting and adding more of this or that – it just ensures all will be pretty well in the end without you having to worry about it.

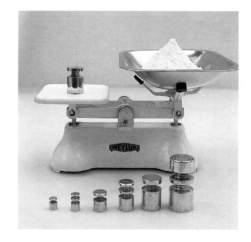

Scales: (*see right*) Let's look at the cowboys first. I, and all the people who work with me, are of one mind about electronic scales: totally unreliable and an absolute no-no. They run out of battery power when you least expect it (such as in the middle of making a cake); if you want to weigh ½ oz (10 g) it's tricky because digital figures don't cope very well with small amounts; and last, but by no means least, they have a limited life, so it's soon time to bin them and start all over again. The other type that gets points for great design but doesn't do the job is scales with a spring mechanism and a needle that points to the correct weight – except the needle often wobbles and wavers and fails. These also have a short life.

All I have to say is, if you want to cook well, there is only one truly accurate way to weigh ingredients and that is to invest in old-fashioned, time-honoured balance scales. It's a small investment for years of worry-free accuracy. With balance scales, everything is instant: you put on the required weight, add the ingredients and can see immediately when the balance of the two has been achieved. You can, as I do, have one set of metric weights and one of imperial. (Anyone over 40 is still likely to think in imperial measures, so if a recipe is all metric you can then proceed without worry.)

Measuring jug: (*see right*) A glass measuring jug (Pyrex is best) shows you in seconds what 3 fl oz (75 ml) looks like, and this is an essential – teacups or half-teacups are not the answer. It is also vital when cooking rice, as this is always measured by volume rather than by weight.

Spoons: (*see left*) Another important aspect of measurement comes in the shape of spoons. I am afraid I can't accept the official version exemplified by sets of (usually) plastic spoons hanging on a metal ring, because a) they can vary in size and b) I think their size is a bit on the mean side. I much prefer to use what was originally intended: real tablespoons, dessertspoons and teaspoons. A useful point to remember is 2 teaspoons equates to 1 dessertspoon, 2 dessertspoons to 1 tablespoon, so long as you use like for like – level, heaped or rounded.

Baking equipment

It could be said that home baking is on the decline. With a million-and-one chocolate bars and a prolific amount of factory-baked goods on offer, why should we *want* to do any home baking? My own theory is that the instinct to be creative – to bake something now and again – is still part of our nature. And while home baking may not be as popular as it was, there are still enough of us who long for that home-baked quality that can never come out of a factory. So, I would like to encourage you to give yourself, as well as family and friends, a home-baked treat now and then.

This list of equipment will stand you in good stead for a lifetime, but don't buy anything – cake tins, baking trays, whatever – unless it looks solid enough to last. They will be more expensive than the flimsy versions but, believe me, it is cheaper to buy something only once. My mother still has the cake tins she used when I was a child! It is obviously not necessary to go out and buy the whole lot at once; perhaps each time you want to give home baking a try you could add to your collection.

Rolling pin: This needs to be wooden, plain and straight, without handles, which get in the way when you want to roll out large sheets of pastry.

Brushes: (*see left*) The flatter brushes, which look like miniature decorator's brushes are the best for large surfaces, while the rounder shape is okay for brushing round rims of pastry. Don't ever put pastry brushes in the dishwasher – they collect nasty bits of grit. Just wash them in warm, running water and a little washing-up liquid and rinse them thoroughly.

Cutters: (*see left*) Fluted or plain or both, these come in tins where all the different sizes fit inside one another, from 3½ inches (9 cm) to 1 inch (2.5 cm). They're essential for making tartlets, biscuits and scones.

Cake tins: (*see photograph on page 10*) Indispensable for making sponge cakes, for me, is a very solid set: a 7 inch (18 cm) tin makes a 2-egg 4 oz (110 g) mixture, double-layer sponge cake, and the 8 inch (20 cm) one is for a 3-egg 6 oz (175 g) mixture. Springform tins are equipped with a metal clip to release the sides, which is excellent for cheesecakes or anything that needs careful unmoulding. For springform and deep cake tins, I would choose the same measurements as the sponge tins (not least because most of my cake recipes fit these sizes).

Loaf tins: (*see photograph on page 10*) Here I always stick to the old-fashioned bread tin shapes. These still have the capacity to hold 1 lb/450 g (6 x 3¾ x 2¾ inches/15 x 9.5 x 7 cm) or 2 lbs/900 g (7¼ x 4½ x 3½ inches/18.5 x 11.5 x 9 cm) of mixture, which, again, all my recipes fit.

Quiche, tart and pie tin: Solid is still the name of the game, and it's good to have at least two sizes of loose-bottomed quiche or tart tin: a 7½ inch (19 cm) one for a small quiche or tart and a 9 inch (23 cm) or 10 inch (25.5 cm) one for family-sized recipes. I also like to have a sloping-sided, deep-rimmed pie tin (*see photograph on page 10*) – one with a 7 inch (18 cm) base and a 9 inch (23 cm) top measurement is the size here.

Baking trays and tins: (*see right*) Sturdy baking trays and tins are, again, a lifetime's investment. Pre-heated in the oven, a baking tray will ensure the pastry base of a pie or quiche will be crisp – just one of its many uses. I use three sizes: 8 x 12 inch (20 x 30 cm), 10 x 14 inch (25.5 x 35 cm) and 11 x 16 inch (28 x 40 cm). Roasting tins come in a host of different sizes, but the key, when roasting meat in them, is that they mustn't be too deep – otherwise the meat will just steam.

Cooling racks: (*see photograph on page 10*) Simple, but so important in baking. Without a rack, cakes and biscuits left to cool on a flat surface become soggy, as steam gets trapped underneath. I think you'll find it useful to have two.

Lattice cutter: This one took the nation by storm when I did my Christmas series, and it is truly innovative. Wheel it across a piece of rolled-out dough and, hey presto, you have a perfect pastry lattice to put on the top of a pie.

Saucepans, frying pans and casseroles

Saucepans: (*see photograph on following page*) These are probably going to be the most important purchase a cook will make. There is so much rubbish out there and millions of pounds spent to beguile you into buying them, so here you really do need some help. What you want is something solid and reliable, and I have spent years searching out what I've now finally come to believe is the best.

There is no doubt that heavy-gauge aluminium is the very best conductor of heat. I have demonstrated in Books One and Two its importance in making omelettes and cooking sauces: no sticking, no catching, no scorching. I would banish the traditional non-stick brigade entirely, having suffered so many peeling, scratched and useless non-stick non-starters. Manufacturers needn't talk to me about being careful – you know, never having the heat high and using plastic spoons and forks etc. I am a cook and if I want to sear a steak, I want the pan to be blasting hot and I don't want to then turn my steak over with some flimsy plastic fork that the heat will melt. Fortunately, about three years ago, I discovered a range of pans produced in Germany, made from heavy-gauge aluminium but with a non-stick surface called titanium, which is forty times harder than

stainless steel. So, at last, high heat, no problem; metal utensils, no problem. Expensive, but one purchase is for life, so cheaper than a long line of dismal failures. All the pans, including the frying pans, have lids, and even the handles can withstand an oven temperature of up to gas mark 10, 500°F (260°C), which means the frying pan can then double up as a shallow casserole or a roasting tray.

Cast-iron ridged griddle: Since it's now fashionable to char-grill so many things, this is a useful addition, and especially good for Bruschetta (see Book One) giving the bread that lovely charred flavour.

Casseroles: I have found that an approximately 4 pint (2.25 litre) capacity flameproof casserole is a good, all-round family size and that a 6 pint (3.5 litre) casserole is a very useful size for entertaining.

Taking care of pans

Sorry, but there is one bit of bad news here. The chemicals in the dishwashing process tend not to be good for saucepans. So, just get into the habit of soaking them in cold water to get rid of any residue, then they will be easy to wash in warm, soapy water – and it will give you much more room in the dishwasher for other items.

Steamers

Clockwise, from top left: double-pan steamer, Chinese bamboo steamer and fan steamer

I do like to steam lots of things so I've got three types of steamer (*see left*). There's the classic double-pan one that stands over a saucepan and will hold a large pudding; a fan steamer that is brilliant for vegetables, even asparagus, which I always trim and lay out horizontally; and finally, a Chinese bamboo steamer I use for fish.

Miscellaneous

Oven thermometer: This is useful for gauging when the temperature is correct, particularly as ovens can vary. It's also crucial for those with an Aga or similar oven, as it can tell you what the temperature is on each shelf in the top and bottom oven.

Sugar thermometer: (*see photograph opposite*) Handy for making sweets and toffee, and an essential item for our Chocolate Fudge on page 232.

Tape measure: If a recipe stipulates the base measurement of a tin or dish, I can never be sure by guessing it, so I always have a tape measure handy.

Kitchen timer: Memories are fallible and a timer can save a lot of hard work from going out of the window.

Pasta tongs: (*see photograph opposite*) These really do lift spaghetti out of the pan very efficiently and quickly without losing any.

Garlic press: (*see photograph opposite*) This one's for speed. It does save time, especially the easy-cleaning version that doesn't clog up.

Apple corer: (*see right*) A simple little tool that makes very quick work of removing the entire core, pips and all.

Melon baller: (*see right*) Useful, not just for melon, but for scraping the centre out of an apple (see Lucy's Tarte Tatin on page 32).

Ice-cream scoop: (*see right*) Gives you a beautifully rounded blob of ice cream in half a second.

Bean slicer: Runner beans are my absolute favourite vegetable and when they're sliced thinly with a slicer (see Book Two), they can be cooked until tender in a matter of moments.

Skewers: (*see right*) Last but definitely not least, the only way I can tell how my meat or fish is cooking, or whether my vegetables are tender. This is an item I don't think I could ever cook without.

What I think you don't need

Because space is always at a premium in any kitchen and everyone has some item of equipment that lurks unused, taking up precious space, now might be a good time to talk about what *not* to put on that wedding list.

Potato ricer: Because the potatoes get cold, and anyway, an electric hand whisk makes a better job of mashed potatoes.

Asparagus steamer: Why give it houseroom when an ordinary steamer does the job perfectly?

Fish kettle: Cooking fish slowly in kitchen foil (see Baked Whole Salmon with Sauce Verte on page 222) produces moister flesh than poaching *and* the flavour isn't all going into the water.

Canelle knife: Because a good potato peeler does the same job.

Piping bags: Simply because life is too short.

Ceramic baking beans: Thankfully, I have pioneered a way to pre-bake a crisp pastry case without them (see Book One).

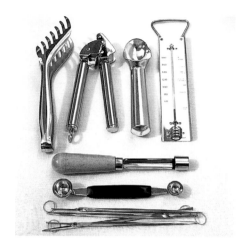

Top row, left to right: pasta tongs, garlic press, ice-cream scoop, sugar thermometer

Bottom row, top to bottom: apple corer, melon baller, skewers

Pepper-Crusted Fillet of Beef with Roasted Balsamic Onions and Thyme

This is one of the easiest ways I know to serve four people something special very quickly and very easily. If you have a first course and a pud, there is enough for six. It goes really well with Potatoes Boulangère with Rosemary (see Book One).

Serves 4-6

1 lb 12 oz (800 g) middle-cut fillet of British beef
1 rounded dessertspoon black peppercorns (or a tablespoon, if you like it really hot)
2 fl oz (55 ml) balsamic vinegar
1 lb (450 g) medium red onions
2 tablespoons chopped fresh thyme
1 tablespoon olive oil, plus a little extra to smear
1 tablespoon molasses sugar
salt

For the sauce:

1 heaped teaspoon plain flour
½ pint (275 ml) red wine
1 tablespoon Worcestershire sauce
1 tablespoon balsamic vinegar

You will also need a large baking tray.

If you can, start this off a couple of hours in advance (or longer, if that suits). All you do is first smear the beef with a little olive oil, then crush the peppercorns coarsely with a pestle and mortar. Tip them into a fine sieve, which will sift out the really hot inner bits and leave you with the fragrant outer bits, and press these all over the surface of the beef.

When you're ready to cook the beef, pre-heat the oven to gas mark 8, 450°F (230°C). Then, to prepare the onions, you first need to mix the sugar and balsamic vinegar together in a large bowl, give the mixture a good whisk, and then leave it to one side for about 10 minutes to allow the sugar to dissolve.

Meanwhile, peel the onions, then, leaving the root intact, cut each one into eight sections through the root, so, in half first, then each half into four. Then add the onions and the tablespoon of oil to the sugar-and-vinegar mixture and toss them around so they get a good coating. After that, spread the onions out on the baking tray, leaving space for the beef in the centre. Then pour the rest of the dressing over them, sprinkle over the thyme leaves and season well with salt.

Now place the beef in the centre of the baking tray, then into the oven on the highest shelf, and cook for 15 minutes; after that, turn the onions over and return the tray to the oven, giving it another 15 minutes, if you like your beef rare. For medium, remove the onions after the 30 minutes, keep them warm, and give the beef another 10 minutes with the oven switched off. If you like it well-done, leave it for another 15-20 minutes. Either way, keep everything warm while you make the sauce.

To do this, put a quarter of the onions into a small saucepan over a medium heat, then stir in the flour to just coat the onions and gradually whisk in the red wine, Worcestershire sauce and balsamic vinegar. Let it just come up to simmering point, then turn the heat down and simmer gently until the sauce has reduced by about a quarter.

To serve, carve the beef, pouring any escaped meat juices into the sauce, and serve garnished with the onions, the sauce poured over.

Braised Beef Goulash with Smoked Pimentón

I've always loved goulash and would definitely list it among my top casserole recipes, but now, since the advent of the spicy, deep-flavoured pimentón (smoked paprika) from southern Spain, goulash has an even greater appeal. I love this served with whole-grain brown rice cooked with onion, and some buttered green cabbage or spicy red cabbage.

Serves 6

2 lb 8 oz (1.15 kg) British chuck steak (braising steak), trimmed and cut into 1½ inch (4 cm) cubes
1 tablespoon each hot and sweet, mild pimentón, plus a little extra to sprinkle
2 tablespoons olive oil
3 large onions, peeled and chopped
2 garlic cloves, crushed
2 tablespoons plain flour
3 bay leaves
1 x 400 g tin Italian chopped tomatoes
1 x 230 g tin chopped tomatoes
2 medium red peppers
salt and freshly milled black pepper

To serve:
8 fl oz (225 ml) soured cream

You will also need a lidded, flameproof casserole with a capacity of 6 pints (3.5 litres).

Pre-heat the oven to gas mark 1, 275°F (140°C).

Begin by heating the oil in the casserole over a highish heat until it is sizzling hot. Then brown the cubes of beef on all sides, cooking a few at a time. They need to be a good, deep nutty brown colour. As they brown, transfer them to a plate, using a draining spoon.

Now, with the heat turned down to medium, stir in the onions and cook them for about 5 minutes, or until they begin to brown and caramelise at the edges. Then stir in the garlic and return the meat to the casserole. Next, sprinkle in the flour and pimentón and give everything a stir to soak up the juices. Now, add the bay leaves and the contents of both tins of tomatoes, and season well with salt and freshly milled black pepper. Let it all come slowly up to simmering point. Then cover the casserole with a tight-fitting lid and transfer it to the middle shelf of the oven to cook very slowly for exactly 2 hours.

Meanwhile, prepare the peppers by halving them, removing the seeds and pith and cutting the flesh into strips roughly measuring 1 x 2 inches (2 x 5 cm). Then, when the 2 hours are up, stir the chopped peppers into the goulash, replace the lid and cook for a further 30 minutes.

Just before serving, take the casserole out of the oven, let it stand for 5 minutes, then stir in the soured cream to give a lovely marbled, creamy effect. Finally, sprinkle over a little more pimentón, and serve straight from the casserole.

Easy Omelette Arnold Bennett

This is an adaptation of a famous omelette created by a chef at The Savoy Hotel for an author who wrote an entire novel while staying there. It's a truly wonderful creation – a flat but very fluffy open-faced omelette made with smoked Finnan haddock.

To begin with, measure the crème fraîche into a medium saucepan and bring it up to a gentle simmer. Add some freshly milled black pepper, but don't add salt yet because the haddock can be quite salty. Then pop in the prepared fish and let it poach gently, uncovered, for about 5 minutes.

Meanwhile, make up the sauce: separate one of the eggs, breaking the yolk into a small bowl and reserving the white in another bowl. Add the cornflour to the yolk and whisk well.

When the fish is cooked, use a draining spoon to lift it out into a sieve placed over the saucepan, to allow all the liquid to drain back. Press lightly to extract every last drop, then place the sieve containing the fish on a plate. At this point, pre-heat the grill to its highest setting.

Now bring the liquid in the pan back up to simmering point, then pour it on to the egg yolk, whisking all the time. Then return the whole mixture to the saucepan and gently bring it back to just below simmering point, or until it has thickened – no more than 1 or 2 minutes. After that, remove it from the heat and stir in the fish, tasting to see if it needs any salt. Next, whisk up the egg white to the soft-peak stage and carefully fold it in.

Now for the omelette. First beat the 4 remaining eggs with some seasoning. Next, melt the butter and oil in the frying pan until foaming, swirling them round to coat the sides and base. When it's very hot, add the eggs, let them settle for about 2 minutes, then begin to draw the edges into the centre, tilting the pan to let the liquid egg run into the gaps.

When you feel the eggs are half set, turn the heat down and spoon the haddock mixture evenly over the surface of the eggs, using a palette knife to spread it. Now sprinkle the Gruyère over the top and place the pan under the grill, positioning it roughly 5 inches (13 cm) from the heat source. The omelette will now take 2-3 minutes to become puffy, golden brown and bubbling. Remove it, garnish with chives, and let it relax for 5 minutes before cutting it into wedges and serving it on warmed plates.

Serves 2 as a supper dish or 3 as a light lunch with salad
8 oz (225 g) smoked haddock, skin and bones removed, cut into ½ inch (1 cm) chunks
2 rounded tablespoons crème fraîche
5 large eggs
½ teaspoon cornflour
½ oz (10 g) butter
1 teaspoon olive oil
2 oz (50 g) Gruyère, grated
freshly snipped chives, to garnish
salt and freshly milled black pepper

You will also need an omelette pan (or frying pan) with a diameter of 8 inches (20 cm).

25

Very Sticky Prune and Date Cake

Cakemaking is really easy, but only when the two major rules are followed: always weigh everything and always use the right-sized cake tin. For a newcomer investing in some balance scales, this cake alone will justify your investment! It's one of the easiest ever, but with a flavour that is really special – dark and caramelised, with lots of luscious fruit, and it keeps really well in an airtight tin.

Begin by placing all the fruit in a largish saucepan (it needs to be large because the mixture splutters a lot), then add the butter, condensed milk and water and bring everything up to the boil, stirring frequently with a wooden spoon to prevent the mixture sticking. Now turn the heat down to low and simmer for exactly 3 minutes, stirring now and then. Don't worry about the appalling look of what will be a very sloppy mixture – this is quite normal. After that, transfer the mixture to a large mixing bowl and let it cool down for about 30 minutes.

While it's cooling, weigh out the flours and sift them into a bowl with the bicarbonate of soda and a pinch of salt. (When sieving wholemeal flour you frequently find small quantities of bran left in the sieve – these can be tipped on to the already-sifted flour.) Pre-heat the oven to gas mark 3, 325°F (170°C).

When the fruit mixture has cooled, stir in the flour using a large metal spoon, then add the tablespoon of chunky marmalade. Now spoon the mixture into the prepared tin and, because this cake does get rather brown on top if not protected, you should cover it with a double square of silicone paper (parchment) with a hole the size of a 50p piece in the centre. Then pop it on to the centre shelf of the oven and bake for 2-2¼ hours.

After removing the cake from the oven, let it cool in the tin for 10 minutes before turning out on to a wire rack. Then, when the cake is completely cold, gently heat the sieved marmalade in a small saucepan with the tablespoon of water and brush the glaze all over the top of the cake to make it lovely and shiny.

Serves 16

6 oz (175 g) ready-to-eat dried
prunes, roughly chopped
8 oz (225 g) pitted dates,
roughly chopped
4 oz (110 g) raisins
4 oz (110 g) currants
10 oz (275 g) butter, plus a little
extra for greasing
1 x 397 g tin condensed milk
10 fl oz (275 ml) water
5 oz (150 g) plain flour
5 oz (150 g) wholemeal flour
¾ teaspoon bicarbonate of soda
1 heaped tablespoon chunky marmalade
2 tablespoons sieved marmalade,
to glaze
1 tablespoon water
salt

You will also need an 8 inch (20 cm) square cake tin, greased, the base and sides lined with silicone paper (parchment), plus extra to cover the cake during baking.

Traditional Lemon Meringue Pie

Everyone on my cookery team agrees that this famous English classic needs a revival. It is supremely light, squashy and fragrant with lemons. How did we ever forget about it?

Serves 6

For the pastry:

4 oz (110 g) plain flour, plus
a little extra for dusting
1 oz (25 g) softened butter, cut
into smallish lumps
1 oz (25 g) softened lard, cut
into smallish lumps
1 tablespoon cold water
salt

For the filling:

grated zest and juice 2 large lemons
10 fl oz (275 ml) water
3 tablespoons cornflour
2 oz (50 g) golden caster sugar
3 large egg yolks
1½ oz (40 g) butter

For the meringue:

3 large egg whites
6 oz (175 g) golden caster sugar

You will also need a 1½ inch (4 cm) deep, sloping-sided, non-stick pie tin with a ½ inch (1 cm) rim, a base diameter of 7 inches (18 cm) and a top diameter of 9½ inches (24 cm); and a baking tray measuring 11 x 16 inches (28 x 40 cm).

Start by making the pastry: first sift the flour and a pinch of salt into a large bowl, holding the sieve up high to give the flour a good airing. Then add the butter and lard and, using only your fingertips, lightly rub the fat into the flour, again lifting the mixture up high. When everything is crumbly, sprinkle in the water. Start to mix the pastry with a flat-bladed knife and then finish off with your hands, adding a few more drops of water until you have a smooth dough that will leave the bowl clean. Then pop the pastry into a plastic food bag and let it rest in the fridge for 30 minutes. Pre-heat the oven to gas mark 5, 375°F (190°C) and pop in the baking tray to pre-heat at the same time.

Next, transfer the pastry to a flat, lightly floured surface and roll it out to a circle about ½ inch (1 cm) larger all round than the rim of the tin. Cut a ½ inch (1 cm) strip from the edge of the pastry, dampen the rim of the tin with water and fix the strip round it, pressing down well. Dampen the strip before lining the tin with the pastry circle, making sure you don't trap any air underneath it. Then prick the base all over with a fork. Place the tin on the baking tray and bake on a high shelf in the pre-heated oven for 20-25 minutes, or until cooked through. After that, remove the pastry case from the oven, and immediately lower the heat to gas mark 2, 300°F (150°C) for the meringue.

Meanwhile, make the filling. Measure the water into a jug, and spoon the cornflour and sugar into a bowl. Add enough of the water to mix the cornflour to a smooth paste, then pour the rest of the water, along with the grated lemon zest, into a small saucepan. Bring this up to the boil, then pour it gradually on to the cornflour, mixing all the time until it's smooth.

Now return the mixture to the saucepan and bring it back to the boil, still mixing. Next, simmer very gently for about a minute, stirring all the time to prevent it from catching. Then remove the pan from the heat and beat in the egg yolks, lemon juice and, finally, the butter. Now pour the lemon mixture into the pastry case.

Finally, for the meringue, use a large, grease-free bowl and in it, whisk the egg whites until they form stiff peaks. Now beat in a quarter of the sugar at a time until it is all incorporated, then spoon the meringue on top, taking it to the very edge of the pastry rim with a palette knife, so it seals the edge completely. (With your knife you can also make a few decorative swirls.) Bake in the oven on the centre shelf for 45 minutes, by which time the meringue will have turned pale beige, and be crisp on the outside and squashy within. Serve warm or cold, but if warm, leave it to settle for about 20 minutes. Chilled pouring cream is a nice accompaniment.

Scottish Semolina Shortbread

This is a very buttery, crumbly shortbread – the real thing, and something that can't be bought, however much you pay for it. Using fine semolina gives it a lovely crunchy texture.

First of all, beat the butter in a bowl with a wooden spoon to soften it, then beat in the sugar, followed by the sifted flour and semolina. Work the ingredients together with the spoon, pressing them to the side of the bowl, then finish off with your hands until you have a smooth mixture that doesn't leave any bits in the bowl.

Next, transfer the dough to a flat, lightly floured surface and roll it out gently to a round (giving it quarter turns as you roll) about the same diameter as the tin, then transfer the round to the tin. Now lightly press in the mixture evenly, right up to the fluted edges. (To make sure it is even, you can give it a final roll with a small glass tumbler.) Finally, prick it all over with a fork – or it will rise up in the centre while it's baking.

Bake the shortbread for 55-60 minutes on the centre shelf of the oven – it should have turned pale gold and feel firm in the centre. Then remove it from the oven and, using a palette knife, mark out the surface into 12 wedges. Leave it to cool in the tin, then, when it's cold, cut it into wedges. Dredge with the remaining golden caster sugar and store in an airtight plastic box or tin until you are ready to serve them.

Note: If you're going to make and serve home-made ice cream, it's nice to serve small, thin shortbread biscuits to go with it. All you do is follow the recipe above, using half the mixture. Roll out the dough thinly, to a thickness of about ⅛ inch (3 mm) and cut it out into approximately 24 shapes using 2 inch (5 cm) cutter. Bake them (at the same temperature) for 15-20 minutes, or until pale gold. Then cool them on a wire rack and, if you want, drizzle some lemon icing (3 oz/75 g icing sugar, 1 tablespoon lemon juice) over them. If you don't want icing, just sprinkle with sugar and, either way, store them in an airtight plastic box or tin.

Makes 12 wedges
3 oz (75 g) fine semolina (or polenta)
6 oz (175 g) butter, at room temperature
3 oz (75 g) golden caster sugar, plus a little extra for dredging
6 oz (175 g) plain flour, sifted, plus a little extra for dusting

You will also need an 8 inch (20 cm) loose-based, fluted flan tin, 1¼ inches (3 cm) deep.

Pre-heat the oven to gas mark 2, 300°F (150°C).

Remove the shortbread from the oven, but don't cut it straightaway – mark the surface into 12 wedges with a palette knife and leave to cool in the tin, right, before storing in an airtight plastic box, far right.

Lucy's Tarte Tatin

Lucy Crabb, the Executive Chef at our restaurant at Norwich City Football Club, makes the very best Tarte Tatin (Caramelised Apple Flan) I've ever tasted. She insists on French apples for this great classic from the Loire Valley, but if you want to use English apples, such as Cox's, it will still be wonderful.

Serves 6

For the pastry:
4 oz (110 g) plain flour, plus a little extra for dusting
1 oz (25 g) unsalted butter, at room temperature, cut into smallish lumps
1 oz (25 g) lard, at room temperature, cut into smallish lumps
2-3 tablespoons cold water

For the filling:
8 large Golden Delicious apples
3 oz (75 g) softened unsalted butter
6 oz (175 g) golden caster sugar

You will also need a non-stick, heavy-based frying pan that is ovenproof (including the handle), with a base diameter of 9½ inches (24 cm), 1½ inches (4 cm) deep.

First of all, you need to make the pastry, so it has time to rest. Begin by sifting the flour into a large mixing bowl from a height, then cut the fats into the flour with a knife, before rubbing the mixture lightly with your fingertips, lifting everything up and letting it fall back into the bowl to give it a good airing. When the mixture reaches the crumb stage, sprinkle in enough water to bring it together to a smooth dough that leaves the sides of the bowl absolutely clean, with no crumbs left. Give it a light knead to bring it fully together, then place the pastry in a plastic food bag and chill it in the fridge for 30 minutes.

To make the filling, peel the apples and then cut them in half vertically and remove the core. (Lucy does this with a melon baller, which works brilliantly and keeps the centre very neat.) Next, spread the softened butter evenly over the base of the pan and sprinkle the sugar over the top. Then, place the apples in concentric circles, cut side up. When you get to the centre, you may have to cut them into quarters to fill any gaps. Now you need to place the pan over a low heat so the butter and sugar melt very slowly together, which will take 8-10 minutes in all. When they have melted, increase the heat slightly, as you now want the sugar to caramelise. Gently shake the pan from time to time, so the apples don't stick and burn on the bottom. (Lucy insists this is not a dessert you can walk away from, as the minute you do, the sugar will burn.) Meanwhile, pre-heat the oven to gas mark 7, 425°F (220°C). It will take about 20-25 minutes for the sugar to reach a rich amber colour and, by that time, the apples should be soft but still retain their shape. When that has happened, remove the pan from the heat.

Now remove the pastry from the fridge, transfer it to a flat, lightly floured surface and roll it out to an 11½ inch (29 cm) round. Fit it over the top of the pan, allowing some to tuck down at the edge, which doesn't have to be too neat. Prick the pastry base all over with a fork so the steam is released when it's cooking and the pastry doesn't go soggy. Next, place the pan on the centre shelf of the oven and bake the tart for 20-25 minutes, or until the pastry is crisp and golden brown.

Remove it from the oven using really thick oven gloves and allow it to cool for about 5 minutes. Now the whole thing gets interesting. Take a plate or tray larger than the pan and place it over the top. Then, using an oven glove to hold the handle, invert the pan on to the plate, giving it a little shake before you do. Serve the tart warm, with lashings of crème fraîche. I have to say, any left over is still wonderful served cold.

Easter Simnel Cake

This is a new and very easy angle on a traditional recipe. Simnel cake was not originally baked at Easter but on Mothering Sunday, as a kind of mid-Lent treat. Somehow or other, it got postponed until the great feast of Easter itself – which, in my book, is precisely where it deserves to be, since it makes the perfect family treat for a bank-holiday weekend. This version is baked with chunks of marzipan interspersed in the cake mixture, which melt deliciously into the fruit.

Serves 12
4 oz (110 g) whole, unblanched almonds
1 lb (450 g) golden marzipan in a block
8 oz (225 g) plain flour
3 teaspoons baking powder
1 rounded teaspoon mixed spice
14½ oz (410 g) mincemeat
12 oz (350 g) mixed dried fruit
2 oz (50 g) whole candied peel, chopped
grated zest 1 orange
grated zest 1 lemon
5 oz (150 g) light soft brown sugar
5 oz (150 g) well softened butter, plus a little extra for greasing
2 tablespoons milk
3 large eggs

To decorate:
a little icing sugar, for dusting
9 oz (250 g) ready-to-roll icing
1 dessertspoon redcurrant jelly
marzipan reserved from the cake
1 large egg yolk, beaten

You will also need a deep, 8 inch (20 cm) round cake tin, the base and sides lined with a double layer of buttered silicone paper (parchment), plus extra to cover the cake during baking.

Pre-heat the oven to gas mark 6, 400°F (200°C).

You need to begin by toasting the almonds to give them some extra crunch and flavour. So, spread them out on a baking tray and pop them into the pre-heated oven for 8-10 minutes. Don't guess the time; please use a timer – they need to be lightly toasted to a golden brown colour and you could end up with an expensive mistake if you try to guess! Now remove the almonds and reduce the oven temperature to gas mark 2, 300°F (150°C). Then, when the almonds are cool, chop them roughly. Next, unwrap the marzipan, cut the block into two halves, re-wrap one of them for use later and chop the remaining half into ½ inch (1 cm) cubes. Toss them in a tablespoon of the flour from the cake.

Now for the cake itself. Take your largest mixing bowl, sift in the flour, baking powder and spice, then simply place all the ingredients, except the squares of marzipan and the decorating ingredients, into the bowl. Then take an electric hand whisk (preferably) or, failing that, a wooden spoon, and give everything a really good mixing – which will take 2-3 minutes – to get it all perfectly and evenly distributed. Finally, gently fold in the squares of marzipan and any remaining flour from tossing them.

Now, using a rubber spatula, spoon the mixture into the prepared tin and level the surface. Place a suitably sized square of double-layered silicone paper (parchment) with a hole the size of a 50p piece in the centre, over the top. Place the cake on the centre shelf of the oven and bake for 2¾-3¼ hours. Have a look at it after 2¾ hours – the cake is cooked when the centre feels springy when lightly pressed. When it is baked, leave it in the tin for 30 minutes before turning it out on to a wire rack to cool.

For the decoration, first dust a work surface with icing sugar and roll out the icing to the same size as the top of the cake. (You can use the base of the tin as a guide here.) Then brush the top of the cake with the redcurrant jelly and fit the icing on top, pressing it securely all round and using a rolling pin to level it as much as possible, and trim off any overhanging pieces.

Next, roll out the reserved marzipan to a rectangle about 9 x 6 inches (23 x 15 cm) and cut it into 12 long strips about ½ inch (1 cm) wide. Assembling the lattice goes as follows: first lay half the strips across the cake, leaving about a ¾ inch (2 cm) gap between each strip. Then begin to thread the rest of the strips, one at a time, under and over the first ones, at right angles. Finally, use some scissors to snip away the overhanging marzipan and press firmly all round to make the edges as neat as possible.

Now pre-heat the grill for at least 10 minutes and, when it's really hot, brush the marzipan strips with the egg yolk and place the cake under the grill, about 4 inches (10 cm) from the heat source. Give it about 30 seconds, watching it like a hawk, until it turns a toasted brown colour. It is now ready to serve or be stored.

2 Gadgets that work

There's something very human about us all being seduced into buying gadgets, and I have to admit, I have had my fair share. But something a lifetime of cooking has taught me is to distinguish between what, in the end, just gathers dust at the back of a cupboard, and what, by contrast, can do a job of work for you and really save you time. My mother always says if you haven't worn something for a whole year you're never going to, so give it to the charity shop. The same applies to gadgets.

Kitchen casualties

While I know what suits one person won't suit another, my own casualties of time – things that take up precious space but are not really needed – are as follows. A slow cooker, because I can cook slowly on top of a stove or in a smaller oven. A pasta machine, because a) I prefer dried pasta and b) I have no time in my life to make my own. A sandwich toaster, which I used once then never took out of its box again (and, in any case, sandwiches can be grilled – see Croque Monsieur in Book One).

Then there's a pressure cooker. No good if you have animals because its high-pitched noise frightens the wits out of them. A deep fat fryer: I really don't need this huge, bulky object, and I also think that deep-frying in general at home is not needed – I find I can shallow-fry things just as easily without large quantities of messy oil. A salad spinner (remember those?): literally a waste of space, and anyway, a clean tea cloth or a wodge of kitchen paper dries salad leaves much more efficiently. Flo Bayley, who has designed this book, chucked her salad spinner in the garage and now uses it to rescue frogs that her cat brings in and to return them to her neighbour's pond. Although I once had an ice-cream maker with a pre-freezing bowl, it never worked for me: either the bowl just took up too much room in the freezer, or, if I didn't keep it in the freezer, I never had time to re-freeze it.

I'm sure there are lots more kitchen casualties that many of you have accumulated, but now let's move on to what, over the years, has really served me well.

Electric hand whisk

I was brought up with something called a rotary whisk, which had a little handle you had to turn furiously to power the blades. Alternatively, there was the smarter and altogether purer way to whisk, which involved a copper bowl and a balloon whisk. Either way, being confronted with a mixing bowl and a mixture needing six minutes of what Victoria Wood's dinner ladies would call 'a bit of wellie' is not my idea of having fun in the kitchen.

But, to be poised by any kind of bowl, electric whisk in hand, to flick a switch and then dream or listen to music while it obeys your every desire – creating volume, whipping to silky smoothness or simply combining things instantly – makes for a much easier and more pleasant life all round.

Hand-held is best. Yes, I know you can buy a grander version, one that is free-standing, has its own bowl and lots of attachments that mean you can walk away while it does its work – so why don't I have one?

(i) Space: free-standing mixers are big, cumbersome things that take up unbelievable kitchen space.

(ii) Air: once the mixture is in the bowl and the whisk head is lowered, it all gets a bit enclosed and not enough air (a most important ingredient) is allowed to circulate.

(iii) Feel: in all my years of cooking I have always liked to get the feel of what I am mixing; under- or over-beating can be avoided as, with experience, you begin to feel when a mixture is right.

The blissful thing about an electric hand whisk is that you can tuck it into a cupboard or drawer, out of sight, and bring it out only when needed. You can use it in a bowl or a saucepan. It is convenient and quick, and afterwards, all you do is pop the beaters in a dishwasher or wash them up by hand. The best one to look for is the most powerful, so look at the wattage. We have found 250W to be powerful enough.

How you can best use an electric hand whisk. Obviously, top of the list is whisking egg whites: a powerful electric whisk and a large bowl (to give you lots of air) will give the best volume in the shortest time.

Mashing potatoes: I have tried ricers, which are very fiddly, and the potato gets cold while you fiddle. Mashers definitely need too much elbow grease, and in a food processor, the mixture just goes gloopy. But the fluffy, creamy mash produced by an electric hand whisk is a joy.

Proper home-made mayonnaise: what a chore this used to be, but it can be made in 7-10 minutes from start to finish using an electric hand whisk.

Cakes: I'm not sure I would actually make a cake that often if I didn't own an electric hand whisk – imagine creaming butter and sugar to that whipped, light, fluffy stage without one. Yes, a wooden spoon can do the job, but oh, the agony and the aching arm – all the more so as you beat the eggs in bit by bit.

Zabaglione

The Italians have invented a beautiful dessert, which is called zabaglione in Italy and sabayon in France. This involves whipping not the whites but the yolks to a voluminous, foamy mass along with some alcohol – in this case, Marsala wine from Sicily.

Serves 6
8 large egg yolks
4 dessertspoons golden caster sugar
75 ml (3 fl oz) Marsala

You will also need an electric hand whisk and six serving glasses.

You need to start this by putting a large saucepan, filled with a couple of inches of water, on a lowish heat to bring it up to a gentle simmer. Then place the egg yolks and sugar in a heatproof mixing bowl large enough to sit over the saucepan without touching the water. Start to whisk them (not on the heat yet) with the electric hand whisk until the mixture is pale and creamy – this will probably take about 4 minutes. Now gradually whisk in the Marsala bit by bit, about a dessertspoon at a time.

Next, transfer the bowl to the saucepan – keeping the heat very low and making sure the bowl doesn't touch the water. Continue whisking until the mixture thickens and becomes foamy. This can sometimes be rather slow (it usually takes 10-15 minutes), but don't be tempted to turn the heat up because, if the mixture becomes too hot, it will curdle. You could do a crossword (one-handed!), listen to the radio or have a natter with someone to pass the time!

When it does thicken, the whisk should leave a clear trail when it is lifted out of the mixture. If you have someone to help, ask them to warm the glasses by dipping them in a bowl of hot water and drying them off just before serving the zabaglione in them.

Note: This recipe contains partially cooked eggs.

Place the yolks and sugar in a bowl and whisk until pale and creamy.

Gradually add the Marsala, then whisk over the heat for 10-15 minutes, until thick.

Once the mixture has thickened, the whisk should leave a clear trail when lifted out.

Food processor

Although this is not an absolutely essential piece of equipment, because you can certainly chop, grate, slice, knead and mix everything by hand, it does do all these things very quickly and efficiently and saves you masses of time and energy. After years of using one myself, I am convinced every serious cook should have a food processor – it's a really great piece of equipment.

There are dozens of different designs and sizes, but I would say that if you invest in the largest, with the most powerful motor, you will have the best of everything. Quality never comes cheap, and beware of what looks like a bargain but may have a short life and not do the job really well. A warning: the blade in a food processor will wear out in time, so if your machine begins to show signs of not performing as it should, it probably needs a sharp new one, which can be ordered from a kitchen shop or direct from the manufacturer. Some top-of-the-range models have either an additional small bowl and blade for reduced quantities, or a blender attachment for making small amounts of, say, hollandaise or pesto.

Know your food processor. When you buy a food processor and begin to use it, you will soon get the feel of how it performs. One of the most common misuses is to overdo it. This was more of a problem before the pulse button was invented, when something chopped could become something liquidised, over-processed nuts became an oily, claggy mess, and puréed meat made hamburgers or rissoles very bouncy! With the pulse button you can see what is happening after each burst, which is important, but care must still be taken not to over-process.

What does a food processor do? First on the list is chopping, particularly large quantities. It can chop a pound of onions in seconds, as well as other vegetables, fruits and nuts. I love my food processor best when I feed it cubes of bread, which it instantly turns into breadcrumbs. (Some of you will be too young to remember the tedious job of grating bread into breadcrumbs by hand.) Also, if you want to make a stuffing, the onions, breadcrumbs and herbs can all be whizzed together – a brilliant time-saver. It can also evenly chop meat much more efficiently than the old-fashioned mincers that squeezed the meat through blades.

Slicing: Yes, it's good at this too. With a special attachment, you can deal with cucumbers, apples, cabbages, potatoes – in fact, whatever needs to be sliced – evenly and precisely. You can even choose thick or thin slices.

Mixing and puréeing: There are a million-and-one things you can mix in a food processor: whole-egg mayonnaise, for instance, can be mixed in moments. It can then be made into chunky tartare sauce, with capers, cornichons (baby gherkins) and parsley chopped in at the end. Taste it and you will never want the shop-bought version ever again. If you are nervous about making pastry, or if the fat from the fridge is too hard to rub in by hand, the food processor will make it extremely well, provided, at the end, you add the water a little at a time to get a good consistency. Sometimes, when you are serving vegetables, it's nice to ring the changes and whip them into a purée – with a little crème fraîche and some butter, it will make a lovely velvety-smooth parsnip purée. I also like to add steamed swede and carrots together to the bowl of the food processor while they are still hot, and whiz them, not to a purée, but to the coarsely chopped stage.

Grating: Grating large quantities – not just of breadcrumbs – can be arduous by hand. A good food processor will have various grating discs so you can grate cheese and vegetables. It makes light work of something really hard, such as fresh coconut (as in the Green Coconut Sambal that accompanies the Spiced Lamb Curry on page 90), and if you need a large amount of freshly grated Parmesan, it is all speedily and easily done.

What doesn't a food processor do? Number one on this list is mashed potatoes. It seems logical that it should, I know, but absolutely not. Something happens to them in the food processor that makes them gloopy and glue-like – not nice at all. Although you *can* use it to make cakes (such as sponge cakes), I feel the space inside the bowl is too confined and doesn't let the air in, so I wouldn't choose to make a cake in mine. The same applies to whisking: there is a whisk attachment that allows you to whisk egg whites but, again, I feel I'm not going to get as much air in, so I always use an electric hand whisk. As for herbs, I feel a good, sharp knife makes a better job of chopping herbs on their own (though herbs added to other mixtures are fine). A food processor can overdo the job and make them rather wet and soggy. Lastly, it's good for puréeing soups if you want a coarser texture, but it can only be done in small quantities or the soup spills over.

Checklist before you buy a food processor: Have you got room to spare? Having it plugged in and ready to go is vital – if it's stashed away in a cupboard you won't want to be bothered. Invest in the best. You could begin with a smaller, cheaper model, but I think a good-sized, powerfully motored, top-of-the-range one will serve you best in the long run. Check the level of the blades as they sit in the bowl – they need to be as low down as possible. The higher they are, the less effective the machine, because a small quantity of ingredients will just sit in the bottom with the blades merrily whizzing about above and the two never meeting!

Belarussian Carrot Salad

This year I was privileged to be invited to a very special family meal in Minsk prepared by Sasha Shidlovskaya and her mother, Irena. Irena gave me her recipe for this simple, but oh-so-good carrot salad, which is perfect for winter when other salad ingredients are not at their best.

Serves 4-6 as a side dish
1 lb (450 g) carrots, peeled
1 dessertspoon coriander seeds
2 tablespoons groundnut or other flavourless oil
1 small onion, peeled and sliced
2 cloves garlic, finely chopped
cayenne pepper

For the marinade:
2 tablespoons cider vinegar
1 teaspoon salt

You will also need a food processor.

First of all, grate the carrot using the fine grater blade on your food processor. After that, transfer it to a bowl, pour over the marinade ingredients and mix to make sure everything is well coated. Then, cover and leave aside for at least 3 hours or, preferably, overnight in the fridge. If the carrots are very fresh, they develop too much juice, which should then be poured away.

Next, you need to dry-roast the coriander seeds. To do this, place them in a small frying pan over a medium heat and stir and toss them around for 1-2 minutes or until they begin to look toasted and start to jump in the pan. Now transfer them to a pestle and mortar and crush them lightly.

After that, heat the oil in the same frying pan. Add the onion and fry until golden. Allow to cool a little, then drain the oil through a sieve on to the carrots and discard the onion, which was there just to give some flavour. Now add the coriander seeds to the carrots, along with the garlic and a pinch of cayenne pepper, and give everything a good stir before serving. Covered, the salad will keep for a couple of days in the fridge.

Return to the blender

When food processors were born, we witnessed a kind of kitchen revolution: it was claimed that sole piece of highly efficient equipment would do absolutely everything – and make blenders redundant. We have already looked at the functions of the food processor and applauded its virtues, but what did not stand the test of time was its ability to blend soups. Even though some had blender attachments, these were too small for the serious soupmaker. In a processor, soupmaking is still a messy business and you never quite achieve a uniform smoothness. Early in the food processor years, blenders disappeared from kitchen shops altogether. Thankfully, they are now back in, in large numbers and every price range.

What will a blender do? It will make very light work of blending soups to a good, smooth, uniform texture – and it can happily cope with as much as 1¾ pints (1 litre) of liquid at a time. This, for me, is its prime function. What else can blenders do? Well, food processors are not always good at blending small quantities, so if you want a small amount of mayonnaise, hollandaise, breadcrumbs, pesto or anything else that needs brief blending, you may find a blender does a better job.

What it *doesn't* do is grate or chop; it pulverises. So herbs, for instance, just get mashed to a pulp, which is okay for pesto but not other recipes. (In this respect, *liquidiser* is probably a more accurate term than blender because it pulverises ingredients almost to a liquid.)

Full-blown blender or hand-held version? With the hand-held blender you have to do a little more work. In the goblet of a full-blown blender, ingredients are pulverised in seconds at the press of a button, though some may find the bother of washing the goblet a chore (even if they are dishwasher-proof nowadays). With a hand-held version, you have to manipulate it into the corners of bowls and pans to make sure the blades are reaching all the parts they need to. Which you use is a matter of personal choice. Indeed, if you don't really enjoy cooking (particularly making and eating home-made soup), you may not need a blender at all. But I feel a serious cook will always appreciate having both a blender *and* a food processor because, together, they provide a useful service in so many different areas of cooking.

Slow-Cooked Celery and Celeriac Soup

Because the vegetables are very slowly cooked, this soup has lots of lovely flavour, and it's quite satisfying and filling, particularly with some Celeriac and Lancashire Cheese Bread (see opposite).

Serves 6

1 lb (450 g) celery stalks (weight after trimming), leaves reserved
1 lb (450 g) celeriac (weight after peeling)
1 medium onion, peeled
2½ pints (1.5 litres) hot stock made with Marigold Swiss vegetable bouillon powder
3 bay leaves
salt and freshly milled black pepper

To garnish:

6 rounded teaspoons natural yoghurt (or crème fraîche)
2 teaspoons celery salt
a few celery leaves

You will also need a blender, and a lidded, flameproof casserole with a capacity of 6 pints (3.5 litres).

Pre-heat the oven to gas mark 1, 275°F (140°C).

Just a word first about preparing the vegetables. You need to use a potato peeler to pare off any really stringy bits from the outside stalks of the celery. The nice thing is that the outside stalks are fine for soups – so if you're using a whole head of celery, once you've weighed out the amount you need, you can keep the tender inside stalks for munching on. Peeling the celeriac will mean you lose quite a bit of the outside, as it's always very fibrous. Once that's done, weigh it and cut it into large chunks. The celery should also be cut into large chunks, and the same with the onion.

All you do now is pop the whole lot into the casserole, then add the stock and bay leaves, along with some salt and freshly milled black pepper. Bring it all up to simmering point on the hob, then put the lid on and transfer it to the oven to simmer very gently and slowly for 3 hours. After that, remove the bay leaves, allow the soup to cool a little, then blend it in batches until smooth. (A large bowl to put each batch in is helpful here.)

Then, return the soup to the casserole and bring it back to a gentle simmer, tasting to check the seasoning before serving. Serve in hot bowls with the yoghurt (or crème fraîche) spooned on top and the celery salt sprinkled over, garnished with a few celery leaves.

Celeriac and Lancashire Cheese Bread

This is yet another version of one of my most favourite and blissfully easy breads (see Goats' Cheese, Onion and Potato Bread with Thyme, in Book One), which is crunchy and crusty on the outside and soft and squidgy within.

All you do is sift the flour into a large mixing bowl, add the spring onions, two-thirds of the crumbled cheese, the cayenne pepper and the salt. Then, using the coarse side of a grater, grate in the celeriac as well.

Now give everything a really good mix. Beat the egg and milk together and, using a palette knife to mix, gradually add it all to the mixture until you have a loose, rough dough.

Now transfer it to the baking tray and, still keeping the rough texture, shape it into a round with your hands. Next, lightly press the rest of the cheese over the surface, sprinkle with a little flour and bake the bread on the middle shelf of the oven for 45-50 minutes, or until golden brown.

Cool on a wire rack and eat as fresh as possible. This is lovely served still warm, and if you have any left over, it's really good toasted.

Serves 6

6 oz (175 g) celeriac (weight after peeling)
4 oz (110 g) Lancashire cheese, roughly crumbled into ½ inch (1 cm) pieces
6 oz (175 g) self-raising flour, plus a little extra for the top of the loaf
4 spring onions, finely chopped, including the green parts
⅛ teaspoon cayenne pepper
1 large egg
2 tablespoons milk
1 teaspoon salt

You will also need a small baking tray, very well greased.

Pre-heat the oven to gas mark 5, 375°F (190°C).

Carrot and Artichoke Soup

This is one of my most favourite soups ever. Firstly, it has an extremely rich, beautiful colour – almost saffron-like, I would say. And secondly, the combination is so unique, people can never quite guess what it is. Jerusalem artichokes don't look user-friendly, but once you've cut off and discarded all the knobbly bits, the flavour is quite outstanding.

Serves 6-8

1 lb (450 g) carrots
1 lb 8 oz (700 g) Jerusalem artichokes
(weight before peeling)
3 celery stalks
3 oz (75 g) butter
1 medium onion, peeled and
roughly chopped
2½ pints (1.5 litres) hot stock made
with Marigold Swiss vegetable
bouillon powder
salt and freshly milled black pepper

To garnish:
6-8 teaspoons crème fraîche
6-8 leaves fresh flat-leaf parsley

You will also need a blender, and a large saucepan with a capacity of about 6 pints (3.5 litres).

Start by peeling and de-knobbling the artichokes and, as you peel them, cut them into rough chunks and place them in a bowl of cold, salted water to prevent them from discolouring. Then scrape the carrots and slice them into largish chunks. Next, use a potato peeler to pare off any stringy bits from the celery and then roughly chop it.

Now melt the butter in the saucepan and soften the onion and celery in it for 5 minutes, keeping the heat fairly low. Then drain the artichokes and add them to the pan, along with the carrots. Add some salt and, keeping the heat very low, put a lid on and let the vegetables sweat for 10 minutes to release their juices.

After that, pour in the stock, stir well, put the lid back on and simmer very gently for a further 20 minutes, or until the vegetables are soft. Now allow the soup to cool a little, then blend it in batches. (A large bowl to put each batch in is helpful here.) Taste to check the seasoning and re-heat the soup very gently until it just comes to simmering point. Serve it in hot bowls, garnishing each one with a swirl of crème fraîche and a few leaves of parsley.

Jerusalem artichokes, far left; Carrot and Artichoke Soup, garnished with crème fraîche and flat-leaf parsley, left.

Ajo Blanco – Chilled Almond Soup

My friend Neville, who has a house in Andalusia surrounded by almond trees, gave me this supremely wonderful recipe for Chilled Almond Soup, generously laced with garlic, that is made by the locals who live there. You can make it up to five days ahead – as Neville says, it goes on improving in flavour.

First you need to blanch the almonds. To do this, place them in a bowl, pour in enough boiling water to cover and leave them aside for 3-4 minutes. Then drain them in a colander and simply squeeze the nuts out of their skins into the bowl.

After that, put the almonds in the blender and pour in the olive oil. (The oil should just cover the almonds – if it doesn't, add a little more.) Then, add the peeled garlic, vinegar and salt and liquidize until everything is smooth. Now, with the motor still running, slowly add the cold water. Pour the soup into a large bowl and if it seems too thick, add a little more water. Then cover the bowl with clingfilm and keep it well chilled until you're ready to serve.

Just before serving, stir in the ice cubes and ladle the soup into the chilled bowls. Garnish with the grapes and apple slices.

Serves 4

7 oz (200 g) unblanched almonds (preferably Spanish almonds – never ready-blanched for this recipe)
7 fl oz (200 ml) Spanish olive oil
3 cloves garlic, peeled
1 dessertspoon sherry vinegar
about 12 fl oz (340 ml) cold water
2 teaspoons salt, or more, to taste

To serve:
8 ice cubes
4 oz (110 g) black grapes, deseeded and halved
1 dessert apple, peeled, cored and thinly sliced

You will also need a blender and four chilled soup bowls.

Breadmaker

I went to great pains to explain the principles of breadmaking in Book One, and I do still feel that it can be a very pleasurable, sometimes therapeutic experience. I also feel it is a very important part of learning how to cook. Having said that, the advent of the automatic breadmaking machine has added a very special experience to day-to-day living. It's quite simply an outstanding invention, almost miraculous, when you think that a freshly baked, crusty, full-flavoured loaf can be delivered to you warm from baking after just a simple assembly of ingredients and the push of a button. Even with your pressured, busy life, your house can be filled with that unique aroma of yeasty earthiness and goodness. That simple pleasure alone can raise your life experience to another level. (If you have any doubts, just think of all that tacky, spongy stuff that comes out of factories in the name of bread.)

Your breadmaker will not only deliver you a finished loaf, you can, alternatively, just use it to do all the hard work of mixing and kneading and let it deliver just the dough, which you can then make into pizzas, or shape into rolls or plaits, and so, enjoy the fun bits of breadmaking.

Breadmaker rules: There are, of course, rules that must be obeyed: Breadmakers are not flexible – they do what they do. Because of this, *they* rule, not you, so you can't be casual about it and not follow the manual precisely. In fact, once you get to know the ropes, you will begin to use it on automatic pilot, without even thinking about it. To familiarise yourself with the process, it's best to start with the manufacturer's own recipes, then move on to others (including mine). The most important rule of all is to add the ingredients in the correct order according to the manual – that one is not negotiable.

What's going on in there? Of course, it's like putting a cake in the oven: the suspense is killing you and you're dying to know what's going on. Well, it's okay during the mixing to lift the lid and have a peek – in fact, it's better if you *do* after about 10 minutes, as it might need a bit more flour if the mixture is too soft, or a bit more water if it's too stiff. After that, when the dough is rising and baking, peeping is strictly not allowed, as it can drastically affect the temperature and spoil everything.

Flour and yeast: The good thing about a breadmaker is producing bread with no additives and from the best-quality flours. (I've also discovered that Carrs Flour Mills – see page 235 – the clever people who invented sauce flour to prevent lumps in sauces, have developed a range of high-quality mixes specifically designed to be used in breadmakers, which come complete with their own sachet of yeast.) There is also a special powdered yeast suitable for use in machines.

Any snags? Yes, if you don't follow the rules! Also, bread doesn't like extremes of temperature, which can kill the yeast, so ingredients need to be at room temperature before you start. They must all be weighed accurately, too, so if you're not the weighing type, don't buy a breadmaker. Lastly, if you're going to leave the machine on a timer, when you place the ingredients in, make sure the yeast is not in contact with the liquid.

To sum up, I think breadmakers are great – the natural flavour of wheat in freshly baked bread with a crisp, crunchy crust is one of life's simplest and best pleasures. Add to that some creamy Normandy butter and home-made preserves (see page 102) and, believe me, eating doesn't come much better.

Pitta Bread

Home-made pitta bread is such a treat, and with a breadmaker to make the initial dough, it's not a lot of bother. I love the way they puff up and become hollow.

Makes 12

1 lb 2 oz (500 g) strong white bread flour, plus 2 tablespoons for dusting
2 teaspoons easy-blend dried yeast
1 oz (25 g) butter, at room temperature, plus a little extra for greasing
11 fl oz (310 ml) water
1½ teaspoons salt

You will also need a breadmaker, and a baking tray measuring 11 x 16 inches (28 x 40 cm), lightly greased.

To make the dough, tip all the ingredients into the breadmaker in the order stated in your manual. Then set the machine to the dough only setting (as the pittas are going to be baked in the oven). Now simply press start and let the machine do all the work.

When you are ready to bake the pittas, pre-heat the oven to gas mark 7, 425°F (220°C). Then transfer the dough from the breadmaker to a flat, lightly floured surface, divide it into 12 equal portions and roll out three of them to oval shapes measuring roughly 4 x 8 inches (10 x 20 cm), covering the remaining dough with a clean tea cloth. Dust the tops lightly with flour and place them on the baking tray. Now pop them into the oven, on a high shelf, and bake them for 8-10 minutes, or until they have become golden and puffy.

Meanwhile, prepare the next three portions and when the first ones are ready, remove them from the oven and wrap them in another tea cloth. (If they're allowed to cool without this, they get too crisp, and a pitta should be soft, not crunchy.) Now just carry on cooking and wrapping the rest of the pittas. It's nice to serve them fresh from the oven with Hummus (page 78) or Tunisian Aubergine Salad (see Book Two), or, if you're making them in advance, warm them through briefly in the oven before serving.

Filled Focaccia with Ham and Melted Fontina

I suppose I would describe this as a kind of hot, home-made sandwich. Lovely to serve straight from the oven for lunch. We've used ham, cheese and sage here, but any kind of filling at all would be fine, including vegetables such as mushrooms or preserved artichokes, or salami – the permutations are endless.

Serves 4

For the dough:
9 oz (250 g) strong white bread flour, plus a little extra for dusting
1 teaspoon easy-blend dried yeast
5 fl oz (150 ml) water
1 dessertspoon olive oil, plus a little extra for greasing
1 teaspoon salt

For the filling:
6 oz (175 g) sliced Parma ham
12 oz (350 g) Fontina (or Gruyère)
3 tablespoons chopped fresh sage leaves
freshly milled black pepper

For the top:
15 small sprigs fresh rosemary
2 tablespoons olive oil
1 teaspoon sea salt

You will also need a breadmaker, and a baking tray measuring 11 x 16 inches (28 x 40 cm), well greased (or a pizza baking stone).

Pop the ingredients for the dough into the breadmaker in the order your manual instructs. Set it to the dough only setting (as the focaccia is going to be baked in the oven) and press the start button.

Meanwhile, towards the end of the time, prepare the filling ingredients, separating the slices of ham and cutting the cheese into thin slices. When the dough is ready, remove it from the machine, turn it out on to a flat, lightly floured surface, divide it into two and then roll out one half to form a rough, rounded rectangle about 11 x 8 inches (28 x 20 cm).

Then place it on the baking tray (or pizza stone) and arrange the slices of ham on top, making sure they go right up to the edge. Follow this with the cheese, right up to the edge again, then scatter over the sage. Now give it a good seasoning of freshly milled black pepper. Then roll out the remaining dough, lay it on top of the first, pinching the edges together all the way round to completely enclose the filling. Now cover it with a clean tea cloth and leave it to puff up again for about 30 minutes. Meanwhile, pre-heat the oven to gas mark 6, 400°F (200°C).

When the dough is ready, make 15 little dimples in it with your finger and press in the sprigs of rosemary. Finally, drizzle over the olive oil and sprinkle with the salt. Bake for 20-25 minutes, or until the dough is crisp and golden. Serve the focaccia, cut into squares or wedges, straight from the oven.

Poppy and Sesame Seed Rolls

This is a very rich dough – so good, in fact, you can eat these buttery-flavoured rolls on their own, without any extra butter.

First of all, put the breadmaker to work by placing all the ingredients for the dough into it in the order your manual instructs. (If it seems like a lot of butter, don't worry, it will all work perfectly well.) Now set it to the dough only setting (as the rolls are going to be baked in the oven), press the start button and let the machine do all the work.

When the dough is ready, turn it out on to a flat, lightly floured work surface and knead and shape it into roughly an 8 inch (20 cm) square.

Now brush the top of the dough with the beaten egg. Next, combine the poppy and sesame seeds in a small bowl and sprinkle them evenly over the top of the dough. After that, take a large, sharp knife and cut the dough into 16 squares, roughly measuring 2 inches (5 cm). Don't worry about getting perfect shapes – they can be quite haphazard.

Now transfer them to the baking tray, leaving a space between each one, as they will prove and rise before baking. Leave them for about 30 minutes. Meanwhile, pre-heat the oven to gas mark 5, 375°F (190°C).

After that bake the rolls on the centre shelf of the oven for 25-30 minutes, or until they're crisp and golden brown. If you're making them in advance, warm them through briefly in the oven before serving.

Makes 16
For the dough:
1 lb 2 oz (500 g) strong white bread flour, plus a little extra for dusting
2 teaspoons easy-blend dried yeast
1 teaspoon golden caster sugar
4 oz (110 g) butter, at room temperature, plus a little extra for greasing
11 fl oz (310 ml) water
1½ teaspoons salt

For the topping:
1 tablespoon poppy seeds
1 tablespoon sesame seeds
1 large egg, beaten

You will also need a breadmaker, and a baking tray measuring 11 x 16 inches (28 x 40 cm), well greased.

Blowtorch

Way back in the 1960s, when Elizabeth David first had her own kitchen shop, I remember being there when a customer was buying a salamander – a heavy, round iron weight on the end of a steel rod. The idea behind it was that if you heated it until it was red hot and then placed it over the sugar surface of a crème brûlée, it would instantly caramelise it (the point being to bypass the British domestic grill, with all its vagaries and unreliability). Mrs David suggested to the said lady (and me, as well, because I couldn't resist buying one, too) that we should practise with ramekins filled with tinned rice pudding first, so as not to waste gallons of cream and eggs. It turned out to be sound advice, as I got through several tins of rice pudding without a single success.

Thus, the art of acquiring that thin, glass-like coating of caramel eluded me. British grills, after all those years, are *still* universally unreliable: until recently, it seemed the only answer was to make up a caramel and pour it on top of the set custard (see Book Two). Then along came the answer and, when the chef's blowtorch first hit the kitchen shops, it was a must-have for all who wanted to cook.

However, the early consignments were not quite the ticket – too faint-hearted by half – so you would spend absolutely ages just getting one ramekin caramelised. Next stop, DIY stores – why not get the genuine article and really give your brûlée a blast? But that was not the answer either, because the heat was too fierce, and I was envisaging hundreds of firefighters up and down the country taking me to task for recommending their use!

But, at last, a great step for mankind: there is now a blowtorch that does the job perfectly. It is self-igniting and makes short shrift of changing sugar into caramel (see Alain's Passion Fruit Brûlée, opposite, and Summer-Fruit Brûlée on page 60). It does a few other jobs as well, such as helping unmould a jelly, skinning tomatoes and giving a smoky, charred taste to aubergines. It is now a standard item in *How To Cook*.

Alain's Passion Fruit Brûlée

My thanks to Alain Benech, our very French chef at the football club, whom I persuaded to part with his delicious recipe for you all to make. Whenever it goes on the menu, it's very popular and always sells out.

Begin by cutting the passion fruit in half and, using a teaspoon, scoop the fruit and seeds out into a large, deep mixing bowl. Then add the egg yolks and 3 oz (75 g) of the sugar to the bowl and, using an electric hand whisk on a high speed, whiz all the ingredients together for about 5 minutes, or until the mixture is frothy and pale in colour. Meanwhile, heat the cream and milk in a saucepan over a medium heat, whisking now and then, until hot but do not boil.

Now, with the whisk on a slow speed, add the hot cream into the mixture, keeping the whisk running as you do so. Then strain the custard through a sieve into a large jug, discarding the passion fruit seeds.

Next, you need to put the ramekins into the roasting tin and fill them with the mixture. Now fill the tin with boiling water from the kettle to about halfway up the sides of the ramekins and place it on the centre shelf of the oven. Let the puddings cook gently for 40 minutes. They are ready when the custard is set but still wobbles when you move them gently. At this point, remove them from the oven and allow them to cool, then cover them with clingfilm and chill them in the fridge for about 2 hours, or, preferably, overnight.

After that, sprinkle each ramekin evenly with some of the remaining 2 oz (50 g) of sugar, dividing it equally. Then very lightly spray the surface with water, using the spray bottle. (This helps melt the sugar, speeding up the caramelising process.) Now use the blowtorch to melt and caramelise the sugar. To do this, hold it over each ramekin, aiming the tip of the flame at the sugar – it will immediately begin to bubble and melt, and soon turn to a golden caramel. As soon as the sugar has reached a dark brown colour, move on to the next one and continue until they've all got a lovely glazed brown surface. It will take about 10 minutes in all. After that, allow to cool before serving.

Serves 8
6 large passion fruit (about 9 fl oz/ 250 ml pulp)
14 fl oz (400 ml) double cream
2 fl oz (55 ml) milk
7 large egg yolks
5 oz (150 g) golden caster sugar

You will also need eight 1½ inch (4 cm) deep ramekins with a base diameter of 3 inches (7.5 cm) (or eight similar-sized heatproof glass bowls); a large roasting tin; a plastic spray bottle; and a chef's blowtorch.

Pre-heat the oven to gas mark 2, 300°F (150°C).

Summer-Fruit Brûlée

Here is another brûlée recipe. If you have invested in a chef's blowtorch, you'll be able to get lots of that lovely, thin, caramelised crust.

Serves 6
1 lb 8 oz (700 g) soft fruits
(including one or more of the following: raspberries, redcurrants, loganberries, blackberries and blackcurrants)
4 oz (110 g) golden caster sugar
10 fl oz (275 ml) whipping cream
10½ oz (295 g) Greek yoghurt
6 oz (175 g) demerara sugar

You will also need a serving dish with a base measurement of 10 x 6½ inches (25.5 x 16 cm), 2 inches (5 cm) deep, a plastic spray bottle and a chef's blowtorch.

First pick over the fruit and place it in a large saucepan (or flameproof casserole). Sprinkle it with the caster sugar and then put the pan (or casserole) over a gentle heat for 3-5 minutes, or until the sugar melts and the juices begin to run, but try not to over-stir, or the fruit will break down to a mush. After that, transfer the fruit to the serving dish with a slotted spoon and allow it to get quite cold. Now whip the cream until thick, fold it into the yoghurt and spread this mixture all over the fruit, taking it right up to the edges of the dish to seal the fruit underneath. Then cover with clingfilm and chill in the fridge for at least 2 hours.

About 2 hours before you want to serve the brûlée, spread the surface thickly and evenly with the demerara sugar, then spray it very lightly with water, using the spray bottle. (This helps melt the sugar and speeds up the caramelising process.) Now use the blowtorch to caramelise the sugar on top. To do this, hold it over the dish, aiming the tip of the flame at the sugar – it will immediately begin to bubble and melt and soon turn to a golden caramel. As soon as that area has reached a dark brown colour, move the blowtorch and continue to caramelise the sugar all over the top. Because the surface is large, it will take about 10 minutes.

Now leave the brûlée to cool, then pop it back in the fridge, uncovered, where the sugar will form a crusty, crunchy surface – wonderful!

Two luxury items

These last two gadgets – an ice-cream maker and an espresso coffee machine (see page 68) – are expensive, unashamed luxuries that are by no means essential. But, if you're anticipating a wedding or having a special birthday, you might like to consider putting them on your list, or treating yourself at some stage in your life when, after years of hard work in the kitchen, you think you deserve them.

Ice-cream maker

It can't be denied that there are now some very good commercially made ice creams available. But that said, it's very satisfying to make your own, to use the purest and best ingredients and to spoil your family and friends with the results.

Making ice cream before the days of refrigeration was honestly a trial, what with hand-cranked churns, packs of ice and so on. Even with modern freezers it's something of a palaver: timing it, hoicking it out, mixing it, then repeating the whole performance over again – not to mention the risks of over- or under-freezing. Yet again, cooks have been truly blessed: there are now fully automatic ice-cream makers with their own in-built freezing and churning unit. So, real home-made ice creams can be made from start to finish in just 30 minutes. What's more, if you like a soft consistency (as I sometimes do) you can serve them straightaway without even putting them in the freezer.

How does it work? Basically, all you need to do is switch the machine on about 10 minutes before you want to use it (or as instructed in your manual) – rather like pre-heating the oven in reverse. (It takes time for the machine to reach the right freezing temperature.) While that's happening, you make up your mixture and just pour it into the container. Then, when you switch on, the motorised paddles automatically churn the ice cream as it freezes, breaking down the ice crystals and producing a velvety-smooth texture and just the right consistency. Because you're in charge of the ingredients, you are also assured of the best possible flavour. Finally, it's as convenient to clean as it is to operate: the removable components are dishwasher-proof or very easy to rinse by hand. Couldn't be simpler.

Any drawbacks? Home-made ice cream is best eaten within a week of being made, but since you can make it as and when you need it in just a few minutes, I don't see this as a problem. Ideally, the machine should be kept out and not transferred in and out of cupboards – it doesn't like being shifted about because it unsettles the intricacies of the freezing unit. So, the only real drawback is one of space. If you have the room and are happy to keep it out on the counter top, you'll get enormous pleasure out of making and eating real ice cream, knowing it doesn't contain additives, emulsifiers, flavourings, stabilisers or preservatives. It also allows you to experiment with so many different recipes – if there's a glut of raspberries, you can make raspberry ice cream, if it's the Seville orange season you can make a sorbet… there's a whole world of ice creams, sorbets and parfaits out there just waiting for you to try them.

Note: If you don't have an ice-cream maker, you can still make ice cream. After you have made up your mixture, transfer it to a lidded plastic box and put it in the coldest part of the freezer for two hours, or until the contents become firm at the edges. At this stage, empty out the box into a mixing bowl and whisk the ice cream with an electric hand whisk to break down the ice crystals. Return the box to the freezer and freeze for another two hours, then repeat the whisking process. Refreeze the ice cream (if making a sorbet that contains a generous quantity of alcohol, as on page 65, freeze overnight) until 30-45 minutes before you want to serve it, at which time you should transfer it to the fridge to soften.

Zabaglione Ice Cream with Biscotti

Once you've mastered the art of Zabaglione on page 40, you've got the perfect base for a brilliant ice cream, and if you fold in some crushed biscotti (hard-baked, brittle biscuits) it all gets very Italian and lovely. It's quite nice to serve some whole biscotti to go with it.

Serves 4
For the zabaglione:
4 large egg yolks
2 oz (50 g) golden caster sugar
2½ fl oz (65 ml) Marsala

For the ice cream:
10 fl oz (275 ml) double cream
3 oz (75 g) almond biscotti, crushed
to crumbs, plus extra biscuits to serve

You will also need an ice-cream maker (pre-frozen according to the manufacturer's instructions), and a lidded plastic box measuring 7 x 5½ x 2½ inches (18 x 14 x 6 cm).
(If you don't have an ice-cream maker, instructions for making ice cream without one are on page 63.)

Begin by whipping the cream to the 'floppy' stage and then transfer to the fridge to chill. Now make the Zabaglione, as described on page 40. Next, remove the bowl from the heat, cover and allow the mixture to cool completely, which will take about 30 minutes.

When the mixture is absolutely cold, gently stir, and fold in the double cream. Then pour the mixture into the ice-cream maker and freeze-churn for 20-30 minutes until the ice cream is soft-set.

Now transfer the mixture to a bowl and stir in the biscotti crumbs. Serve straightaway, or freeze in the plastic box for 1-2 hours until firm, transferring to the fridge 30 minutes before serving to allow the ice cream to soften and become easy to scoop.

Note: This recipe contains partially cooked eggs.

Spike's Apple Sorbet

Spike is the nickname of our friend Galton Blackiston, who is the owner and chef of the Michelin-starred country-house hotel Morston Hall in Norfolk. He's a fanatical Norwich City supporter, so we always end our meals there with lots of football tales until the early hours. He has generously allowed me to adapt his brilliant apple sorbet recipe.

First of all, chop the apples into ½ inch (1 cm) cubes and place them in a food processor, along with the lime juice, membrillo (or jam), sugar and Calvados, and process everything to a fine purée. Now set a large, fine nylon sieve over an equally large bowl and pour the puréed mixture through it, pushing it with the back of a spoon to get as much apple pulp through as possible. All that should be left in the sieve are the tiny flecks of apple peel, which can be discarded.

Now you need to be fairly swift or the apple will discolour. Pour the mixture into the ice-cream maker and freeze-churn. This may take a little longer than usual, due to the generous quantity of alcohol. Either serve straightaway or spoon it into the plastic box and freeze for later. From the freezer, it will need 20 minutes in the fridge to soften before serving.

Serves 6
8 Granny Smith apples, washed and cored (no need to peel)
juice 4 limes
4 oz (110 g) membrillo (quince paste) or apricot jam
4 oz (110 g) golden caster sugar
4 fl oz (120 ml) Calvados

You will also need an ice-cream maker (pre-frozen according to the manufacturer's instructions), and a lidded plastic box with a base measurement of 8 x 5 x 2 inches (20 x 13 x 5 cm).
(If you don't have an ice-cream maker, instructions for making ice cream without one are on page 63.)

Preserved Ginger Ice Cream

This is one of the creamiest ice creams I know, and it provides a perfectly luscious backdrop to the strong, assertive flavours of stem ginger. Serve in some crisp Molasses Brandy Snap Baskets (see opposite), with a little of the ginger syrup poured over – a great combination.

Serves 4-6

4 pieces preserved stem ginger, chopped into ¼ inch (5 mm) cubes
2 tablespoons stem ginger syrup
10 fl oz (275 ml) double cream
10 fl oz (275 ml) single cream
4 large egg yolks
1 oz (25 g) golden caster sugar
2 slightly rounded teaspoons cornflour
3-4 drops pure vanilla extract

To garnish:
2 pieces preserved stem ginger, chopped
a little extra stem ginger syrup

You will also need an ice-cream maker (pre-frozen according to the manufacturer's instructions), and a lidded plastic box measuring 7 x 5½ x 2½ inches (18 x 14 x 6 cm). (If you don't have an ice-cream maker, instructions for making ice cream without one are on page 63.)

First of all, whip the double cream until it reaches the 'floppy' stage but isn't too thick, then pop it into the fridge to chill.

Now make a custard – first pour the single cream into a saucepan, then carefully heat it to just below boiling point. Meanwhile, beat together the egg yolks, sugar and cornflour in a bowl until absolutely smooth.

Next, pour the hot cream on to this mixture, whisking as you pour. Now return the custard to the pan and continue to whisk it over a medium heat until it has thickened and come up to boiling point again. (Ignore any curdled appearance, which may come about if you don't keep whisking and have the heat too high. The cornflour will stabilise it, so don't worry – it will regain its smoothness when cooled and whisked.)

Now rinse the bowl and pour the custard into it. Then place it in another, larger bowl of cold water, with a few ice cubes, stirring it now and then until absolutely cold. Next, fold into the custard the chilled, whipped cream, ginger syrup and vanilla extract. Now pour the whole lot into the ice-cream maker and freeze-churn for 20-30 minutes until the ice cream is soft-set. Quickly fold in the chopped stem ginger, then spoon it into the plastic box and freeze until firm, which will take 1-2 hours.

Transfer the ice cream to the fridge 45 minutes before serving to allow it to soften and become easy to scoop. Garnish with the stem ginger and serve with a little of the syrup poured over.

Serve the Preserved Ginger Ice Cream in the Molasses Brandy Snap Baskets, with a little stem ginger syrup poured over.

Molasses Brandy Snap Baskets

I think these are really fun to make, and the crunchy caramel flavour is the perfect partner to any ice cream – particularly Preserved Ginger Ice Cream (see opposite).

Measuring golden syrup is a sticky business, and the easiest way to deal with it is to first weigh out the sugar and then weigh the golden syrup on top, so it sticks to the sugar and not the scale pan. Next, put the whole lot into a medium-sized, heavy-based saucepan, together with the butter, and heat gently for about 5 minutes, or until all the sugar has dissolved, there are no granules left and the mixture is completely smooth. (The way to test this is by looking at some on the back of a spoon.) Then remove the pan from the heat and beat in the flour and ginger, followed by the brandy.

Now place 2 tablespoons of the mixture on to the lined baking tray, allowing space for them to spread as they cook to make two circles roughly 7 inches (18 cm) in diameter. Bake on the middle shelf for 7 minutes, keeping a close eye on them for the last 2 minutes' cooking time.

When they're ready, remove the tray from the oven and allow the brandy-snap circles to cool for a couple of minutes before lifting one from the tray and moulding it over the upturned, greased jam jar, pressing the edges out to get a frilly basket shape. If they get too cool to mould, don't worry about it – just pop them back in the oven for a minute and then try again. If you're unsure of yourself, have several goes at it – but it *is* easier than it sounds!

As soon as the first basket is ready – it only takes about a minute – place it on a cooling rack and quickly mould the second one. Then repeat the whole process in twos until they're all complete. The brandy snap baskets can be made several hours in advance and stored in an airtight tin.

To serve, place them on a plate and fill with a large scoop of ice cream. If it's the Preserved Ginger Ice Cream, pour a little ginger syrup over and decorate with a few pieces of chopped preserved ginger.

Makes 6
1 teaspoon brandy
2 oz (50 g) molasses sugar
1½ oz (40 g) golden syrup
2 oz (50 g) butter, plus a little extra for greasing
1½ oz (40 g) plain flour, sifted
¾ teaspoon ground ginger

You will also need a baking tray measuring 11 x 16 inches (28 x 40 cm), lined with silicone paper (parchment), and a jam jar with a base diameter of about 2 inches (5 cm), well-buttered.

Pre-heat the oven to gas mark 4, 350°F (180°C).

Mould the brandy-snap circles over an upturned, greased jam jar, pressing the edges to get a frilly shape.

Espresso coffee machine

Obviously, this is neither essential nor part of a *batterie de cuisine* for cooks, except that, if you're slaving away in the kitchen, you deserve a really good cup of coffee now and then. The machine I have offers unashamed luxury. You can choose espresso, regular black or cappuccino, and the coffee comes in neat little capsules with lots of blends to choose from. When you have made the coffee, you just throw the capsules out, which means no messy washing-up, no coffee grounds, no plungers that get stuck halfway. (In contrast, cleaning the plunger-type coffee-makers is a nightmare.)

Initially, this machine did seem quite expensive, particularly as the coffee has to be delivered. But, when I remember all the cold leftover coffee we used to throw away, I'm sure there is far less waste. The machine is easy to clean and has a transparent water chamber at the back that enables you to see quite clearly when it needs topping up. Because we live in a hard-water area, ours needed to be serviced after about a year and the company efficiently sent a special container to ship it back for servicing – so full marks for after-sales service. It is expensive, but when something really serves you well and gives so much pleasure to you and all those you serve coffee to, then, over a period of time, it's cheap at the price.

Vanilla Bean Ice Cream with Espresso

This is my long-standing, classic vanilla ice cream recipe, which I think is much improved of late, having incorporated a whole vanilla pod, with its speckly seeds, and crème fraîche, with its slightly acidic but very dairy flavour. However, it's also excellent if you replace the crème fraîche with double cream. I also love it made with untreated Jersey cream, which I get from my local farmers' market.

First of all, you need to make the custard, so begin by splitting the vanilla pod lengthways and, using the end of a teaspoon, scoop out the seeds into a mixing bowl. Next, pour the single cream into a saucepan, add the pod and then carefully heat the cream up to just below boiling point. While that's happening, place the vanilla seeds, egg yolks, custard powder and sugar in a mixing bowl and whisk until absolutely smooth.

Next, pour the hot cream on to this mixture, discarding the pod, and whisking as you pour. Now return the custard to the pan and continue to whisk it over a medium heat until it has thickened and come up to boiling point again. (Ignore any curdled appearance, which may come about if you don't keep whisking and have the heat too high. The custard powder will stabilise it if you pour it into a bowl and whisk, and it will become quite smooth.)

When the custard is ready, place the bowl in another, larger bowl of cold water, with a few ice cubes, stirring it now and then until it's absolutely cold. Then fold the crème fraîche into the custard, pour the whole lot into the ice-cream maker and freeze-churn until the mixture is soft-set. If you prefer it set a little firmer, or you want to eat it later, freeze it in the plastic box for 1-2 hours until firm – but whenever you come to remove it from the freezer, transfer it to the fridge for 30 minutes to soften before serving. Then scoop it into heatproof glasses or serving bowls and pour some hot espresso over each one just before serving.

Note: Little thin Shortbread Biscuits (see page 31) are good with this ice cream.

Serves 6

1 vanilla pod
12 fl oz (340 ml) hot espresso coffee
10 fl oz (275 ml) single cream
4 large egg yolks
2 slightly rounded teaspoons custard powder
2 oz (50 g) golden caster sugar
10 fl oz (275 ml) crème fraîche

You will also need an ice-cream maker (pre-frozen according to the manufacturer's instructions); a lidded plastic box measuring 7 x 5½ x 2½ inches (18 x 14 x 6 cm); and six heatproof glasses (or serving bowls).
(If you don't have an ice-cream maker, instructions for making ice cream without one are on page 63.)

3

How to cook pulses

Pulses have somehow managed
to re-invent themselves. Whereas
once they were discounted
and ridiculed as being food fit
only for the poor, now they've
become chic, occupying premier
position on the shelves of the
very smartest food shops, and
firmly re-established as a vital part
of new-age cooking and eating.

The kind of dismissive comments we used to hear about pulses included describing the poorest of meals as a 'beanfeast', and someone having nothing at all as 'not having a bean'. The reason for this is that what we call first-class protein – meat, fish, eggs, cheese and so on – is usually expensive, while pulses are cheap. Nonetheless, they are highly nutritious and therefore, the next best thing. In fact, if you combine them with grains (as in the Creole dish of rice and red beans), what you get is something nutritionally equal to first-class protein. Our most popular snack in Britain, beans on toast, fulfils all the criteria of a highly nutritious meal. I think this reincarnation of pulses is for the most part due to the rise of vegetarianism, and along the way, meat-eaters, too, have come to appreciate pulses, with or without meat.

What are pulses?

It is the generic term for a whole family of fresh, dried or canned vegetables – beans, peas and lentils – a gift of nature, providing an abundance of produce through the summer to last the winter months. After harvesting, the fresh vegetables are dried and stored, and to cook them (with the exception of lentils and split peas), they have to be pre-soaked and reconstituted.

What's good about them? First of all, apart from their nutritional value, what I like about them is that they're always sitting in my cupboard offering me plenty of choice and variety. No time to shop for vegetables? Just cook some pulses. Secondly, pulses collectively have one very great virtue – an enormous capacity to absorb other flavours. They may have little to offer plain-boiled but, magically, when you marry them with other, stronger flavours, they are transformed. A chilli con carne, for instance, needs very little meat because the red kidney beans absorb the beefy flavour, making a small amount go a very long way.

What's not good? With the exception of lentils and split peas, pulses have to be pre-soaked and need quite long cooking, so you have to think ahead. You can be spontaneous with a bag of frozen peas, but, with pulses, you do need to plan. It's not a big deal, though: it just means popping them into cold water before you go to bed at night or, alternatively, quick-soaking them (see opposite). The only other thing you have to consider is how old they are. A year on your shelf is their maximum – after that, throw them out because they will never soften during the cooking.

What about tinned pulses? Yes, you *can* be spontaneous with tinned pulses, but, with a couple of exceptions, I'm against them, because they're simply inferior – often over-sweet and slimy. At a pinch, they can be used in short-cut, no-cooking dishes, but for food lovers, they do need to be freshly cooked. The two exceptions to this are tinned marrowfat peas and flageolets, which I think respond best to the canning process.

What about soaking? All pulses need to be washed under cold, running water and any broken ones or alien bits discarded. Then, with the exception of lentils and split peas, they need soaking. If it is convenient, soak them overnight in 4 pints (2.25 litres) of cold water per 8 oz (225 g). If you need them today and haven't the time for this, simply bring them up to the boil (using the same quantity of water), boil for 10 minutes and leave them to soak for two hours.

If you are soaking pulses overnight, some, such as kidney beans, still need 10 minutes' fast-boiling to purify them before cooking. This is because they sometimes contain toxins in their outer skins, which are destroyed by the fast-boiling.

Cooking pulses

Being tough and hard, pulses need long, slow cooking (and this long, slow marrying with other flavours is what they're particularly good at), but the key is *careful* cooking – over-cooking results in their skins splitting and the pulses disintegrating. It used to be said that salt should not be added during cooking, as it encourages liquid out of and not into dried things, but I believe this was the legacy of pulses being kept for too long (before we had date-stamping). Now I always add salt during the cooking as it really does give a better flavour. It may, in some cases, mean a little longer cooking, but it's worth it – salt never seems to be absorbed properly when added at the end. Lastly, don't forget pulses are great in salads and salsas – again, they absorb the flavours of the other ingredients and the dressings.

Varieties of pulses

With so many varieties from all round the world, it's not possible to include them all here, so what I've aimed to do is introduce you to those pulses most widely available in this country. Anyway, in most recipes you can ring the changes and experiment with other varieties that will need roughly the same treatment and cooking times. For instance, try using black beans in a chilli instead of red, or red beans in a soup in place of white.

Adzuki beans: These look like little, shiny red pills, with a white line running down one side. I have used them successfully in salads, but when I visited Japan, I was fascinated to discover they are used in sweet dishes, where they seem to have a texture and flavour similar to chestnuts. I was so impressed I brought back a recipe – Sesame Blancmange with Sweetened Compote of Adzuki Beans – that you'll find on page 93.

Black beans: Very good-lookers, these are shiny, ebony-black, kidney-shaped beans. They make a luscious, dark, velvety soup, but can be used in any kidney-bean recipe – I love spicy Black Bean Chilli (in the *Winter Collection*) with Avocado Salsa stirred in at the end.

Black-eyed beans: These are pale and creamy in colour, kidney-shaped with little black 'eyes'. I have made them into Mashed Black-Eyed Beancakes (also in the *Winter Collection*), popular in the Caribbean. They are also very much part of traditional cooking in the Deep South of America.

Top row, left to right: butter beans, black beans, chickpeas
Second row: marrowfat peas, green split peas, green lentils
Third row: yellow split peas, borlotti beans, kidney beans
Fourth row: Puy lentils, haricot beans, pinto beans
Fifth row: cannellini beans, red split lentils, judion beans
Sixth row: adzuki beans, flageolet beans, black-eyed beans

Borlotti beans: These are definitely the aristocrats of the bean world, both in looks and in flavour. They are grown in Italy and I would describe their appearance as pale pinky-beige, with dark red, marbled veins. They are not quite so widely available as some of the other varieties, but you can find the name of an Italian stockist on page 235. I have used them in Tuscan Bean and Pasta Soup with Rosemary on page 84.

Butter beans: Just coming back into their own, having suffered from being boiled dry and tasteless in the frugal canteen-cookery of my schooldays. However, put them into a slowly cooked, Old-Fashioned Shin of Beef Stew (see page 88) and they become something else altogether: fat, plump, mealy and full of meaty flavour. I also discovered them served in a salad in Paris, with lots of chopped shallots and flat-leaf parsley, in a wonderful garlicky vinaigrette. The best butter beans, if you can find them, are the Spanish judion beans (for a Spanish stockist, see page 235).

Cannellini beans: The upper-class version of the humble haricot (see below). These are so pretty – rather elongated and like pale, creamy, translucent porcelain. Lovers of Italian cooking will instantly recognise them in Tonno e Fagioli, the white bean and tuna fish salad (see Book Two). They have a great affinity with pork, bacon and Italian sausages, and the ability to soak up all their richness.

Chickpeas: These are definitely from the top drawer of the pulse family, with a firm texture that doesn't disintegrate, and a lovely nutty flavour. One of my all-time best soup recipes – Chickpea, Chilli and Coriander (in the *Winter Collection*) – is made with chickpeas, I have included them in a Moroccan Baked Chicken dish (also in the *Winter Collection*), and here I have used them in a Spiced Chickpea Cakes recipe (see page 86). Finally, I simply had to include Hummus in this chapter (see page 78), as home-made, it knocks the socks off anything out of a supermarket.

Flageolet beans: Beautiful to look at, these small, pastel green beans are actually under-developed cannellini beans, harvested while still young. They have their own distinctive yet delicate flavour and a smooth, silky texture. They are a wonderful match for lamb – either braised along with it, as in Lamb with Flageolets (in the *Winter Collection*), or cooked separately with onion, garlic and herbs, to serve alongside roast lamb.

Haricot beans: Fine in a can of baked beans, they are small and squat and the poorer cousin to the cannellini. I would stick with serving them on crisp, buttered toast and not choose them for cooking.

Lentils: The easiest of all the pulses, because they don't need pre-soaking. The tiny, French, greeny-black Puy lentils have far and away the best flavour and I always keep some in my store cupboard for when there's no time to shop for vegetables. They are excellent cooked with an onion first sweated in olive oil with rosemary or thyme, and simmered in red wine.

I love them equally in salads, and there's a recipe for Lentil Salsa on page 128. Then there are the green-brown lentils (with a hint of terracotta), which, although they don't have the depth of flavour of the Puy, are still excellent and can be used in exactly the same way. They're particularly good in soups or made into little cakes with vegetables, as in my recipe for Chilladas (in *The Illustrated Cookery Course*). The best recipe ever for these is the Lentil Sauce on page 79. Split orange lentils are really only good for soups, having very little intrinsic flavour, as their outer skins have been removed; I would therefore always recommend using whole lentils.

Dried peas: Can't tell you how much I love these. I love peas at all stages of their development: from the young and tender, to be eaten raw or lightly cooked, to older peas, braised with lettuce and onion, to our friends here – dried whole peas, and split peas, yellow and green. Let us salute here our famous mushy peas, the essential accompaniment to fish and chips in the north of England. In this chapter, I have revived another great northern dish, Pease Pudding, a thick, luscious combination of marrowfat peas and onions simmered alongside a Smoked Collar of Bacon (see page 80). Split peas of both varieties make extremely good soup, as they are still as flavoursome as whole dried peas, with the added advantage of not needing any soaking.

Pinto beans: Very pretty, cream-coloured beans with red veins, a staple food in Mexico – so I've used them here in a Mexican Chicken Chilli dish (see page 87). They can, in fact, be used in virtually any dish that calls for beans and, when borlottis are hard to find, I always use pintos instead.

Red kidney beans: A suitable grand finale to this list, they are a great favourite everywhere – but please, *not* out of tins, because they will be but pale shadows of the freshly cooked ones. They are the star turn in chilli con carne. What a shame that sublime combination of meat, chillies and red kidney beans has become so bastardised in restaurants the world over. Home-made, it provides me with one of my best pleasures in cooking – lifting the lid and catching a whiff of the simmering beans, with their own quite distinctive, seductive aroma.

Others: There are many more variations from around the world you might like to try. (The soaking/cooking methods are the same for most pulses.) Among these are Soy beans (best, I think, for soy sauce and not for cooking), Ful medames (small brown beans used in Middle Eastern cooking), and Brown beans (a larger version popular in Scandinavian cooking). Then there are Dried broad beans, dark brown and similar – though, in my opinion, not as good as – butter beans. And finally, Dhals: a whole array of various forms of lentils in their whole or split guises. Note: All the recipes from my previous books are also available on my website, www.deliaonline.com.

Braised Lamb Shanks with Cannellini Beans

This is delightfully simple as everything goes into one pot, no accompaniments are needed, and it provides a complete menu for two people. It is also very good with flageolet or borlotti beans to ring the changes.

Serves 2

2 lamb shanks (each weighing about
1 lb/450 g)
4 oz (110 g) dried cannellini beans,
pre-soaked and drained (see page 72)
4 medium-sized, ripe tomatoes
1 large stick celery
2 tablespoons olive oil
2 cloves garlic, chopped
1 large onion, peeled and cut into
eighths through the root
1 large carrot, peeled and chopped
into 2 inch (5 cm) chunks
15 fl oz (425 ml) red wine
1 fresh bay leaf
2 tablespoons fresh rosemary bruised
in a mortar, then chopped, plus 4
sprigs, to garnish
salt and freshly milled black pepper

You will also need a lidded, flameproof casserole with a capacity of 4 pints (2.25 litres).

Begin by skinning the tomatoes. Place them in a heatproof bowl and pour boiling water on to them. Leave them for exactly a minute, then remove them and slip off their skins (protecting your hands with a tea cloth if they are hot). Then chop them fairly roughly. Next, using a potato peeler, remove the worst of the stringy bits from the celery and cut it into 2 inch (5 cm) chunks. Now pre-heat the oven to gas mark 1, 275°F (140°C).

After that, you need to heat the oil in the casserole over a highish heat. Then, season the lamb shanks with salt and freshly milled black pepper and, when the oil is really hot, brown them on all sides, holding them at the bone end while protecting your hand again with the tea cloth, and turning them round in the hot oil.

When they're nicely browned, remove them to a plate and, keeping the heat high, add the celery, onion and carrots and brown them as well, turning and tossing them around for about 6 minutes. Now stir in the garlic, cook for one minute, then add the drained beans and give everything another good stir.

Next, add the tomatoes, wine, bay leaf, chopped rosemary and some seasoning. Then, finally, place the lamb shanks on top and when everything is beginning to simmer, cover with the lid and transfer the casserole to the oven to braise very slowly for 3 hours. Serve garnished with the sprigs of rosemary.

Hummus bi Tahina

Couldn't have a chapter on pulses without this famous favourite. Yes, I do know it's sold absolutely everywhere but let me tell you, this home-made version is way above anything you will have bought. It is also an essential accompaniment to our gorgeous Pitta Bread on page 54.

Serves 6
4 oz (110 g) dried chickpeas, pre-soaked (see page 72), then drained and the water discarded
5 fl oz (150 ml) tahina paste
juice 2 lemons
2 fat cloves garlic
4 tablespoons olive oil, plus a little extra for drizzling
cayenne pepper
black olives and Greek-style pickled chillis, to serve
salt

You will also need a blender.

To begin with, put the chickpeas in a medium-sized saucepan, cover them with fresh water and bring them to the boil, along with a pinch of salt. Then reduce the heat to low, cover and simmer gently for 1½-2 hours, or until they are tender.

Then, drain them, reserving the cooking liquid, and put them into a blender, together with the lemon juice, garlic, olive oil and 5 fl oz (150 ml) of the liquid. Switch on and blend, adding the tahina paste to the mixture as the blades revolve, stopping the blender every now and then to push the mixture down into the goblet. The consistency should be something like mayonnaise so, if you think it's too thick, add a little more of the cooking liquid. Then season to taste with cayenne pepper and salt.

Now place the hummus in a serving bowl and drizzle with olive oil. Serve with olives, pickled chillis and warm pitta breads.

Shaun Hill's Sautéed Scallops with Lentil Sauce

Everyone I know in the world of cooking and catering agrees unanimously that this is the best lentil recipe ever invented. Shaun Hill, one of Britain's most outstandingly gifted chefs, serves this in his restaurant, The Merchant House, in Ludlow, and he has generously allowed me to adapt it and use it here.

To cook the lentils for the sauce, place them in a saucepan with the stock and a pinch of salt and simmer gently with a lid on for 40-45 minutes, until they're really soft and beginning to break up. Then drain them, reserving the cooking liquid.

Now heat half the oil in the medium-sized frying pan over a medium heat, add the onion, garlic and ginger and fry until pale golden – about 8 minutes. Meanwhile, skin the tomatoes. To do this, place them in a heatproof bowl and pour boiling water on to them. Leave them for exactly a minute, then remove them, slip off their skins (protecting your hands with a cloth if they're hot) and finely chop them.

Next, remove the pan from the heat, add the cardamom seeds, stir for a few seconds, then add the tomatoes, two-thirds of the cooked lentils and all the cooking liquid. After that, whiz the whole lot to a purée in a food processor, then add the remaining lentils. All this can be done in advance.

When you are ready to finish the dish, re-heat the lentil purée, whisk in the butter, crème fraîche and lemon juice, and taste and season with salt and freshly milled black pepper. Finally, add the coriander and keep the lentil mixture warm while you cook the scallops.

To do this, heat the large frying pan over a high heat without adding any fat. Dry the scallops and corals with kitchen paper. When the pan is searing hot, lightly brush them on both sides with the remaining oil and season with salt and freshly milled black pepper.

Now add them to the pan and let them cook without moving for about one minute, until the underside is dark brown and caramelised, then use a small palette knife to flip them over. Continue to cook for 30 seconds on the other side, but no more. What you are aiming for is a golden, caramelised outside, with a soft and barely cooked inside. It's important to have your frying pan really hot to get the dish right – if the scallops boil or steam, they will lose the concentrated flavour needed to balance the sauce.

To serve, arrange the scallops on warmed serving plates or in clean scallop shells, then spoon over the lentil sauce and garnish with the sprigs of coriander.

Serves 6 as a starter
18 plump, fresh scallops, cleaned, with the corals attached
2 oz (50 g) green lentils (no need to soak), rinsed
10 fl oz (275 ml) hot stock made with Marigold Swiss vegetable bouillon powder
2 dessertspoons groundnut or other flavourless oil
½ medium onion, peeled and chopped
1 fat clove garlic, crushed
1 inch (2.5 cm) fresh root ginger, peeled and finely grated
2 large, ripe tomatoes
1 dessertspoon cardamom pods, seeds removed and husks discarded
2 oz (50 g) unsalted butter
1 tablespoon crème fraîche
juice ½ lemon
¾ oz (20 g) fresh coriander, chopped, plus 6 sprigs, to garnish
salt and freshly milled black pepper

You will also need one medium-sized and one large, heavy-based frying pan.

Smoked Collar of Bacon with Pease Pudding and Creamy Onion Mustard Sauce

Let me explain the appeal of this delightfully unfashionable, totally forgotten delicacy. First, collar of bacon has more flavour than the leaner, middle-cut gammon. Secondly, I'm sure many people have forgotten – or never actually tasted – dried marrowfat peas with their mealy texture and concentrated flavour. Then, when we add an onion and mustard sauce, the combination of the whole is utterly sublime. What you can do after boiling the bacon is reserve and freeze the stock to make the recipe called The London Particular – Green Split Pea Soup (see page 82).

Serves 6

1 smoked bacon collar joint (weighing about 3 lb/1.35 kg), all packaging and string removed
1 small onion, peeled and studded with a few cloves
2 fresh bay leaves
1 small carrot, peeled
6 black peppercorns

For the pease pudding:

6 oz (175 g) dried marrowfat peas, pre-soaked and drained (see page 72)
1 small onion, peeled and quartered
1 fresh bay leaf
1 sprig fresh thyme
1 oz (25 g) butter
1 large egg, beaten
whole nutmeg
salt and freshly milled black pepper

For the sauce:

1 large onion, peeled and finely chopped
1 rounded teaspoon mustard powder
1 rounded teaspoon wholegrain mustard
1½ oz (40 g) butter
1 oz (25 g) plain flour
6 fl oz (175 ml) milk
salt and freshly milled black pepper

You will also need a lidded, flameproof casserole with a capacity of 6 pints (3.5 litres), a 16 inch (40 cm) square piece of muslin, and some kitchen foil and string.

Start off by cooking the pease pudding. To do this, place the peas in a pan, pour in just enough fresh water to cover, then add the onion, bay leaf and thyme (but no salt). Bring it up to a gentle simmer, put the lid on and cook for about an hour, or until the skins split and the peas are tender – they will be having some more cooking so they don't need to be absolutely smashed.

Next, drain off the cooking water, discarding the thyme and bay leaf, then put the peas and the onion into a bowl and mash them with a large fork, along with the butter, beaten egg, a seasoning of salt and freshly milled black pepper and a few gratings of nutmeg. Now transfer the mixture to sit in the centre of the square of muslin, gather the edges into the centre, then, leaving a bit of room for it to expand, tie with string.

What you need to do next is place the bacon in the casserole along with the small onion studded with cloves, the bay leaves, carrot and peppercorns, then tie the pease pudding to the handle of the pan so it sits alongside the bacon. Cover with cold water and bring the whole lot up to a gentle simmer. Put the lid on and let it cook very gently for 1¼ hours.

When the bacon is cooked, transfer it to a dish, cover with kitchen foil and let it rest. Leave the pudding in the casserole but ladle out 6 fl oz (175 ml) of the cooking water into a measuring jug. If you want to make The London Particular, reserve and freeze the rest of the stock. Next, make up the sauce: in a smallish saucepan, melt 1 oz (25 g) of the butter and add the onion, and when you've stirred it so it's nice and buttery, let it cook on the lowest possible heat for about 20 minutes. It's important not to let it colour, so give it a stir from time to time.

Now, using a wooden spoon, stir in the flour and the mustard powder until smooth, then, add the milk a little at a time, followed by the stock, switching to a balloon whisk, and whisking well after each addition. Now season the sauce with salt and freshly milled black pepper to taste, and let it barely simmer for 5 minutes. After that, stir in the grain mustard and the rest of the butter, then pour the sauce into a warmed serving jug.

Carve the bacon joint into slices to serve with the pease pudding, and have some extra mustard on the table. I serve this with mashed potatoes and boiled, buttered Savoy cabbage, but smaller steamed potatoes, such as Anya or Charlotte, would also be good.

The London Particular – Green Split Pea Soup

This soup, made with the bacon stock from the Smoked Collar of Bacon (see page 80), is so named because of the thick 'peasouper' London fogs that were so prevalent during the first half of the last century.

Serves 6

12 oz (350 g) green split peas
(no need to soak), rinsed
3½ pints (2 litres) stock from the
Smoked Collar of Bacon (see page 80),
with added water if needed
1 large celery stalk, destringed
and chopped
4 oz (110 g) butter
6 oz (175 g) smoked streaky bacon,
rind removed, diced
1 medium onion, peeled and
roughly chopped
1 large carrot, peeled and sliced
salt and freshly milled black pepper

To garnish:

2 oz (50 g) crustless white bread cut
into ⅓ inch (8 mm) cubes for croutons
2 oz (50 g) crisp bacon, reserved from
the soup

You will also need a very large
saucepan.

First strain off 3½ pints (2 litres) of the stock into the saucepan and bring it just up to simmering point, then add the split peas, stir well, cover, and simmer very gently for about 30 minutes.

Meanwhile, heat 1 oz (25 g) of the butter in a medium-sized saucepan and add 4 oz (110 g) of the bacon, along with the prepared vegetables. Then cook them over a medium heat until softened and nicely golden – this will take about 15 minutes.

After that, the bacon and softened vegetables can be transferred to join the stock and split peas. Then put the lid back on and simmer very gently for a further 40-50 minutes.

In the meantime, heat a large frying pan (without any fat in it) and fry the remaining bacon until it is really crisp, then transfer it to a plate, using a draining spoon. Next, add 2 oz (50 g) of the butter to the pan, and as soon as it begins to foam, add the cubes of bread and fry these, tossing them around for about 5 minutes, until they are also nice and crisp. Then remove them to join the bacon, using a draining spoon.

When the soup is ready, either process or blend it, then return it to the saucepan. Taste to check the seasoning, adding a little more of any reserved stock if it seems a little too thick. Just before serving, melt the remaining butter into it, then ladle into hot soup bowls and sprinkle each one with the croutons and crispy bacon bits.

Vegetarian Shepherd's Pie with Goats' Cheese Mash

Although I am not a vegetarian, I really love this alternative version to meat, with its diverse combination of dried pulses and fresh vegetables. It's also extremely popular with veggie customers in our restaurant.

First put the drained beans into a saucepan with the split peas and lentils. Add the boiling water and some salt, cover and simmer gently for 50-60 minutes, or until the pulses have absorbed the water and are soft. Then remove them from the heat and mash them just a little with a large fork.

Now pre-heat the oven to gas mark 5, 375°F (190°C), and put the potatoes on to steam. Next, roughly chop all the vegetables, pile the whole lot into a food processor and process until chopped small. Next, melt the butter in a large frying pan over a medium heat, add the vegetables and cook gently for 10-15 minutes, stirring now and then until they're softened and tinged gold at the edges.

Meanwhile, skin the tomatoes. Place them in a heatproof bowl and pour boiling water on to them. After exactly a minute (or 15-30 seconds, if they are small), remove them (protecting your hands with a cloth if the tomatoes are hot), slip off their skins and slice them.

After that, add the vegetables to the pulses mixture, along with the herbs, spices, and salt and freshly milled black pepper to taste. Then spoon the mixture into the baking dish and arrange the tomatoes in overlapping slices on the top.

As soon as the potatoes are cooked, place them in a bowl, add the butter, milk and goats' cheese, whisk to a smooth purée, season with salt and freshly milled black pepper and spread the potato over the rest of the ingredients in the dish. Finally, sprinkle over the Pecorino and bake the pie on the top shelf of the oven for 20-25 minutes, or until the top is lightly browned. If you want to prepare this in advance, it will need about 40 minutes in the oven.

Serves 4
4 oz (110 g) dried black-eyed beans, pre-soaked and drained (see page 72)
3 oz (75 g) green split peas (no need to soak), rinsed
3 oz (75 g) green lentils (no need to soak), rinsed
1¼ pint (725 ml) boiling water
2 oz (50 g) peeled carrots
2 oz (50 g) peeled swede
2 oz (50 g) peeled celeriac
1 large onion, peeled
1 small green pepper, deseeded
2 oz (50 g) butter, plus a little extra for greasing
1 heaped tablespoon chopped mixed fresh herbs, such as sage, rosemary, thyme and parsley
¼ teaspoon ground mace
¼ teaspoon cayenne pepper
salt and freshly milled black pepper

For the topping:
4 oz (110 g) soft goats' cheese
1 lb 8 oz (700 g) potatoes, peeled
8 oz (225 g) tomatoes
2 oz (50 g) butter
2 tablespoons milk
1 oz (25 g) Pecorino cheese, grated
salt and freshly milled black pepper

You will also need a steamer; and a round baking dish with a diameter of 9 inches (23 cm), 2 inches (5 cm) deep, buttered.

Tuscan Bean and Pasta Soup with Rosemary

This is Tuscany in a bowl, with all those lovely Italian flavours in a big, hefty soup – perfect for the winter months with a light main course to follow. Alternatively, it is a complete lunch, with just some cheese and a salad to follow.

Serves 4

8 oz (225 g) dried borlotti beans, pre-soaked and drained (see page 72), soaking liquid reserved

4 oz (110 g) short-cut macaroni

1 heaped tablespoon fresh rosemary, bruised in a mortar, then very finely chopped

2 tablespoons olive oil

1 large onion, peeled and finely chopped

2 cloves garlic, crushed

2½ tablespoons tomato purée

Parmesan (Parmigiano Reggiano), grated or shaved, to serve

salt and freshly milled black pepper

You will also need a blender.

First heat the oil in a large saucepan, add the onion and let it cook gently for about 10 minutes without colouring. Then add the garlic and cook for another minute. Now add the tomato purée and rosemary, stir for a minute and then pour in the beans, together with 3 pints (1.75 litres) of the reserved water (topping up the liquid, if necessary) and some salt. Now bring everything up to simmering point and simmer very gently, partially covered, for about an hour, or until the beans are tender.

After this time, taste and season with salt and freshly milled black pepper, then pour half the soup into the blender and liquidise until it's absolutely smooth. Now return the puréed half to the pan to join the rest of the beans, bring back to a gentle simmer, then add the macaroni and simmer for a further 10-12 minutes, stirring from time to time, until the pasta is cooked. Serve in hot soup bowls with lots of the Parmesan.

Spiced Chickpea Cakes with Red Onion and Coriander Salad

Serves 6 as a starter or 4 as a main course

8 oz (225 g) chickpeas, pre-soaked (see page 72)

1 heaped teaspoon each coriander and cumin seeds, dry-roasted (see page 90)

1 teaspoon ground turmeric

2 oz (50 g) butter

1 small green pepper, deseeded

2 small red chillies, deseeded

1 small onion, peeled and finely chopped

3 fat garlic cloves, finely chopped

½ oz (10 g) fresh coriander, plus a few sprigs to garnish

1 lb 2 oz (500 g) Greek yoghurt

grated zest ½ lemon

1 dessertspoon lemon juice

1 large egg, beaten

3 tablespoons wholemeal flour or chickpea flour (gram flour)

2 tablespoons groundnut or other flavourless oil

salt and freshly milled black pepper

For the salad:

1 medium red onion, peeled and thinly sliced into half-moon shapes

3 tablespoons fresh coriander leaves

1 teaspoon grated lemon zest

juice 1 lemon

At Norwich City Football Club, we're always trying out new ideas for vegetarians. This one's a real winner and can hold its own against any meat or fish recipe. If you're serving it as a main course, it's nice with some nutty brown rice.

Drain the chickpeas, then cover them with fresh water and add a pinch of salt. Bring to a simmer and cook for 30 minutes. Then drain in a sieve.

Meanwhile, prepare the salad. All you do is mix the onion with the lemon zest, juice and coriander in a small bowl and then set it aside for at least 30 minutes.

Next, transfer the roasted coriander and cumin seeds to a pestle and mortar and crush them to a powder. Now finely chop the pepper and the chilli and gently fry them, along with the onion and garlic, in the butter in a saucepan for 5 minutes, until they have softened and begun to turn brown. Then stir in all the spices and continue to cook for 30 seconds.

Next, process the chickpeas, along with the coriander, until everything is evenly chopped, but not to a purée – the chickpeas should still have some of their texture. Then transfer them to a bowl and stir in the onion mixture, 3 tablespoons of the Greek yoghurt, and the lemon zest and juice. Now give it all a really good mix, taste, and add plenty of seasoning.

As soon as the mixture is cool enough to handle, form it into 12 cakes about 2 inches (5 cm) in diameter and ½ inch (1 cm) thick for a starter, or eight larger cakes if you are serving them for a main course.

Now coat each cake with the beaten egg and dust with flour. Next, heat the oil in a large frying pan over a high heat and when it's really hot, fry them in two batches to a golden brown colour for about a minute on each side. Drain them well on kitchen paper and serve as soon as possible with the red-onion salad and 2 tablespoons of yoghurt per person. Garnish each one with a sprig of coriander.

Mexican Chicken Chilli with Yellow Tomato Salsa

I have to admit they probably won't have heard of this in Mexico, but I've so named it because it's a dish based on a couple of Mexican themes: firstly, there are the delightful pinto beans, and secondly, the cheese is melted into the sauce. Anyway, Mexican or not, it's a great recipe.

Start by stripping the coriander leaves into a small bowl, then cover it with clingfilm and pop it into the fridge. Now chop the coriander stalks very finely. Next, heat the oil in the casserole and, over a gentle heat, cook the onions, garlic, chillies and coriander stalks for about 10 minutes, stirring once or twice until softened.

Meanwhile, grind the roasted cumin seeds to a powder in a pestle and mortar, then add them, along with the drained beans, to the casserole and stir. Now sprinkle in the flour and give it another good stir. Next, gradually add the stock, followed by the Tabasco sauce and a little salt, bring everything to a simmer and cook, covered, on the lowest heat possible for 1¼-1½ hours, until the beans are tender.

In the meantime, make the salsa. Simply combine half the reserved coriander leaves and the rest of the salsa ingredients and add seasoning. Mix well, then cover and leave aside to allow the flavours to develop.

When the chilli has had its initial cooking time, deseed the pepper and cut it into ½ inch (1 cm) pieces. Then stir the chicken and pepper into the casserole, season well with salt and freshly milled black pepper, cover, and simmer for a further 30 minutes.

In the meantime, mix the Mozzarella with the cream, then, when the 30 minutes are up, add it to the casserole. Simmer gently, uncovered, for a further 20-25 minutes, stirring now and again, by which time the cheese should have melted and formed a smooth sauce. Finally, stir in the lime juice and the remaining coriander leaves. Serve with a little rice and a green vegetable, such as runner beans, and hand the salsa round separately.

Serves 6

2 lb 4 oz (1 kg) skinless, boneless chicken thighs, cut into bite-size chunks
6 medium-sized green chillies, deseeded and finely chopped
1 oz (25 g) fresh coriander
2 tablespoons olive oil
2 large onions, peeled and sliced
4 cloves garlic, crushed
1 heaped teaspoon cumin seeds, dry-roasted (see page 90)
9 oz (250 g) pinto beans, pre-soaked and drained (see page 72)
1 tablespoon plain flour
1 pint (570 ml) hot chicken stock
1 teaspoon Tabasco sauce
1 large green pepper
8 oz (225 g) Mozzarella, grated
2½ fl oz (65 ml) double cream
juice ½ lime
salt and freshly milled black pepper

For the salsa:

9 oz (250 g) yellow (or red) tomatoes, skinned (see page 79), deseeded and finely chopped
½ small red onion, peeled and very finely chopped
half the reserved coriander leaves, roughly chopped
juice ½ lime
few drops Tabasco sauce
salt and freshly milled black pepper

You will also need a lidded, flameproof casserole with a capacity of 6 pints (3.5 litres).

Old-Fashioned Shin of Beef Stew with Butter Beans and Crusted Onion Dumplings

The good old-fashioned family stew – meat and vegetables simmering gently and slowly together, and in this slowness, releasing precious juices that mingle to provide intense yet mellow flavours and the tenderest of textures. Let's not be duped into thinking we don't have the time. This stew actually takes very little time – you'll be amazed. The time it does take is not yours. Tucked away in the oven, it will leave you free to go out for a couple of hours if you want to, ready to greet you with evocative, comforting aromas when you come home. I have included some dumplings in this recipe (because I like them!), but even without them it is perfectly good.

Serves 6

3 lb (1.35 kg) shin of British beef or stewing beef, in 2 inch (5 cm) chunks
12 oz (350 g) butter beans (or judion beans), pre-soaked and drained (see page 72)
2 oz (50 g) plain flour
8 oz (225 g) each celery, carrots, swede
6 small onions (12 oz/350 g)
4 sprigs fresh thyme
3 bay leaves
1½ pints (850 ml) premium dry cider
1 tablespoon Worcestershire sauce
salt and freshly milled black pepper

For the dumplings:
1 small onion, peeled and finely chopped
a teaspoon groundnut or other flavourless oil
8 oz (225 g) self-raising flour, plus a little extra for dusting
1 heaped teaspoon mustard powder
4 oz (110 g) suet
1 tablespoon freshly snipped chives
3 tablespoons cold water
salt and freshly milled black pepper

You will also need a lidded, flameproof casserole with a capacity of 8 pints (4.5 litres).

Pre-heat the oven to gas mark 1, 275°F (140°C).

Start off by placing the flour in a large bowl and seasoning it with 1½ teaspoons of salt and some freshly milled black pepper. Now dip each chunk of meat into it to get a good coating, then transfer them to a plate. Next, prepare the vegetables. Use a potato peeler to pare the worst of the stringy bits from the celery, then cut it into 2 inch (5 cm) chunks. Peel the carrots and swede and cut them into similar size chunks. Lastly, peel the onions but leave them whole. Now toss them all in the remaining flour and transfer them, along with the meat and the beans, to the casserole, layering the ingredients alternately and sprinkle in any flour still in the bowl. Add the thyme and bay leaves, season with salt and freshly milled black pepper, then pour in the cider, plus the Worcestershire sauce. Put the casserole on the hob and bring it up to a gentle simmer before covering with the lid, placing a sheet of kitchen foil under it to ensure a tight seal. After that, place it on the middle shelf of the oven to cook for 4½ hours.

After this time, remove the casserole from the oven, set it aside, turn the temperature up to gas mark 6, 400°F (200°C) and make the dumplings. Fry the onion in the oil until brown and caramelised, then allow to cool. After that, sift the flour, mustard powder and a little salt together, then add the suet, chives and onion, and season with freshly milled black pepper and a bit more salt. Now sprinkle the water over all the ingredients and then, using first a knife and then your hands, bring it all together to form a soft dough, adding a little more water if you need to.

Next, transfer the dough to a flat, lightly floured surface, divide it into 12 portions and roll each one into a little round, using the palms of your hands. Add them to the casserole so that a part of each one can be seen just above the surface of the stew. Return the casserole to the top shelf of the oven and cook, without the lid, for a further 25-30 minutes, until the dumplings are golden brown and crusty.

Spiced Lamb Curry with Chickpeas, Green Coconut Sambal and Tomato-and-Red-Onion Pickle

There is, I have to admit, some work involved in this one, but I absolutely promise the depth and flavour of fresh coconut is really worth that bit of extra time. If you're serving this to guests, the good thing is that all the work can be done in advance, so all you have to do is cook some plain basmati rice to accompany it (see Book One).

Serves 6

2 lb (900 g) neck of British lamb, trimmed and cut into 1 inch (2.5 cm) cubes
1 rounded teaspoon cumin seeds
1 rounded teaspoon coriander seeds
6 cardamom pods, crushed
1 rounded teaspoon ground fenugreek
1 rounded teaspoon ground turmeric
8 oz (225 g) dried chickpeas, pre-soaked (see page 72), drained and soaking liquid reserved
3 medium onions, peeled
1 fat clove garlic
4 bird eye chillies, deseeded
4 tablespoons groundnut or other flavourless oil
1 inch (2.5 cm) fresh root ginger, peeled and grated
milk from 1 fresh coconut
grated flesh ½ fresh coconut (weighing about 3 oz/75 g)
3 oz (75 g) creamed coconut, grated
salt and freshly milled black pepper

You will also need a lidded, flameproof casserole with a capacity of 6 pints (3.5 litres).

First chop the onions, garlic and bird eye chillies quite small in a food processor, then heat 2 tablespoons of the oil in the casserole and cook them gently for 5 minutes to soften. Now heat the remaining oil in a large frying pan and when it's nice and hot, quickly brown the cubes of meat. (You will have to do this in about three batches.) Next, sprinkle the ginger and the spices over the onion mixture in the casserole and stir to soak up the juice, then cook gently for 2 minutes. Now pre-heat the oven to gas mark 2, 300°F (150°C).

To prepare the coconut, first push a thick skewer into the three holes in the top, then drain out the milk and reserve it for the recipe. Next, place the coconut in a plastic bag and sit it on a hard surface – a stone floor or an outside paving stone. Then give it a hefty whack with a hammer – it won't be that difficult to break. Now remove the pieces from the bag and, using a cloth to protect your hands, prise the tip of a kitchen knife between the nut and the shell. You should find you can force the whole piece out in one go. After that, discard the shell and take off the inner skin using a potato peeler. Once you have rinsed it, the coconut will now be ready to use.

The best way to grate coconut flesh is with the fine grating disc of a food processor, but a hand grater will do the job, too. Grate it, reserving half for the sambal.

Next, pour the coconut milk into a measuring jug and make it up to 1½ pints (850 ml) with the chickpea-soaking liquid. Slowly pour this into the casserole, stirring all the time. Next, stir in the grated fresh and creamed coconut and then transfer the browned meat to the casserole, along with the chickpeas. Finally, season with salt and freshly milled black pepper, then bring everything up to simmering point, cover and cook in the centre of the oven for 2 hours.

To make the sambal, first dry-roast the cumin seeds. To do this, place the seeds in a small frying pan over a medium heat and stir and toss them around for 1-2 minutes, or until they begin to look toasted, smell fragrant and start to jump in the pan. Now use a pestle and mortar and crush them to a powder.

Next, grate the shallots using the fine grater blade of the food processor, then remove them to a bowl. Process the remaining ingredients, this time with the chopper blade, until they are all finely chopped. Add this mixture, along with the cumin and the reserved grated coconut, to the shallots.

Next, make the tomato-and-red-onion pickle. All you do is mix the tomatoes with the onion, coriander, lime juice and chilli powder in a small bowl and set the mixture aside to marinate for at least 15 minutes.

Serve the sambal as an accompaniment to the curry, along with the tomato-and-red-onion pickle and some plain basmati rice that has been cooked with a cinnamon stick and bay leaf.

For the sambal:
grated flesh ½ fresh coconut, reserved from the curry
3 shallots, peeled
½ oz (10 g) fresh coriander leaves
1 tablespoon fresh mint leaves
1 medium-sized green chilli, deseeded
½ inch (1 cm) fresh root ginger, peeled
½ teaspoon cumin seeds

For the pickle:
3 medium-sized ripe but firm tomatoes, skinned (see page 79), deseeded and thinly sliced
1 medium red onion, peeled and sliced into thin half moons
1 dessertspoon chopped fresh coriander leaves
juice 1 large lime
a few pinches chilli powder

Clockwise, from left: Spiced Lamb Curry with Chickpeas, basmati rice, Green Coconut Sambal, and Tomato-and-Red-Onion Pickle

91

Braised Sausages with Borlotti Beans, Rosemary and Sage

You can use any beans in this recipe, but borlotti are the best of all. The smokiness of the pancetta is also important, but if you can't get it, use smoked bacon.

Serves 2-3

1 lb (450 g) good, meaty pork sausages
8 oz (225 g) dried borlotti beans, pre-soaked and drained (see page 72), soaking liquid reserved
1 heaped teaspoon chopped fresh rosemary, plus 2-3 sprigs to garnish
1 heaped teaspoon chopped fresh sage, plus 2-3 leaves to garnish
1 tablespoon olive oil
4 oz (110 g) sliced smoked pancetta (or smoked bacon), chopped
1 large red onion, peeled and chopped
2 cloves garlic
10 fl oz (275 ml) dry white wine
salt and freshly milled black pepper

You will also need a lidded, flameproof casserole with a capacity of 4 pints (2.25 litres).

Pre-heat the oven to gas mark 1, 275°F (140°C).

First of all, heat the oil in the casserole over a medium heat and carefully brown the sausages, turning them occasionally so they are a nice golden brown colour on all sides – this will take 8-10 minutes.

After that, remove them to a plate, then add the pancetta to the frying pan, turn up the heat and toss it around for about 5 minutes, or until it's golden brown at the edges. Now, using a draining spoon, transfer it to join the sausages, then turn the heat down again to medium and soften the onion for 10 minutes in the juices left in the pan, stirring it around from time to time. Then add the garlic and cook for another minute.

Next, add the drained beans to the casserole, along with the herbs, then the sausages and pancetta, tucking them in among the beans, and finally, add the wine and 10 fl oz (275 ml) of the reserved water. Season with salt and freshly milled black pepper and bring everything up to simmering point on the hob. Now put a lid on the casserole and transfer it to the centre shelf of the oven to cook slowly for 3 hours. Serve garnished with the sprigs of rosemary and sage.

I don't think this needs any other vegetable but a green salad, and some Italian cheese would be nice to follow.

Sesame Blancmange with Sweetened Compote of Adzuki Beans

This dish is delightfully cool and intriguing. It's quite interesting to ask whoever you're serving it to to guess what it's flavoured with! I think it's a great dessert to serve if your main course has a Japanese theme.

The compote can be prepared well in advance. All you do is place the beans and their soaking liquid in a medium-sized saucepan over a medium to high heat and bring to the boil. Boil for 10 minutes, turn the heat down, cover with a lid and let them simmer for 30 minutes, topping up with a little more water if necessary. Then drain, reserving the cooking liquid, and make this up to 16 fl oz (450 ml), using cold water.

Next, return the liquid and the beans to the pan, add half the sugar, stir to dissolve it and continue to simmer for 10 minutes, this time without a lid. Then add the remaining sugar and salt and simmer until you have a nice syrupy consistency, which will take 15-20 minutes.

Meanwhile, pre-heat a large, heavy-based frying pan over a medium heat. Add the sesame seeds, stirring and keeping them on the move for 1-2 minutes, until they start to pop. Watch them like a hawk – be careful not to let them brown too much or burn. Remove them from the pan to a plate and leave to cool.

Next, transfer the compote to a bowl and, in the rinsed saucepan, bring the milk up to the boil, add the sesame seeds and leave them to infuse until the milk is completely cold.

To make the blancmange, put the water and sugar into a small saucepan over a medium heat, stir to dissolve the sugar, boil for a minute, then remove the pan from the heat and sprinkle in the gelatine, stirring until it has completely dissolved.

Now strain the sesame seeds and milk through a fine sieve into a large jug. (It does need to be very fine, as you don't want to push them through. If your sieve is not a fine one, line it with muslin or gauze.) When you've strained the milk through, you'll need to use the bowl of a ladle to press the sesame seeds to extract all the milk.

Now add the gelatine-and-sugar mixture to the milk, whisking to combine it all thoroughly, then pour into the pudding basins. Cover with clingfilm and chill in the fridge until set.

To serve, briefly dip the bottom of the basins into hot water, then invert them on to serving dishes and spoon the compote around them, reserving a few adzuki beans for decoration.

Serves 4
For the blancmange:
4 oz (110 g) sesame seeds
1 pint (570 ml) whole milk
5 fl oz (150 ml) water
1½ oz (40 g) golden caster sugar
1 x 11 g sachet powdered gelatine

For the compote:
4 oz (110 g) adzuki beans, pre-soaked (see page 72) in 1 pint (570 ml) water, soaking liquid reserved
3 oz (75 g) golden caster sugar
½ teaspoon salt

You will also need four mini pudding basins with a capacity of 6 fl oz (175 ml), or a pudding basin with a top diameter of 6 inches (15 cm), a bottom diameter of 3 inches (7.5 cm) and a capacity of 1¼ pints (725 ml).

4

First steps in preserving

Why would anyone want to make preserves in these modern times? After all, in the shops, there's a wealth of real jams with high fruit content, and chutneys and pickles from around the world. It was okay when our ancestors grew too much for their immediate needs and had to put things by to liven up the dreariness of winter. But our problem now is too much choice, too much food every single month of the year. My answer, as I embark on teaching you how to preserve fruit and vegetables, is that for all the choice available, not a lot of it measures up to home-made.

I hate over-sweet chutney and factory-made piccalilli (I've not found a good commercial one yet), and no manufacturer has ever been able to make Seville Orange Marmalade with all the chunkiness, depth and tangy flavour of the home-made (see page 100). Yes, there are a few exceptions and I confess to being a keen fan of farmers' markets, where you can buy some fabulous preserves. In fact, I have an excellent recipe for runner-bean chutney in my *Summer Collection*, but now that my local farm shop (Alder Carr in Needham Market) sells one every bit as good, I never bother to make it.

Nevertheless, these are exceptions and there's a great deal of creative satisfaction in seeing a row of shiny jars filled with good things stored away ready to enliven all kinds of meals. I particularly love it at Christmas, with all those cold cuts crying out for what has become a ritual in our house – chunky sautéed potatoes and an array of lovely pickles and chutneys. I'm a romantic and confess to wanting to keep alive our country's great tradition of preserving, so I am anxious for you to learn the basic techniques, which are not difficult once you understand them. If you've been strawberry-picking and have an over-abundance, or (as I did once, honestly) climbed a tree and hand-picked a basket of damsons, then a mouthful of summer in the depths of winter in some strawberry preserve spread over hot, buttered crumpets, or a bowl of Spiced Damson Chutney (see page 105) to dip your jacket potato skins into will give that pleasurable edge to everyday life.

Equipment

Preserving pan: Not strictly necessary unless you want to make really large quantities – actually, for beginners, it's better to make small quantities just to get the feel of preserving. Having said that, I do have one – when I make Spiced Damson Chutney, I like to make a lot because, not only am I crazy about it, I always want to give some to friends. There's no point in buying a really big pan. Buy the smaller size, because modern domestic hobs are simply not powerful enough to bring a huge pan of marmalade, or similar, to what used to be called a rolling boil. Stick to a heavy-gauge aluminium pan – it is the best conductor of heat and is not as expensive as stainless steel (but don't leave acid fruit in the pan after it cooks). The capacity of the pan in the photograph on page 99 is 15¾ pints (9 litres).

Funnel: (*see left*) A simple little thing, but so important when you are trying to fill the jars. It prevents sticky blobs spilling over the edges and down the sides.

Jars: (*see left*) Ideally, you should invest in some proper preserving jars because they have their own tight-sealing lids that make life much simpler. Look after them and they will serve you year after year and easily justify the initial cost. You can, of course, use commercial jars, but one thing to remember is that the lids for pickles and chutneys must be plastic-coated, as the vinegar can corrode metal. Either way, lids are essential. Cellophane covers won't work for pickles and chutneys. Also, it is important to remember to fill the jars as full as possible, not leaving any gaps.

Waxed discs: Preserves should always be sealed while still hot, and the seal is provided by waxed discs – little circles of paper covered with a thin layer of wax – placed over the surface of chutneys or jams, waxed side down. They are widely available in kitchen shops and stationers, or by mail order.

Muslin: You can now buy ready-made squares of muslin in various sizes, and these are what are needed to wrap the pickling spices that are suspended in a pan of chutney or the orange pips that are needed in marmalade. Ordinary gauze, available at chemists, does just as good a job.

Labels: Personally, I don't bother with the rather badly designed fancy brigade. I just buy stationers' self-adhesive, plain white labels. Labelling and dating is important – you might like to know you still have some preserve left from a vintage year!

Sterilised jars: Vital – because preserves that are going to be kept for long periods need to start off in spanking clean, sterilised jars – but perfectly simple. Just wash the jars and lids in warm, soapy water, rinse well (again in warm water), then dry them thoroughly with a clean tea cloth, place them on a baking tray and pop them in a medium oven, gas mark 4, 350°F (180°C) for a minimum of 5 minutes. Add their contents while they are still hot.

How to make jams, marmalade and preserves

Home-made jams are made from just two ingredients, fruit and sugar, unlike some of their cousins on the supermarket shelves. In fact, I am a passionate studier of labels and have rarely come across any commercially made jam or marmalade that contains only fruit and sugar. So, both in terms of quality and economy, it makes sense to make them at home and add that touch of luxury to everyday eating.

Jam is essentially preserved fruit. The fruit, if it's in good condition (and slightly under-ripe) contains in its cell walls a natural setting agent called pectin. This, together with the natural acid from the fruit, is released when the fruit is boiled with sugar. As it boils, the sugar concentrates and all three – sugar, acid and pectin – combine to form a mass that eventually reaches 'setting point'.

The fruit should be dry, since the water content of damp fruit will dilute the pectin and the acid and render them less active. Any dusty fruit should only be wiped with damp kitchen paper, and anyway, the boiling will effectively purify the fruit. Slightly under-ripe fruit actually contains more pectin and fruit acid than over-ripe fruit (which should therefore be avoided). With those fruits that contain less acid than others, this deficiency is made up by adding lemon juice.

The proportion of sugar to fruit varies according to the type of fruit used. I believe really sharp fruits, such as damsons or loganberries, make the best jams because they are not overpowered by the sweetness of the sugar, and the fruit flavour is predominant. This is also why I think Seville oranges make the best marmalade, tasting of oranges rather than sugar. Of course, other fruits also make good jams – providing the fruit content is high and there's not too much sugar.

Ten steps to jam-making

1 Sugar has a hardening effect, so tough-skinned fruits should always be simmered *before* the sugar is added to the pan.

2 Conversely, soft-skinned fruits, such as strawberries, which tend to disintegrate when cooked, should be soaked in sugar *first,* to harden them and help keep the fruit whole in the finished jam.

3 The sugar should be completely dissolved before the jam reaches the boil, otherwise it will be difficult to set and the finished jam will be sugary. To test if the sugar has dissolved, dip a wooden spoon in, turn it over and if no sugar crystals are visible in the liquid that coats the back of the spoon, it has indeed dissolved. (To be quite sure, stir well and repeat this test a couple of times.) To speed up the dissolving process, you can warm the sugar in a bowl in the oven before adding it.

4 Don't try to make too large a quantity of jam in one go. It will take far too long to come to the boil, and then will not boil rapidly enough to produce a good set.

5 How to test for a set: at the same time as you begin cooking the fruit, place three or four saucers in the freezing compartment of the fridge. When you have boiled the jam for the given time, remove the pan from the heat and place a teaspoonful of the jam on to one of the chilled saucers. Let it cool back in the fridge, then push it with your finger: if a crinkly skin has formed on the jam, then it has set. If it hasn't, continue to boil for another 5 minutes, then do another test.

6 Don't worry about any scum that rises to the surface while the jam is boiling – if you keep skimming it off, you'll finish up with no jam at all! Instead, wait until you have a set, then remove the jam from the heat and stir in a small lump of butter, which will disperse the scum.

7 Once the jam has set, leave it to settle for 15 minutes or so – particularly with jam containing whole fruit, such as strawberry or damson, or chunky marmalade – to prevent the fruit from rising to the top when it's poured into the jar. Then pour into clean, dry, hot jars, filling them as near to the top as possible. Straightaway, place a waxed disc over the surface, then seal with a lid. Wipe the jars with a warm, damp cloth.

8 Don't put the labels on until the jam is cold – otherwise the heat will prevent them sticking properly and they'll fall off for sure.

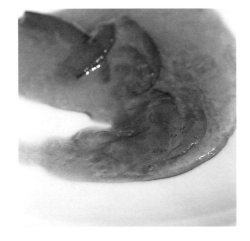

To test for a set, place a teaspoonful of the preserve on to a chilled saucer, cool in the freezer, then test by pushing with your finger to see if a wrinkly skin forms. If so, the preserve is set.

9 Store in a cool, dry and preferably dark place. Too much light is not good for storage, while a damp or steamy atmosphere can cause mould to develop on the surface of the jam.

10 If things go wrong: if the jam hasn't set after cooling and potting, tip it all back into the pan and boil again, adding the juice of a small lemon; if mould develops on the surface of jam in a jar, remove it with a spoon, along with about half an inch (1 cm) of the jam underneath – rest assured, the remainder of the jam will not be affected – and place a waxed disc dipped in brandy on top.

How to make chutneys and pickles

I have always thought of chutneys and pickles as an essentially English thing, but of course, like so many of our seemingly traditional foods, they actually have their origins in our long history as a trading nation. The word 'chutney' is Hindustani, and what we are familiar with now is the result of our earlier efforts to reproduce in this country the exotic recipes brought back by our traders in India in the 18ᵗʰ century. They were a great hit at the time and have since become virtually an indigenous part of our cuisine – in a way that the food of no European country ever has.

I'm a total devotee. I just love the idea of putting food by for later. Actually, I love all the things we eat with pickles and chutney, too: cold cuts, pork pies, Scotch eggs, ploughman's lunch and, of course, curries! Over the years I have been cooking, I have acquired a long list of recipes, and those in this chapter are a few of my established favourites, as well as some of my latest discoveries. But first, a few notes to help you get started.

What is chutney? What are pickles? Chutney is a combination of chopped fruits or vegetables (or both) that has been simmered with vinegar, sugar and spices until reduced to a thick purée, which is then potted and sealed, and should last for ages. Pickles, on the other hand, are not minced or chopped, but fruits and vegetables preserved whole or in chunks.

How do I know when the chutney is ready? There's a very simple test (*see photograph, right*). When the chutney appears thick enough, make a channel with a wooden spoon across its surface. If it leaves a channel imprinted for a few seconds without being filled by spare vinegar, it is ready.

The cardinal rule: Unless a recipe says otherwise, never eat chutneys or pickles until they have matured and mellowed – you need to store them for at least three months before eating. Freshly made, they taste harsh and vinegary – I'll never forget a letter I received when I first started publishing recipes: 'I've just made your chutney and it's disgusting!' I now know to warn you to be patient. Both pickles and chutneys need to be stored in a cool, dry, dark place – a cupboard under the stairs would be ideal, or else in a box in the garage or under a bed in the spare room.

To test if the chutney is thick enough, make a channel across the surface, if it leaves an impression for a few seconds without being filled by spare vinegar, it is ready.

Traditional Seville Orange Marmalade

You can find some very good shop-bought marmalade now, but it's still never ever like home-made. The intensely sharp, bitter Seville oranges here hold their own, conquering the sweetness of the sugar; that fresh, intensely orange fragrance and flavour is unmatched in any preserve anywhere in the world.

Makes six 1 lb (350 ml capacity) jars
2 lb (900 g) Seville oranges
4 pints (2.25 litres) water
1 lemon
4 lb (1.8 kg) golden granulated sugar, warmed
½ teaspoon butter

You will also need a preserving pan or a large, heavy-based saucepan; a 9 inch (23 cm) square of muslin (or gauze); some string; a funnel; and six 1 lb (350 ml capacity) jars, sterilised (see page 97).

Simmer the marmalade gently for two hours, uncovered, to allow the liquid to reduce and the orange peel to become completely soft.

Begin by measuring the water into the pan, then cut the oranges and lemon in half and squeeze the juice out of them. Now add the juice to the water, and place the pips and any bits of pith that cling to the squeezer on the square of muslin (or gauze), laid over a small bowl. Now cut the orange peel into quarters with a sharp knife, and then cut each quarter into thinnish shreds. As you cut, add the shreds to the water; any pips or spare pith you come across should go on the muslin (or gauze). The pith contains a lot of pectin, so don't discard any and don't worry about any pith and skin that clings to the shreds – it all gets dissolved in the boiling.

Now tie up the pips and pith loosely in the muslin (or gauze) to form a little bag, and tie this on to the handle of the pan with string, so that the bag is suspended in the water. Then bring the liquid up to simmering point and simmer gently, uncovered, for 2 hours, or until the peel is completely soft – test a piece carefully by pressing it between your finger and thumb. At this point, pop three or four saucers into the freezer compartment of the fridge to chill.

Next, remove the bag and leave it to cool on a saucer. Then pour the sugar into the pan and stir it now and then over a low heat, until you can see all the crystals have melted when you test the liquid on the back of a spoon – check this carefully, as it's important. Now increase the heat to very high and squeeze the bag over the pan to extract all the sticky, jelly-like substance that contains the pectin. You can do this by pressing the bag between two saucers or by using your hands. As you squeeze, you'll see it ooze out. Stir or whisk it into the rest.

As soon as the mixture reaches a fast boil, start timing. After 15 minutes, remove the pan from the heat, spoon a little of the marmalade on to one of the chilled saucers and pop it back in the freezer compartment for a few seconds. You can tell if it is set by pushing the mixture with your finger: if the surface wrinkles, it is; if not, continue to boil the marmalade and give it the same test at about 10-minute intervals until it does set.

After that, remove the pan from the heat. (If there's a lot of scum, most of it can be dispersed by stirring in the half teaspoon of butter, and the rest can be spooned off.) Leave the marmalade to settle for 20 minutes.

Pour it into the hot, sterilised jars with the aid of the funnel, filling them as full as possible, cover straightaway with waxed discs and seal while still hot. Label when cold and store in a dry, cool, dark place. Then hurry up and make some toast to try some!

Dark Apricot and Almond Conserve

Most fruit conserves are made in summer, so it's good to be able to make this one in the depths of winter when it's too cold to go out. Serve it on some warm scones (see Book Two) or toasted crumpets.

Makes three 1 lb (350 ml capacity) jars
1 lb (450 g) dried apricots
2 oz (50 g) whole unblanched almonds, roughly chopped
1 pint (570 ml) water
1 lb (450 g) dark soft brown sugar
juice 4 lemons

You will also need a preserving pan or a 6 pint (3.5 litre) heavy-based saucepan; a funnel; and three 1 lb (350 ml capacity) jars, sterilised (see page 97).

You need to begin this the night before because the apricots need to be soaked, so put them in a bowl and pour the water over them.

The next day, pop three or four saucers into the freezer compartment of the fridge (for testing the setting point later on). Then, place the apricots, along with their soaking water, in the pan and simmer them very gently for about 30 minutes or until they're really tender when tested with a small skewer. Now add the sugar and, keeping the heat very low, allow it to melt and all the granules of sugar to completely dissolve – if not, the conserve will be grainy in texture. To test this, dip in a wooden spoon, and as the liquid runs off the back of it, you will be able to see clearly if there are any granules left. When the sugar has dissolved, turn the heat up to high. Next, add the lemon juice and almonds and boil rapidly for 15 minutes, stirring from time to time to prevent the conserve catching on the base of the pan.

When the time is up, remove the pan from the heat and place a teaspoonful of the conserve on one of the chilled saucers. Allow it to cool for about 30 seconds by putting it back in the fridge, then push it with your little finger: if a crinkly skin has formed, then the conserve has set. If not, boil it again for another 5 minutes and do another test, repeating three or four times if necessary, then remove the pan finally from the heat. Let it stand for 15 minutes to allow the conserve to settle. After that, pour it through the funnel into the hot, sterilised jars, filling them as full as possible, and seal straightaway with waxed discs and tight-fitting lids. Wait till the conserve is cold before putting on the labels and then store it in a cool, dry, dark place.

Lemon Curd

Lots of lovely recipes call for lemon curd and, once again, it's something that is never quite the same when shop-bought.

Begin by lightly whisking the eggs in a medium-sized saucepan, then add the rest of the ingredients and place the saucepan over a medium heat. Now whisk continuously using a balloon whisk until the mixture thickens – about 7-8 minutes. Next, lower the heat to its minimum setting and let the curd gently simmer for a further minute, continuing to whisk. After that, remove it from the heat.

Now pour the lemon curd into the hot, sterilised jars, filling them as full as possible, cover straightaway with waxed discs, seal while it is still hot and label when it is cold. It will keep for several weeks, but it must be stored in a cool place.

Makes three 1 lb (350 ml capacity) jars
grated zest and juice 4 large
juicy lemons
4 large eggs
12 oz (350 g) golden caster sugar
8 oz (225 g) unsalted butter, at room
temperature, cut into small lumps
1 dessertspoon cornflour

You will also need three 1lb (350 ml capacity) jars, sterilised (see page 97).

Spiced Cranberry and Claret Jelly

Even if it's not Christmas, it's such a treat to always have some home-made cranberry jelly on standby in your cupboard to serve with game or roast chicken or pâté – it livens up so many things and gives you a taste of luscious cranberries all year round.

Makes about one 17½ fl oz (500 ml) preserving jar
3 lb 8 oz (1.6 kg) cranberries
1 cinnamon stick
a few juniper berries
2 cloves
18 fl oz (510 ml) good claret
18 fl oz (510 ml) water
golden granulated sugar

You will also need a nylon sieve with a top diameter of 9½ inches (24 cm) (or 2 smaller sieves); some muslin (or gauze); and a 17½ fl oz (500 ml) preserving jar, sterilised (see page 97).

First of all, place the cranberries, cinnamon stick, juniper berries, cloves and water in your largest saucepan and simmer them over a gentle heat for 25-30 minutes, or until the cranberries have burst and become tender and mushy. Then empty the entire contents of the pan into the sieve, lined with the muslin (or gauze) and placed over an equally large bowl or jug, and leave it to drip for a minimum of 8 hours or, preferably, overnight. Do not be tempted to press the cranberries; the juice may become cloudy, but it's important to leave it alone to drip away.

The next day, chill three or four saucers in the freezer compartment of the fridge. Now measure the juice and, for every 1 pint (570 ml), weigh out 10 oz (275 g) of sugar. Pour the juice back into the rinsed pan, add the sugar and stir over a gentle heat until all the sugar has completely dissolved. Then add the claret, bring the mixture up to a fast, rolling boil and boil hard for about 10 minutes. (I always use a timer.)

After 10 minutes, test for a set. Remove the pan from the heat while you do so. Put a teaspoonful of jelly on to one of the chilled saucers, pop it back into the fridge for a few seconds, then push a finger gently through it. If the surface of the jelly wrinkles, setting point has been reached. If not, continue to boil and re-test at 5-minute intervals. Once the jelly has set, leave it to settle for 15 minutes or so, then pour it into the hot, sterilised jar, filling it as full as possible, cover straightaway with a waxed disc, then seal tightly and label when cold. Store in a cool, dry, dark place.

Note: It is never practical to state the exact yield in a jelly recipe because it all depends on the ripeness of the fruit and the time allowed for dripping.

Spiced Damson Chutney

There are chutneys and chutneys, but this one is simply the best of all. It is something I couldn't live without, having it permanently on my shelf. I love it with cold cuts, with cheese, but best of all, sausages and jacket potatoes – dipping crisp, crunchy potato skins into this dark, spicy, deeply flavoursome preserve is one of life's great pleasures.

You've got two options here. One is to halve the damsons, slitting them down the natural line of the fruit and twisting out the stones – very tedious. The other is to stew them gently with ½ pint (275 ml) of the vinegar and then, wearing rubber gloves, remove the stones as they separate themselves from the flesh – also tedious but, either way, it will only take about 25 minutes and I promise you it is well, well worth it. Place them in a preserving pan, then core the apples but leave the peel on, and finely chop them in a processor. Then process the onions, adding both these to the pan.

After that, crush the garlic and add that, followed by the ginger, raisins, sugar and the (remaining) vinegar. Then sprinkle in the salt and stir everything thoroughly. Now wrap the cinnamon, allspice and cloves in the muslin (or gauze) and tie the top loosely with the string to form a little bag, which should then be tied on to the handle of the pan and suspended among the rest of the ingredients.

Now bring everything to the boil, then lower the heat and let the chutney simmer very gently for 2-3 hours, stirring it occasionally and rather more often towards the end to prevent it sticking to the bottom. When almost all the vinegar has disappeared and the chutney has thickened to a soft consistency, do the channel test – if it is ready, when you draw a channel with a wooden spoon across its surface, it will leave an imprint for a few seconds without filling up with vinegar. While it is still warm, pour it into the hot, sterilised jars, filling them as full as possible. Cover each with a waxed disc and seal tightly with a vinegar-proof lid. Label when cold and store the chutney in a cool, airy cupboard, leaving it to mellow for at least 3 months before eating.

Makes six 1 lb (350 ml capacity) jars
3 lb (1.35 kg) damsons
2 heaped teaspoons ground ginger
2 small cinnamon sticks
1 oz (25 g) allspice berries
1 dessertspoon cloves
2 pints (1.2 litres) malt vinegar
1 lb (450 g) cooking apples (no need to peel)
3 largish onions, peeled
3 cloves garlic
1 lb (450 g) seedless raisins
1 lb (450 g) dark soft brown sugar
1 lb (450 g) demerara sugar
2 tablespoons sea salt

You will also need a preserving pan, or a very large, heavy-based saucepan; a 12 inch (30 cm) square piece of muslin (or gauze); some string; and six 1 lb (350 ml capacity) jars, sterilised (see page 97).

Spiced Pickled Agen Prunes in Armagnac

It's great to have a jar of these pickles in the cupboard to serve with cold meats or pâtés, but I think they also make a wonderful accompaniment to Crisp Roast Duck (in Book Two).

Makes five 1lb (350 ml capacity) jars
2 lb (900 g) Agen prunes, pitted
6 cloves
2 blades mace
6 allspice berries
5 small sticks cinnamon
5 tablespoons Armagnac
1 tablespoon Lapsang Souchong tea
1 pint (570 ml) good-quality red wine vinegar
8 oz (225 g) light muscovado sugar

You will also need five 1lb (350 ml capacity) jars, sterilised (see page 97).

You need to begin this the night before. Measure 2 pints (1.2 litres) of boiling water into a measuring jug, then stir in the tea and allow it to steep for 3 minutes. Meanwhile, put the prunes into a large, non-metallic bowl. Now strain the tea and allow it to cool completely before pouring it over the prunes. Then cover the bowl with a clean tea cloth and leave them to soak overnight.

Next day, put the vinegar, along with the sugar and spices, into a medium-sized saucepan, bring everything slowly up to the boil, and allow to simmer for 15 minutes. Meanwhile, drain off the tea and pack the prunes into the hot, sterilised jars, filling them as full as possible. Now transfer the liquid from the pan to the jug and carefully pour it over the prunes, swivelling the jars to make sure they are completely covered. Finally, spoon a tablespoon of Armagnac into each jar, then cover straightaway with a waxed disc and seal tightly with a vinegar-proof lid. When the pickles are cold, label the jars and store in a cool, dry, dark place for at least 3 months – the prunes will go on getting better as they mature.

Clockwise, from top: Spiced Mustard Pickle (Piccalilli), Spiced Pickled Agen Prunes in Armagnac, and Smoky Tomato Chutney

Smoky Tomato Chutney

Pimentón – smoked paprika – gives a smoky flavour to this dark, luscious, red tomato chutney. Great to serve with hamburgers and sausages, and lovely with sharp Cheddar cheese. If you prefer a milder chutney just use the sweet, mild pimentón.

Makes four 1 lb (350 ml capacity) jars
4 oz (110 g) sun-blush (or mi-cuit) tomatoes
2 lb 8 oz (1.15 kg) red, ripe tomatoes
1 tablespoon hot pimentón
1 tablespoon sweet, mild pimentón
1 dessertspoon coriander seeds
1 dessertspoon mustard seeds
2 fat cloves garlic, peeled
2 large onions, peeled and quartered
4 oz (110 g) light muscovado sugar
½ pint (275 ml) good-quality red wine vinegar
1 heaped teaspoon salt

You will also need a preserving pan or large heavy-based saucepan; a funnel; and four 1 lb (350 ml capacity) jars, sterilised (see page 97).

First of all, drain the sun-blush tomatoes of excess oil and pat dry with kitchen paper. (If using mi-cuit tomatoes, there will be no need to drain them.) Then heat a small, heavy-based frying pan and dry-roast the coriander and mustard seeds over a medium heat, turning them over and stirring them round for 2 minutes to draw out their flavour. Then crush them together with a pestle and mortar – not very much; they just need to be broken up.

Now, making the chutney is going to be a lot easier if you have a food processor. In the past, an old-fashioned mincer was used for chutneys, and a processor is even faster, but if you have neither, then you just need to chop everything uniformly small.

Add the sun-blush (or mi-cuit) tomatoes to the food processor and chop till roughly ¼ inch (5 mm) in size. Then add the fresh tomatoes and process briefly until they are the same size. Now pour the whole lot into the pan. Next, add the garlic and onions to the processor and process these to about the same size. Then transfer them to join the tomatoes and add the crushed spices, pimentón, sugar, vinegar and salt.

Bring everything up to simmering point, stirring all the time, then, when you have a gentle simmer, reduce the heat to low and let it cook very gently, uncovered, for 3-3½ hours. It doesn't need a great deal of attention – just come back now and then to give it a stir to prevent it sticking.

The chutney is ready when all the liquid has been absorbed and the mixture has thickened to a nice soft consistency. The way to test for the right moment is by using a wooden spoon to make a trail all the way across the top of the chutney – if the trail fills with the vinegary juices, it's not ready; when the spoon leaves a trail that does not fill with juice, it is.

You need to watch the chutney carefully at the end because undercooking will make it too sloppy and overcooking will make it dry. When it is ready, allow it to cool a little and pour it through the funnel into the hot, sterilised jars, filling them as full as possible. Cover each one straightaway with a waxed disc and seal with a vinegar-proof lid while it's still hot, but don't put a label on until it's cold. Store the chutney in a cool, dry, dark place for 8 weeks to mellow before using.

Spiced Mustard Pickle (Piccalilli)

I love autumn, and one of the things I love most about it is that it's the time to make some pickles to have at Christmas, to serve with cold cuts. Good piccalilli is something you can't buy factory-made – it's never really successful. So, why not make your own? It's also lovely with sharp English cheeses and perhaps, best of all, with a fresh, crusty pork pie.

You need to begin this the day before. What you do is place the prepared cauliflower and onions in a non-metallic bowl, and the cucumbers and beans in another. Then whisk the salt into 4 pints (2.25 litres) of cold water to make a brine, and pour this over the vegetables. Now put a plate with a weight on it on top of each one to keep them submerged and leave them for 24 hours.

The next day, drain away the salt water and briefly rinse the vegetables. Now place the cauliflower, onions and the 2 pints (1.2 litres) vinegar together in the pan. Then add the nutmeg and allspice, bring it up to the boil, cover and simmer for 8 minutes. Next, take off the lid and stir in the cucumbers, beans, sugar, garlic and ginger. Now bring the mixture up to simmering point again, cover and cook for a further 4-5 minutes. The vegetables should still be slightly crisp, so don't go away and forget them.

Next, set a large colander over a large bowl, pour the contents of the pan into it and leave it all to drain, reserving the vinegar. Then mix the mustard powder, turmeric and flour together in another bowl. Gradually work in the additional 5 tablespoons of vinegar and the water so the mixture becomes a fairly smooth paste. Now add a ladleful of the hot vinegar liquid drained from the vegetables, stir again and transfer the sauce mixture to a saucepan.

Bring it to the boil, gradually whisking in the remaining hot vinegar. Simmer gently for about 5 minutes, then transfer the vegetables from the colander back to the large bowl, and pour over the sauce. Stir really well now to mix everything evenly, then spoon the piccalilli into the hot, sterilised jars. Cover straightaway with waxed discs, seal with vinegar-proof lids and when cold, label and store the piccalilli in a cool, dry, dark place to mellow for 3 months before eating.

Makes seven 1lb (350 ml capacity) jars and one ½ lb (175 ml capacity) jar

2 oz (50 g) dry mustard powder
½ whole nutmeg, grated
½ teaspoon ground allspice
1 oz (25 g) ground turmeric
2 medium cauliflowers, divided into 1 inch (2.5 cm) florets
1 lb (450 g) small pickling onions, peeled and halved, through the root
2 small cucumbers (each weighing about 9 oz/250 g), peeled, cut into ¼ inch (5 mm) rounds, then each round quartered
1 lb (450 g) dwarf green beans, topped and tailed and cut into 1 inch (2.5 cm) lengths (or 1 lb/450 g runner beans, destringed and cut into 1 inch/ 2.5 cm diagonal slices)
2 pints (1.2 litres) malt vinegar, plus 5 extra tablespoons
6 oz (175 g) golden caster sugar
2 cloves garlic, crushed with 3 teaspoons salt
1 dessertspoon fresh root ginger, peeled and grated
1 oz (25 g) sauce flour
2 tablespoons water
4 oz (110 g) sea salt

You will also need a preserving pan, or a heavy-based saucepan with a capacity of 8¾ pints (5 litres); seven 1 lb (350 ml capacity) jars and one ½ lb (175 ml capacity) jar, all sterilised (see page 97).

Giardiniere Pickles (Italian Garden Pickles)

I had a spell of work in Italy when I was 21, and one of my abiding memories of all those Italian meals was that Sunday lunch always began with a plate of salamis, prosciutto and mortadella served with pickled vegetables. I loved the way the pickles cut through the richness of the meats. So, here is another recipe by our chef Lucy Crabb, which she calls Italian Garden Pickles.

Makes four 17½ fl oz (500 ml) preserving jars

8 oz (225 g) red onions, peeled
8 oz (225 g) courgettes
12 oz (350 g) aubergine
9 oz (250 g) trimmed fennel bulb
1 medium red pepper
1 medium yellow pepper
4 oz (110 g) button mushrooms
4 oz (110 g) cherry tomatoes
(or small vine tomatoes)
6 cloves garlic, thinly sliced
7 tablespoons olive oil
1¼-1½ pints (725-850 ml) good-quality white wine vinegar
8 fresh bay leaves
8 small sprigs each fresh rosemary and thyme
16 black peppercorns
6 oz (175 g) sea salt

You will also need four 17½ fl oz (500 ml) preserving jars, sterilised (see page 97).

This has to begin the night before with the normal salting process. Work your way through the list of vegetables until they are all prepared: cut each onion into eight wedges through the root; next, cut the courgettes and aubergine into thick matchsticks, and the fennel bulb into wedges; lastly, core and deseed the peppers and cut them into 2 inch (5 cm) chunks. Now layer all the vegetables, except the tomatoes and garlic, in a non-metallic bowl, and as you pile them in, sprinkle salt between the layers. Now pour over 3 pints (1.75 litres) of water, cover with a plate with a weight on it to submerge the vegetables, and leave the bowl in a cool place overnight.

Next day, drain the vegetables in a colander, then rinse them well under cold, running water. Now shake off the excess water, dry them in a clean tea cloth, and leave them spread out for about 3 hours on another clean tea cloth to thoroughly dry off.

After that, tip the vegetables into a bowl and stir in the garlic, along with the tomatoes and olive oil. Next, pour a thin layer of vinegar into the bottom of the hot, sterilised jars and add a bay leaf, a sprig of rosemary and a sprig of thyme. Then pack in the vegetables, adding the remainder of the herbs and peppercorns as you go, and pour in enough vinegar over each layer to ensure the vegetables are covered completely. Now swivel the jars to make sure the air is expelled and really press the vegetables down under the liquid before you cover with vinegar-proof lids. Label when cold and store the pickles in a cool, dry, dark place to mellow for a month before eating. They will keep for up to 6 months.

Pickled Okra

This is one of my most favourite pickles. The recipe was given to me by a very talented artist, Deborah MacMillan, whose paintings (I have three) I am very attached to. When I bought my first one, Night Swimmer, *she offered me a glass of wine and some pickled okra, then, as I was so taken with it, kindly gave me the recipe.*

Makes two 17½ fl oz (500 ml) jars
1 lb (450 g) small okra
4 cloves garlic, peeled
1¼ pints (725 ml) distilled vinegar
4 oz (110 g) light soft brown sugar
1 tablespoon sea salt

You will also need two 17½ fl oz (500 ml) preserving jars, sterilised (see page 97).

Begin this the night before. First of all, wash the okra, put it into a colander and sprinkle it with the salt. Cover with a clean tea cloth, put a large bowl underneath it to catch the juices and leave it overnight.

Next day, rinse the okra, then press them to get rid of the excess moisture and dry them with the cloth. Then leave them spread out on it to thoroughly dry off. After that, pack the okra into the hot, sterilised jars, along with the garlic. Next, in a saucepan, slowly bring the vinegar to the boil with the sugar, boil for 3 minutes, then pour it over the okra and garlic, covering them completely. Now swivel the jars to make sure the air is expelled and really press the vegetables down under the liquid before you place waxed discs on top. Seal tightly with vinegar-proof lids, label when cold and store in a cool, dry, dark place to mellow for 3 months before eating.

Pickled Peppers and Courgettes

*This is adapted from an old Cordon Bleu recipe for pickled cucumber.
It's one of the best, in my opinion, for serving with pâtés, as it provides
a bit of crunch and acidity to cut through the richness.*

Begin this the night before. First, deseed the peppers, cut out any pith
and slice them into 2 inch (5 cm) strips. Next, trim and slice the courgettes
into diagonal ½ inch (1 cm) slices. After that, halve the onions and cut
them into ¼ inch (5 mm) slices. Now pack the vegetables into a large
colander in layers, sprinkling each layer with salt, put a dish underneath
it to catch the juices and another with a weight on it on top, and leave
them overnight.

Next day, rinse the vegetables under cold, running water, really press
them to get rid of any excess moisture, and pat them dry with a clean tea
cloth. Then leave them spread out on the cloth for about 2 hours to
thoroughly dry off.

After that, place the vinegar, sugar and spices, including the chillies, in
a saucepan and stir them together over a medium heat until the sugar has
completely dissolved. Let it all simmer for about 3 minutes and then add
the vegetables, simmering for another 3 minutes. Then divide the pickle
between the hot, sterilised jars, packing it right up to the top. Swivel them
to make sure the air is expelled and really press the vegetables down under
the liquid before you place waxed discs on top. Then seal tightly with
vinegar-proof lids, label the jars when cold and store the pickles in a cool,
dry, dark place. They are supposed to be kept for 3 months to mellow
before eating (if you are patient), but I've found them to be very good in
about a month.

*Makes four 17½ fl oz (500 ml)
preserving jars*
2 large red peppers
2 lb 8 oz (1.15 kg) courgettes
(no need to peel)
12 oz (350 g) red onion (about
3 onions), peeled
1½ pints (850 ml) good-quality
white wine vinegar
8 oz (225 g) demerara sugar
1 oz (25 g) mustard seeds
1 teaspoon celery seeds
1 rounded teaspoon ground turmeric
½ teaspoon ground mace
2 medium-sized red chillies, deseeded
and thinly sliced
1½ oz (40 g) sea salt, lightly crushed

You will also need four 17½ fl oz
(500 ml) preserving jars, sterilised
(see page 97).

113

Sour Dill Pickles

Supermarket dill-pickled cucumbers are always a bit on the sweet side for me, so this is my attempt at capturing that lovely sour New York deli-type pickle.

Makes two 17½ fl oz (500 ml) preserving jars
¾ oz (20 g) fresh dill, stalks removed, broken into sprigs
1 lb (450g) ridge cucumbers (small cucumbers)
4 shallots
1 pint (570 ml) good-quality white wine vinegar
1 heaped teaspoon coriander seeds
1 heaped teaspoon black peppercorns
1 oz (25 g) sea salt

You will also need two 17½ fl oz (500 ml) preserving jars, sterilised (see page 97).

You need to begin this the night before. First of all, cut the cucumbers in half lengthways and then in quarters lengthways, then cut them on the diagonal into 1 inch (2.5 cm) chunks. After that, peel and slice the shallots in half through the root, then into three. Next, you need to place the cucumbers and shallots in layers in a non-metallic colander and sprinkle with the salt between each layer, making sure they are fairly evenly coated. Then place a plate over them, press it down with a scale weight, or something equally heavy, and leave them overnight so the salt can draw out the excess moisture. Put a dish underneath the colander to catch the drips.

Next day, rinse the vegetables under cold, running water and dry them in a clean tea cloth, then spread them out on the cloth for about an hour to thoroughly dry off. After that, pack them into the hot, sterilised jars.

Now place the vinegar and spices in a saucepan, along with the dill, bring it up to the boil and simmer for about 30 seconds, then pour the whole lot over the vegetables, covering them completely. Swivel the jars to make sure the air is expelled and really press the vegetables down under the liquid before you place waxed discs on top. Then seal tightly with vinegar-proof lids, label when cold and store the pickles in a cool, dry, dark place to mellow for 3 months before eating.

5

Waist watchers

This chapter is included by overwhelming popular demand. On my website it is the most requested subject. There are, it seems, millions of waist watchers out there asking for help: please can we have recipes that taste good but are not fattening; can you help us to eat well but stay slim? I've never been one to turn down a challenge and, I have to say, it is a subject that has occupied my thoughts and a great deal of my time for months. I have concluded what we need to do first is stand back, rid ourselves of the myths and confusion, and focus on what the basic problem is.

Let me say from the outset that I am not a qualified nutritionist; I can only offer you my own views and thoughts, and what has been helpful to me personally over the years.

The problem. Simply that we eat too much and do too little. During the war and for a while afterwards we had fewer food choices than today and didn't have cars, so we did a hell of a lot of walking or cycling to get around. Nowadays, we ride everywhere and consume far more snack-type foods and chocolate bars. If sweets and crisps and snacks are a regular part of your daily diet, then me offering you low-fat recipes won't help one bit.

The myth of healthy foods. I'm thoroughly fed up of hearing about 'healthy' foods. It's an absolute con. What we have to grasp is there's *no* such thing. *All* food, if it is pure and natural, is good for you: it provides pleasure, comfort, community – all that's important in life. Imagine Mother Nature saying, here are all the good things of the earth to give you pleasure, and then rapping you on the knuckles, saying, but don't eat this or that – it's bad for you!

What *is* unhealthy is too much of something. I know it's not sexy advice, but it does boil down to one thing, and that's balance. A doughnut is not unhealthy, neither is a KitKat or a steak-and-kidney pudding or even half a pint (275 ml) of double cream. If you're not eating too much, you can eat anything. Those things (if they existed at all) were treats during the war, not something available every hour of every day. Cookery presenters like me are always in the firing line. How, people ask, can you be using all that butter, all that cream? But the point is, I'm not saying, eat roast buttered chicken every day or even every week. I'm saying, if I'm not eating butter the rest of the week, why not have some on Sunday? I have always had an uphill struggle with my own weight, and what's helped me is treating Sundays or dinner with friends as a feast day. I will always make a dessert or a cake for weekends, but I very rarely eat sweet things on other days – it also gives me something to look forward to!

The big fat question. Just as we've been duped into thinking some foods are unhealthy, so we are also victims of the commercial low-fat lobby. Yes, we may well need to cut down our fat intake overall (and if we're not getting any exercise, we certainly do), but buying so-called low-fat products containing a load of other undesirable ingredients is sometimes not the way to do it. There is too often an unhealthy obsession with fat that regards it as poison. Spare me from egg-white omelettes, for instance, in which we are not allowed even the relatively small amount of fat contained in an egg yolk – it's bordering on madness. So, despite what you might have heard, fat isn't all bad, and we do need some in our diet.

The other culprit. Cutting down on *excessive* fat is one way to lose weight, but there's another ingredient that is often hidden away in all those manufactured low-fat foods and recipes. Carbohydrates, once consumed, are themselves converted into sugar, so any *added* sugar is going to be extra to that. (Also, lots of sugary foods contain lots of fat, too.) Not that having extra is necessarily a bad thing, but think about it – are you a person who *needs* sweetness every day? Really enjoying something sweet is different to actually *needing* it. That need may not be a problem if you're not overweight, but, if you are, it could be. Enjoying sweet things now and then is part of the joy of eating. But if you need to lose weight, they have to be restricted, and sometimes it's helpful to use a sweetener, but, again, not every day. Some of our weight problems can be put down to this addiction to unnatural sweetness.

Sugar is a highly refined, concentrated form of sweetness and if you were to remove it (along with artificial sweeteners) from your diet, a minor miracle would happen: you would eventually cease to be an addict. In fact, in about six weeks, you would begin to discover how wonderfully sweet an apple or a glass of milk is. When I gave up adding sugar to tea and coffee I hated it for weeks, but when I put it back I hated it more, and understood how the sweetness had been masking the real flavour. Once you've managed to kick the habit, you'll find most commercial products too sweet and you won't want them. (It's my theory that chocoholics may not be addicted to cocoa, but simply to sweetness.)

Getting the right balance. The now famous advice to eat five portions of fruit and vegetables every day is a sound one, and should also lessen the desire for sugary snacks – an excellent way of beginning to cut down on the wrong sorts of food. It's also important to remember that you can have something of everything, but not too much of anything. As a seasoned dieter myself, I now feel that one of the best ways to achieve that balance and lose weight sensibly is the Weight Watchers™ programme. I like the fact that with the points system no foods are taboo, and several of my friends – even if they're not continuing to diet – have been helped to re-educate themselves into a much more sensible pattern of eating.

The recipes. The question remains, what can the home cook do to make losing a few pounds more interesting? What I have attempted to do here is provide recipes that contain the minimum amount of fat and hardly any sugar. In some cases, there may be a minimal quantity of sweetener, and I'm aware of the controversy surrounding its use, but soft drinks and most yoghurts contain it and I would be far more worried about those being consumed on a daily basis than I am about its appearance in the occasional, once- or twice-a-week dessert.

You'll find that cooking non-fattening dishes is a lot easier if you stock up on a number of basic ingredients. Some of these items have been written about in Book Two, but, in addition, you'll find the following useful.

Diet products

Fromage frais: The best low-fat versions I've found are one from Isigny in Normandy (a version with 8 per cent fat), and La Faisselle, the strained fromage frais. Both are divine eaten just as they are, or with fruit, or even spread on bread instead of butter – you'll be amazed how this can give you a real dairy taste without all the fat. I also use fromage frais a lot in cooking in place of cream. There is, if you are seriously cutting down, an Isigny fromage frais with virtually no fat at all.

0 per cent Greek yoghurt: A brilliant product – still thick and 'creamy', with no fat, no sugar and no artificial flavour. This, together with fresh fruit, is a delight for breakfast.

Natural low-fat yoghurt: Although I prefer the Greek yoghurt for eating, I have found natural low-fat yoghurt is sometimes better for cooking.

Quark: A soft, white, skimmed-milk, very low-fat cheese. For an instant snack, try it spread on sesame Ryvitas with Marmite, or add it to scrambled eggs or mashed potato.

Cottage cheese: The slimmer's friend, sprinkled with chives and served with a salad, or in low-fat Cappuccino Cheesecakes (see page 146).

Buttermilk: Since embarking on this chapter, I have discovered that buttermilk makes a wonderful marinade ingredient. Both fish and chicken respond beautifully to it, becoming moister and more luscious.

Semi-skimmed milk: I'm afraid I can't cope with skimmed milk, so I opt for semi-skimmed, which still has some residual creaminess. When I've really needed to cut down, I have allowed myself 5 fl oz (150 ml) per day.

Light evaporated milk: Great for cooking, as it's the nearest thing to cream without all the fat (see Slimmers' Wild Mushroom Risotto on page 139).

Half-fat crème fraîche: Useful, but do add it sparingly, as it contains more fat than the ingredients above.

Oriental ingredients: In my recipes I have included Japanese soy sauce, mirin (Japanese sweet rice wine), Shaosing (Chinese brown rice wine) and Thai fish sauce (make sure you buy an authentic one, as some of the fish sauces available are over-salty). All these are really helpful as you can add lots of flavour with little or no fat. Even toasted sesame oil, though it *is* an oil, is so strong and assertive you need only a minimal amount.

Oil, butter and cheese: Not, as you might have thought, banned totally, but to be used in minute quantities – I've confined myself to using no more than a teaspoon of oil or butter per person when creating the diet recipes in this chapter. Strong-flavoured cheeses, such as Parmesan and Pecorino, give a fair amount of cheese flavour without too many calories.

Bloody Mary Soup with Vodka Tomato Salsa

More of a Virgin Mary really, but there's nothing to stop you adding a shot of vodka if you have the mind to. Honestly, though, it won't need it because it has a lovely spicy kick of its own, and the very best news is it must easily be the fastest soup to make on record, although it tastes as though it took hours!

First place the tomatoes (including the one for the salsa) in a heatproof bowl, pour boiling water over them and count 60 seconds. After that, pour off the water and slip off their skins (protecting your hands with a cloth if the tomatoes are hot). Reserve the tomato for the salsa and chop the others very finely, adding them to a medium-sized saucepan. Bring them up to a gentle simmer and let them cook for about 3 minutes.

Meanwhile, make the salsa. Cut the reserved tomato in half, then squeeze out the seeds and dice the flesh. Now mix the tomato and the celery with the remaining ingredients.

Next, pour the tomato juice and the rest of the soup ingredients into the saucepan and season. Taste and add more Tabasco or lime, if needed. Now bring everything back up to simmering point. Then ladle the soup into hot bowls and spoon half the salsa on to each one before serving.

Serves 2
3 large ripe tomatoes (weighing about 6 oz/175 g)
18 fl oz (510 ml) fresh tomato juice
1 tablespoon Worcestershire sauce
1 tablespoon balsamic vinegar
juice 1 lime
4 drops Tabasco sauce
salt and freshly milled black pepper

For the salsa:
2 teaspoons vodka
1 medium-sized ripe tomato
3 inch (7.5 cm) piece celery, destringed and diced
¼ teaspoon celery salt
2 dashes Tabasco sauce

Marinated Chicken Brochettes with Green Couscous

Buttermilk makes a superb marinade – so much so you'll wonder why you ever needed oil. The chicken will be luscious and tender and, with all the other wonderful flavours, you'll forget this is in any way a diet recipe. This is also good served with the Coriander Chutney from Book One.

Serves 2

2 x 6 oz (175 g) boneless chicken breasts, skin removed
6 fresh bay leaves, cut in half
½ medium red onion, peeled, halved and separated into 8 layers
½ large yellow pepper, deseeded and cut into 8
1 teaspoon groundnut or other flavourless oil
salt and freshly milled black pepper

For the marinade:
1 clove garlic
1 teaspoon peeled, grated fresh root ginger
1 medium-sized green chilli, deseeded
1 tablespoon fresh coriander leaves
1 teaspoon ground turmeric
6 fl oz (175 ml) buttermilk
salt and freshly milled black pepper

For the couscous:
5 oz (150 g) couscous
9 fl oz (250 ml) boiling chicken or vegetable stock
4 spring onions, including the green parts, finely chopped
2 tablespoons chopped fresh coriander
1 oz (25 g) rocket, leaves finely chopped
2 limes: juice of 1, 1 cut into wedges, to garnish
salt and freshly milled black pepper

You will also need two wooden skewers, about 10 inches (25.5 cm) long.

First of all, you need to make the marinade. To do this, use a pestle and mortar to crush the garlic with about ½ teaspoon of salt until it becomes a purée. Next, add the grated ginger. Then chop the chilli and coriander and mix these with the garlic and ginger, along with the turmeric and some freshly milled black pepper. After that, pour the buttermilk into a bowl and whisk the other ingredients into it.

Now cut each chicken breast into five pieces, add them to the bowl and give everything a good stir. Then press the chicken down well into the marinade, cover the surface with clingfilm and pop the bowl into the fridge for a few hours or, preferably, overnight.

When you are almost ready to cook the chicken, soak the skewers in hot water for 30 minutes (to prevent them burning). Pre-heat the grill to its highest setting for at least 10 minutes and line the grill pan with kitchen foil.

Next, dry the skewers in a clean tea cloth and thread half a bay leaf on to each one, then a piece of chicken, a piece of onion and a piece of pepper. Carry on alternating the bay leaf, chicken, onion and pepper until you have threaded five pieces of chicken on to each skewer, finishing with half a bay leaf on each. Make sure you pack everything together as tightly as possible, then season with salt and freshly milled black pepper and brush the vegetables with a minute amount of oil. Lay the brochettes on the grill rack and place them under the grill, about 4 inches (10 cm) from the heat source. Brush liberally with some of the remaining marinade and grill them for 10 minutes, before turning them over and grilling them for a further 10 minutes, brushing them with more of the marinade as they cook, and watching them carefully so they don't burn.

While the chicken is cooking, place the couscous in a largish bowl, then pour the boiling stock over it, add some salt and freshly milled black pepper and stir it with a fork. Then leave it on one side for 5 minutes, by which time it will have absorbed all the stock and softened. After that, fluff it up by making cutting movements across and through it with a knife. Then stir in the remaining couscous ingredients and season to taste.

When the chicken is ready, pop the brochettes on top of the couscous and serve straightaway on warmed serving plates, garnished with the wedges of lime.

PER SERVING
CHICKEN: 260 kcal, FAT 4.2 g, SATURATES 1 g, PROTEIN 46.3 g, CARBOHYDRATE 10.3 g
COUSCOUS: 178 kcal, FAT 0.9 g, SATURATES 0 g, PROTEIN 4.9 g, CARBOHYDRATE 39.5 g

Swordfish Ceviche

Ceviche is a dish in which fish is 'cooked' in lime or lemon juice with lots of other gutsy flavours. I love to serve it on a hot summer's day, but it's good at any time of year when you want something really interesting that doesn't contain any added fat.

Serves 4

1 lb 4 oz (570 g) skinned swordfish, cut into ½ inch (1 cm) cubes
8 oz (225 g) tomatoes, preferably yellow
6 oz (175 g) red onion (about 1 medium onion), peeled and very thinly sliced
1 fat clove garlic, finely chopped
½ oz (10 g) chopped fresh coriander leaves, plus 1 tablespoon coriander leaves to garnish
1 tablespoon chopped fresh mint leaves
juice 6 limes (about 6 fl oz/175 ml)
1 teaspoon black peppercorns, crushed
1 teaspoon sea salt

You will also need a shallow serving dish with a base measurement of 6½ x 8 inches (16 x 20 cm).

Begin by skinning the tomatoes. Place them in a heatproof bowl and pour boiling water on to them. After exactly a minute (or 15-30 seconds if the tomatoes are small), remove them from the water and slip off their skins (protecting your hands with a cloth if they are hot). Then cut them in half, squeeze out the seeds and cut them in half again to make quarters.

Next, layer the swordfish, tomatoes, onion, garlic, and chopped coriander and mint leaves in the serving dish, sprinkling with the salt and freshly crushed black pepper. Now simply pour over the lime juice and press down with your hands so that everything is well covered with juice. Then cover the dish with clingfilm and refrigerate for 12 hours, turning the fish over once during that time.

Serve with salad leaves and garnished with the remaining coriander.

PER SERVING: 187 kcal, FAT 6.2 g, SATURATES 1.3 g, PROTEIN 27 g, CARBOHYDRATE 6.2 g

This is probably the most difficult challenge in low-fat cooking (apart from creating a low-fat chocolate dessert). If I'm watching the fat content in my diet, I often just squeeze lemon or lime juice over my salad, or sometimes, particularly with tomatoes, I use balsamic vinegar. However, that can become boring, so here are three very low-fat dressings to enliven your salads and, hopefully, help you forget the word 'diet'.

A low-fat version of a classic dressing.
Crush the garlic and salt with a pestle and mortar until creamy, and then work in the mustard and some freshly milled black pepper. Next, add the oil, wine and vinegar and blend well with a small whisk. Whisk again before dressing the salad.

PER SERVING: 29 kcal, FAT 2 g, SATURATES 0.3 g, PROTEIN 0.6 g, CARBOHYDRATE 0.5 g

This is popular in America, but normally mega-calorific!
You'll need to start off by making the Almost Mayonnaise on page 126 and then chill it for a couple of hours in the fridge. All you do now is mix all the remaining ingredients into the mayonnaise, whisk the whole lot together until well blended and sprinkle with the cayenne pepper.

PER SERVING: 56 kcal, FAT 1.5 g, SATURATES 0.4 g, PROTEIN 3.4 g, CARBOHYDRATE 7.5 g

Yes, it does contain cheese, but very little gives a lot of flavour!
This one's even speedier! Just whiz everything together in the small bowl of a food processor, or in a small mixing bowl, using an electric hand whisk (in which case, you'll need to crush the garlic first). Sprinkle with the chives and it's ready to serve.

PER SERVING: 34 kcal, FAT 2.7 g, SATURATES 1.6 g,
PROTEIN 2.1 g, CARBOHYDRATE 0.7 g

*Clockwise, from left: Almost Vinaigrette,
Thousand Island Dressing and Blue-
Cheese Dressing*

Almost Vinaigrette
Serves 2
1 teaspoon olive oil
1 small clove garlic
1 teaspoon wholegrain mustard
1 tablespoon wine (any colour)
1 tablespoon balsamic vinegar
¼ teaspoon sea salt
freshly milled black pepper

Thousand Island Dressing
Serves 2
2 tablespoons Almost Mayonnaise
(see page 126)
2 tablespoons tomato-and-chilli relish
1 cornichon (baby gherkin),
finely chopped
a pinch of cayenne pepper
salt and freshly milled black pepper

Blue-Cheese Dressing
Serves 3-4
1 oz (25 g) Gorgonzola Piccante,
at room temperature
5 oz (150 g) 0 per cent Greek yoghurt
1 small clove garlic
1 tablespoon semi-skimmed milk
a few freshly snipped chives
salt and freshly milled black pepper

Almost
Mayonnaise

This is adapted from Eliza Acton's recipe for English Salad Sauce, written in the 1840s. While hers used double cream, the recipe below uses eight per cent fat fromage frais. The vote from the team when we were testing this is that it's every bit as good as the original.

Serves 4-6
3 large eggs
1 tablespoon cold water
2 pinches cayenne pepper
5 fl oz (150 ml) 8 per cent fat
fromage frais
4 teaspoons white wine vinegar
¼ teaspoon salt

First, place the eggs in a saucepan and cover completely with plenty of cold water. Bring the water up to simmering point and give them exactly 9 minutes from the time it starts boiling. Then cool them under cold, running water to stop them cooking any further. Now peel away the shells, cut the eggs in half and place the yolks only in a mixing bowl.

Add the tablespoon of cold water and pound the yolks to a smooth paste with a wooden spoon. Then add the cayenne pepper and salt, and stir in the fromage frais, bit by bit, mixing it smoothly as you go. When it's all in, add the vinegar, check the seasoning and add more if it needs it. If you think the mixture's far too runny at this stage, don't worry. Cover the bowl and leave it for a couple of hours in the fridge, after which time it will have thickened. (It should, in any case, have the consistency of thickish cream, rather than mayonnaise.)

Note: To make a low-fat Tartare Sauce, after chilling the Almost Mayonnaise, add 1 small garlic clove, chopped; ½ teaspoon mustard powder; 1 dessertspoon lemon juice; 1 tablespoon chopped fresh flat-leaf parsley; 1 heaped tablespoon salted capers and 4 cornichons (baby gherkins), both chopped; and mix together.

PER SERVING: 65 kcal, FAT 3.7 g, SATURATES 1.1 g, PROTEIN 6.1 g, CARBOHYDRATE 1.8 g

Sea Bass with Puy Lentil Salsa

This is an extremely fast supper dish for two people that is full of colour and flavour. Some small new potatoes would make a good accompaniment, but for serious waist watchers, I don't think it really needs it.

Serves 2

2 sea bass fillets (each weighing
7-8 oz/200-225 g)
1 teaspoon olive oil
½ lime, cut into wedges
salt and freshly milled black pepper

For the lentil salsa:

1½ oz (40 g) Puy lentils (no need
to soak), rinsed
4 fl oz (120 ml) water
1 large tomato
¼ medium red onion, peeled
1 small red chilli, halved and deseeded
2 tablespoons fresh coriander leaves
juice 1 lime
salt and freshly milled black pepper

Begin by making the lentil salsa. Place the lentils in a small saucepan with the water and some salt. Next, bring them up to simmering point and gently simmer without a lid for about 30 minutes, or until they are tender but still have some bite and retain their shape, by which time, most of the water will have been absorbed.

While the lentils are cooking, skin the tomato. Do this by placing it in a heatproof bowl and pouring boiling water on to it. After exactly a minute, remove it from the water and slip off the skin (protecting your hands with a cloth if the tomato is hot), then halve it and squeeze out the seeds. Now chop it into small pieces. After that, chop the onion and chilli very small, add the tomato and coriander, and keep all this aside, covered in clingfilm, until needed.

When the lentils are cooked, empty them into a bowl and while they are still warm, toss them in the lime juice. Now taste to check the seasoning and add the rest of the prepared salsa ingredients. Mix well and leave aside in a cool place.

To cook the fish, you need to pre-heat the grill to its highest setting for at least 10 minutes. Next, line a grill tray with kitchen foil, brush the fish fillets on both sides with the oil and place them on the tray flesh-side up. Season with salt and freshly milled black pepper, then grill for 5-6 minutes, turning halfway through, or until just cooked through. Serve straightaway with the salsa and some lime wedges to squeeze over.

Note: Sometimes farmed sea bass fillets are very small, in which case, use two per person.

PER SERVING: 311 kcal, FAT 7.5 g, SATURATES 1.2 g, PROTEIN 47 g, CARBOHYDRATE 14.9 g

Chinese Steamed Trout with Ginger and Spring Onions

As with salmon, trout is slightly higher in fat, but still very low compared with meat. The fat in both trout and salmon is the good kind we all need to include in our diets. If you're wondering what the pink bits are in the photograph, they're pink spring onions, which looked very pretty the day we took the picture!

Serves 2

2 whole trout (each weighing about 8 oz/225 g), gutted
1 inch (2.5 cm) piece of fresh root ginger, peeled and cut into thin strips
4 spring onions
1 clove garlic, sliced thinly
1 dessertspoon crushed sea salt

For the sauce:

1 teaspoon peeled, grated fresh root ginger
1 clove garlic, chopped
3 tablespoons Japanese soy sauce
3 tablespoons Shaosing (Chinese brown rice wine)
1 teaspoon toasted sesame oil
½ teaspoon dark soft brown sugar

You will also need a steamer.

First of all, rinse the trout and dry it with kitchen paper, then sprinkle the outside of the fish with salt and leave aside for half an hour to help firm up the flesh. Meanwhile, place all the sauce ingredients in a small saucepan, then bring them up to simmering point and simmer for 5 minutes.

Next, the spring onions should be cut in half where the green and white parts meet, and the very green part cut in diagonals (making diamond shapes when opened out). The rest should be thinly shredded lengthways.

When you're ready to cook the trout, wipe the salt away with some more kitchen paper and place the fish in the steamer, with the ginger and garlic scattered inside and all over. Place it over boiling water and steam with a lid on for exactly 15 minutes.

Serve the trout with the re-heated sauce poured over and garnished with the spring onions. Plain basmati rice would be a good accompaniment.

PER SERVING: 319 kcal, FAT 13.3 g, SATURATES 2.7 g, PROTEIN 45.5 g, CARBOHYDRATE 4.8 g

Eggs and Leeks en Cocotte

This can be a starter or a light snack for one person, providing something very special for the bored dieter. You can ring the changes, too – instead of leeks, use steamed asparagus tips or lightly cooked, chopped spinach. For a low-fat accompaniment, serve with wholemeal bread spread with a little Greek yoghurt instead of butter.

First of all, cut the leek vertically, fan it under cold, running water to get rid of any dirt, then chop it quite finely. Now place a small pan over a medium heat, add the leeks and some seasoning, stir, then turn the heat down to low. Cover and let them cook gently in their own juices for about 5 minutes, shaking the pan and stirring two or three times. After that, use a draining spoon to transfer them to the ramekin (or dish).

Next, carefully break the egg in on top of the leeks and add some seasoning. Then gently spoon the yoghurt over, spreading it out with a knife so it covers the egg completely. Finally, sprinkle with the Parmesan.

Now pour about 1 inch (2.5 cm) of boiling water into the roasting tin, place the ramekin (or dish) in it and pop the whole lot in the oven to bake for 15-18 minutes, depending on how you like your egg cooked (bearing in mind it will go on cooking after it has been removed from the oven).

Serves 1
1 large egg
2 oz (50 g) leeks (about 1 medium leek), trimmed
2 rounded tablespoons 5 per cent Greek yoghurt
½ teaspoon freshly grated Parmesan (Parmigiano Reggiano)
salt and freshly milled black pepper

You will also need a ramekin 1½ inches/4 cm deep, with a base diameter of 3 inches/7.5 cm (or a small, round ovenproof dish), smeared with a trace of butter from a butter paper; and a small roasting tin.

Pre-heat the oven to gas mark 4, 350°F (180°C).

Turkey
Saltimbocca

This is a variation on the famous Italian recipe made with thin escalopes of veal – but turkey is usually easier to find. However, you can ring the changes by using veal, or even slices of pork fillet.

Serves 2
2 turkey steaks (weighing about 10 oz/275 g in total – choose fairly equal-sized steaks)
6 slices Parma ham (weighing about 3 oz/75 g in total)
8 large fresh sage leaves
8 fl oz (225 ml) dry Marsala
1 teaspoon olive oil
salt and freshly milled black pepper

You will also need a medium-sized frying pan and eight cocktail sticks.

First of all, prepare the turkey steaks, which need to be flattened out. So, place one of them between two large pieces of clingfilm and gently pound it using a rolling pin, being careful not to break the meat. It needs to be flattened out to a shape measuring about 6 x 7 inches (15 x 18 cm), ⅛-¼ inch (3-5 mm) thick. Repeat this with the second turkey steak, between two fresh pieces of clingfilm. Then cut each flattened steak into four pieces measuring about 3 x 3½ inches (7.5 x 9 cm).

Next, you need to separate the slices of Parma ham, trim away the fat and cut a 1½ inch (4 cm) strip off the end of each slice. (You'll need these smaller pieces of ham to finish off two of the turkey pieces.) Now place a piece of ham on each slice of turkey, folding and creasing it up to fit, if necessary, then divide the six smaller pieces of ham between the last two turkey slices. Finally, top each one with a sage leaf and secure the whole thing together with a cocktail stick. Then season each piece on both sides with salt and freshly milled black pepper.

Next, measure the Marsala into a small saucepan and heat it gently until it begins to bubble. While that's happening, cook the turkey: heat the oil in the frying pan over a fairly high heat and when it's really hot, put in half the pieces of turkey, sage-side down, reduce the heat to medium and fry for 2-3 minutes, until crisp and golden. Then turn them over and give the other side about a minute before removing them to a warmed serving dish. Do the same with the remaining pieces and when they're done, keep them warm with the others. Now pour the warmed Marsala into the frying pan, turn the heat right up again and let it bubble and reduce to a syrupy sauce, which should take 4-5 minutes. Return the turkey pieces to the pan and turn in the sauce. Serve on warmed plates (not forgetting to remove the cocktail sticks!) with the syrupy sauce poured over.

PER SERVING: 352 kcal, FAT 7.5 g, SATURATES 2.3 g, PROTEIN 44.1 g, CARBOHYDRATE 7.3 g

Oriental
Chicken

It's hard to believe something so simple and easy can, firstly, be low-fat and secondly, taste so very good. I guarantee that once you've made this once, you'll go on making it forever.

Serves 2

4 plump free-range chicken thighs
5 fl oz (150 ml) Shaosing (Chinese brown rice wine)
3 fl oz (75 ml) Japanese soy sauce
2 fl oz (55 ml) water
1 heaped teaspoon peeled, grated fresh root ginger
4 cloves garlic, crushed
5 whole star anise
1 teaspoon toasted sesame oil

To garnish:
1 small red chilli, deseeded and cut into fine shreds
1 spring onion, cut into fine shreds

To serve:
5 fl oz (150 ml) rice, cooked

You will also need a small flameproof casserole.

Pre-heat the oven to gas mark 6, 400°F (200°C).

I'm afraid you're first going to have to remove the skin from the chicken, but because of all the lovely flavours, you won't miss it. Then place the skinned chicken thighs in the casserole. Now mix the rest of the ingredients together in a bowl and pour this mixture over the chicken, place the casserole over a medium heat and bring the liquid to the boil. Now transfer it to the oven (no need to cover) and bake on the centre shelf for 40 minutes, turning the chicken halfway through the cooking time.

Serve the cooked chicken on a bed of plain rice with the sauce poured over and the shreds of chilli and spring onion sprinkled on top.

PER SERVING
CHICKEN: 146 kcal, FAT 4.5 g, SATURATES 1.1 g, PROTEIN 22.8 g, CARBOHYDRATE 4.5 g
RICE: 287 kcal, FAT 2.7 g, SATURATES 0.7 g, PROTEIN 5.5 g, CARBOHYDRATE 64.3 g

Oriental Green Beans with Red Chillies and Toasted Sesame Seeds

This is a vegetable dish that will accompany any oriental recipe, or can be served with a bowl of rice or noodles all on its own.

First toast the sesame seeds. Place a small saucepan over a medium heat to heat through, then add the sesame seeds. Shake and keep them on the move until they have turned golden and begin to splutter – about a minute. Then remove the pan from the heat and allow it to cool. After that, add the rest of the sauce ingredients, return the pan to the heat and simmer for 5 minutes.

All this can be done well in advance, then, when you're ready to cook the beans, steam them over simmering water for about 6 minutes, or until tender, then toss them quickly in the sauce just before serving.

Serves 2, or 4 as an accompaniment
8 oz (225 g) dwarf beans (or fine green beans), topped, but tails left on

For the sauce:
1 small red chilli, deseeded and very finely chopped
1 heaped teaspoon sesame seeds
2 tablespoons Japanese soy sauce
2 tablespoons Shaosing (Chinese brown rice wine)

You will also need a steamer.

Steamed Cod with Nori and Soba Noodle Salad

This is a wonderful combination of flavours and textures – and only contains half a teaspoon of oil between two people! In the photograph, we used green tea soba noodles – buckwheat noodles made with green tea – but if you find these difficult to get, ordinary soba noodles are fine. Most of the other ingredients are readily available in all supermarkets, but we also have a stockist on page 235.

Serves 2

10 oz (275 g) skinless cod fillet
2 sheets toasted nori seaweed
1 tablespoon Japanese soy sauce
1 tablespoon Thai fish sauce
2 tablespoons cold water
2 tablespoons Japanese pickled ginger, to serve

For the noodle salad:

7 oz (200 g) dried soba noodles
3 tablespoons Japanese soy sauce
3 tablespoons lime juice
½ teaspoon toasted sesame oil
about 6 sprigs watercress
a pinch salt

You will also need a Chinese bamboo steamer or a fan steamer.

First of all, cut the cod into eight equal pieces measuring about 1½ x 2 inches (4 x 5 cm), then mix these with the soy sauce, fish sauce and water in a medium-sized bowl. Now stir the cod around, cover it with clingfilm and leave it to marinate in the fridge for about an hour, stirring it around once or twice more in that time.

While the fish is marinating, make the soba noodle salad. What you do here is – as for pasta – have plenty of water boiling in a largish saucepan with a little salt added. Boil the noodles for exactly 3 minutes, then drain them in a colander and let the cold tap run on them while you lift and shake them with your hands. (They need to be cooled down quickly, otherwise the heat makes them sticky.) After that, shake off all the excess water and place the noodles in a bowl. Now whisk the soy sauce, lime juice and sesame oil together and pour this over the noodles, mixing well so they are all coated in the dressing.

Now for the fish. Towards the end of the marinating time, place the steamer over a pan of boiling water. (Pre-heating it will prevent the nori sticking.) When you're ready to cook the fish, cut each of the nori sheets into quarters, then take one of them and lay it, shiny-side down on a clean, flat surface. Now take a pastry brush, dip it into the fish marinade and brush the nori. Then place a piece of cod in the centre, First fold in two opposite sides, then brush the two remaining flaps with a little more of the marinade and wrap them over the fish, too, to form a tight parcel. (Don't worry if some of the fish is not covered.)

Then repeat this with the remaining seven pieces of fish and quarters of nori. To cook them, place all the parcels seam-side down in the steamer, put a lid on and steam them for 5 minutes. Then serve them with the noodles, garnished with the watercress, and hand the pickled ginger around separately.

After brushing the surface of the nori with the fish marinade, fold the sides around the fish to form a tight parcel.

PER SERVING: 545 kcal, FAT 8 g, SATURATES 0 g, PROTEIN 42 g, CARBOHYDRATE 81 g

Slimmers' Wild Mushroom Risotto

This is an oven-baked risotto with the deep, fragrant flavour of mushrooms. It's extremely creamy and luscious but – can you believe it? – it contains no cream, no butter and, what's more, no cheese. The secret of all this lies in one simple ingredient – low-fat evaporated milk. Hard to believe, I know, but try it and see.

First of all, give the dried mushrooms a quick rinse in a sieve under cold, running water, then place them in a heatproof bowl and pour 1 pint (570 ml) boiling water over them. Then just leave them to soak and soften for about 30 minutes. Meanwhile, chop the fresh mushrooms into chunks – not too small, about ½ inch (1 cm), as they shrink quite a bit in the cooking. Now pre-heat the oven to gas mark 2, 300°F (150°C).

Next, put the shallots and the Madeira into a medium-sized saucepan, bring it up to simmering point and simmer gently for 10-15 minutes, until the shallots have softened and the Madeira has reduced down to about 2 tablespoons. Then remove the pan from the heat, add the fresh mushrooms, stir well and then leave the pan on one side.

When the dried mushrooms have softened, line a sieve with a double layer of absorbent kitchen paper, place it over a bowl and strain them, reserving the liquid. Squeeze them to remove any excess liquid, then chop them fairly finely.

Next, put the rice into the baking dish, along with the dried and fresh mushrooms and shallots, then season well with salt and freshly milled black pepper. Now whisk the evaporated milk into the reserved mushroom-soaking liquid, pour it over the rice and give it all a good stir. Place the dish on the centre shelf of the oven without covering, set a timer and give it exactly 20 minutes.

After that, gently stir and turn over the rice grains. Put the timer on again and give it a further 20-25 minutes' cooking – when ready, the risotto should be very slightly soupy, and the longer you leave it to stand, the thicker it will get, so, immediately it is ready, remove it from the oven and serve as soon as possible.

Serves 2-3

½ oz (10 g) dried porcini mushrooms
8 oz (225 g) fresh mixed mushrooms, such as dark-gilled open-cap, chestnut or girolles
6 fl oz (175 ml) carnaroli rice (use a measuring jug)
2 shallots, peeled and finely chopped
7 fl oz (200 ml) dry Madeira
7 fl oz (200 ml) Carnation Light (evaporated semi-skimmed) milk
salt and freshly milled black pepper

You will also need a 2½ inch (6 cm) deep baking dish, with a diameter of 9 inches (23 cm).

Thai Crab Salad with Mango

This is a low-fat variation of the Thai Grilled Beef Salad with Grapes in Book Two. In Thailand they serve it with pomelo, which is very similar to grapefruit. When they're not available, I use mango, but you could ring the changes with grapes or small segments of pink grapefruit.

Serves 4 as a light lunch or 6 as a starter
12 oz (350 g) each white crab meat and brown crab meat (or 2 medium-sized, ready-dressed crabs in the shell)
grated zest 1 lime (juice reserved for dressing)
3 tablespoons chopped fresh coriander
3 tablespoons chopped fresh mint

For the salad:
1 large mango, peeled and sliced into strips (see Book Two)
1 teaspoon sesame seeds
4 oz (110 g) rocket leaves, stalks removed
3 stems lemon grass, ends trimmed and tough outer layer discarded, then very finely sliced
6 kaffir lime leaves (if available), rolled into a cigar shape and very finely shredded
1 teaspoon freshly snipped chives

For the dressing:
2-3 medium-sized red chillies, halved and deseeded
2 cloves garlic
1 inch (2.5 cm) piece fresh root ginger, peeled
6 sprigs fresh coriander
1 sprig fresh mint
1½ tablespoons Thai fish sauce
juice 2 limes (about 3 tablespoons)
1 teaspoon light (or dark) soft brown sugar

First pre-heat a small frying pan over a medium heat, then add the sesame seeds. Keep them on the move until they're golden and begin to splutter – about a minute. Then remove the pan from the heat and allow it to cool.

Meanwhile, make the dressing. Blend the chillies, garlic, ginger, and sprigs of coriander and mint in a food processor or blender until finely chopped, then add the fish sauce, lime juice and sugar and whiz again.

Next, put the crab meat into a bowl and pour over three-quarters of the dressing, then add the lime zest and most of the chopped coriander and mint (saving some to sprinkle over later), and toss so it's well coated.

Now put the rocket leaves into a large serving bowl, toss them in the remaining dressing and pile the crab meat on top, along with slices of mango here and there. Then sprinkle over the lemon grass, lime leaves (if using), remaining coriander and mint, chives and sesame seeds.

PER SERVING: 161 kcal, FAT 5.7 g, SATURATES 0.8 g, PROTEIN 18.6 g, CARBOHYDRATE 9.5 g

Pasta with Pepper Relish

The great thing about this is that, because the flavour of the peppers and garlic is so intense, the pasta honestly doesn't need any cheese.

First dry-roast the cumin seeds in the frying pan for about a minute, until they become fragrant. Now add the oil and when it's hot, stir in the peppers, garlic and chillies and turn the heat down as low as possible. Then cover and cook slowly for about 40 minutes, stirring from time to time, until the peppers are really soft.

After that, add the tomatoes and the sun-dried tomato paste to the softened peppers. Season and continue to cook, uncovered, over a highish heat, until the mixture is reduced and thickened slightly – about 5 minutes.

Next, keep the sauce warm and cook the pasta – for a minute less than the pack instructions advise. Then drain it and quickly return it to the hot pan, along with the sauce, and place it over a gentle heat. Stir, and continue to cook for about another minute, to allow the pasta to absorb the sauce. Serve straightaway in hot bowls, garnished with the basil.

Serves 4
1 lb (450 g) pasta: rigatoni or spaghetti

For the relish:
1 lb (450 g) mixed red and yellow peppers (about 3 peppers in total), quartered, deseeded and cut into ¼ inch (5 mm) strips
1 rounded teaspoon cumin seeds, lightly crushed
1 dessertspoon olive oil
5 cloves garlic, chopped
2 medium-sized red chillies, deseeded and chopped
4 medium-sized ripe tomatoes, skinned (see page 121) and roughly chopped
2 tablespoons sun-dried tomato paste
4 sprigs fresh basil, to garnish
salt and freshly milled black pepper

You will also need a lidded frying pan with a 10 inch (25.5 cm) diameter.

Teriyaki Grilled Marinated Salmon with Marinated Cucumber and Sesame Salad

Serves 4

4 x 5 oz (150 g) skinless salmon fillets
½ teaspoon groundnut or other flavourless oil for greasing
a few freshly snipped chives, to garnish

For the marinade:
4 tablespoons each Japanese soy sauce, sake (Japanese rice wine) and mirin (Japanese sweet rice wine)
1 teaspoon golden caster sugar
1 tablespoon peeled, grated fresh root ginger
2 fat cloves garlic, crushed

For the salad:
1 cucumber
2 tablespoons sesame seeds
3 tablespoons Japanese soy sauce
2 teaspoons each sake, mirin and rice vinegar
1 teaspoon golden caster sugar

You will also need a large baking tray.

Like Chinese Steamed Trout (see page 130), this has a slightly higher fat content than the other Waist Watcher recipes because I'm using salmon, which works best, but it can be made with other fish, such as cod or haddock fillet, too.

To begin with, make the marinade. All you do is whisk together the soy sauce, sake, mirin, sugar, ginger and garlic. Next, place the salmon fillets in a small, shallow dish and pour the marinade over. Now cover them and leave in a cool place, turning them once, halfway through the marinating time.

To make the cucumber salad, begin by toasting the sesame seeds. Do this by pre-heating a medium-sized, heavy-based frying pan over a medium heat, then add the sesame seeds, moving them around in the pan to brown evenly. As soon as they begin to splutter and pop and turn golden, they're ready. This will take 1-2 minutes. Then remove them to a plate.

Next, cut the cucumber in half, then into quarters and then into eighths (all lengthways). Remove the seeds, then chop each piece on the diagonal into 3 inch (7.5 cm) strips and place them in a bowl.

After that, measure the soy sauce, sake, mirin, vinegar and sugar into a screw-top jar, shake them together thoroughly, then pour this mixture over the cucumber wedges and leave them to marinate for about an hour – again, giving them one good stir at half-time.

When you're ready to cook the salmon, pre-heat the grill to its highest setting for at least 10 minutes. Brush the baking tray with the oil and put it under the grill to pre-heat as well. When the grill is really hot, remove the tray, using a thick oven glove. Now take the salmon steaks out of the marinade (reserving it) and shake them slightly before placing them on to the baking tray. (They should sear and sizzle as they touch the hot metal.) Then position the tray about 3 inches (7.5 cm) from the heat source and grill them for 6 minutes exactly. I advise you to use a kitchen timer here, as the timing is pretty crucial.

Meanwhile, pour the marinade into a small pan and bring it up to simmering point, allowing it to bubble, until the mixture has reduced by about a third, or until it is syrupy. Strain this sauce through a sieve.

Serve the salmon with the sauce poured over, garnished with the chives. Sprinkle the sesame seeds over the cucumber salad and hand it round separately on a plate.

PER SERVING: 334 kcal, FAT 20.3 g, SATURATES 3.4 g, PROTEIN 32.6 g, CARBOHYDRATE 5.4 g

Grilled Venison Steaks with Red Onion, Grape and Raisin Confit

Venison steaks are very lean and tender and, so, perfect for a low-fat supper dish. A confit to serve with them is, I think, far nicer than a sauce containing lots of cream and butter. Having made the confit once, you might want to serve it again with other meats, such as lean gammon steaks or low-fat, very meaty sausages.

Begin by making the confit. You can make it at any time – even the day before. What you do is put all the ingredients together in a medium-sized saucepan, bring everything up to a very gentle simmer, then let it cook as gently as possible, without a lid, for 45-60 minutes – you'll need to give it a gentle stir from time to time – until all the liquid has reduced to a lovely sticky glaze.

When you are ready to cook the steaks, season them with freshly milled black pepper. Then pre-heat the grill to its highest setting for about 10 minutes. Brush the steaks lightly on both sides with the oil and grill them for about 4 minutes on each side if you like them medium-rare, otherwise for a little longer. Meanwhile, gently re-heat the confit. Serve the venison on warmed plates with the confit and a crisp salad.

Serves 4

4 venison steaks (each weighing about 5 oz/150 g)
2 teaspoons groundnut or other flavourless oil
a few salad leaves, to garnish
freshly milled black pepper

For the confit:

1 medium red onion, chopped, but not too small
6 oz (175 g) black grapes, halved and deseeded (no need to peel)
3 oz (75 g) raisins
10 fl oz (275 ml) red wine
2 fl oz (55 ml) red wine vinegar
1 teaspoon dark soft brown sugar

Baked Apple Meringues with Orange-Soaked Raisins

This is the perfect dessert for someone watching their waistline. I'm quite proud of the fact this tastes so sublime without any fat or sugar, but, depending on you and what you're trying to cut down on, you could use sugar instead of sweetener.

Serves 4
2 medium Bramley apples, washed and cored (no need to peel)
4 large egg whites
grated zest and juice 1 orange
4 oz (110 g) raisins
2 tablespoons granulated sweetener
a little butter for greasing

You will also need a small baking tray, lightly buttered.

Pre-heat the oven to gas mark 5, 375°F (190°C).

First mix the raisins and the orange zest and juice in a bowl and then leave them to soak for about 30 minutes.

Meanwhile, using a sharp knife, cut each apple in half horizontally, arrange the halves on the baking tray and pop them on to the centre shelf of the oven for 30 minutes. After that, slide the shelf half out, spoon the soaked raisins over each apple half and bake for another 15 minutes.

Towards the end of that time, place the egg whites into a grease-free bowl and, using an electric hand whisk, whisk them until they form soft peaks that just tip over when you lift the whisk. Then whisk in, bit by bit, all but a teaspoon of the sweetener. Now pile up the fluffy egg white on top of each baked apple, sprinkle with the remaining sweetener, and return them to the oven for another 10-15 minutes, until the egg white has just set and is tinged golden brown.

PER SERVING: 113 kcal, FAT 0.2 g, SATURATES 0 g, PROTEIN 3.7 g, CARBOHYDRATE 25.8 g

Tropical Fruit Jellies

This is a cheat's recipe. The tropical fruit juice comes freshly squeezed – in a bottle from the supermarket. And, what's more, this really beautiful dessert contains virtually no fat.

First of all, put ¼ pint (150 ml) of the tropical fruit juice into a shallow dish. Add the gelatine, pressing it down so the liquid covers it, and set it aside to soften – about 10 minutes.

Now put another ¼ pint of the fruit juice into a small saucepan and bring it up to simmering point. Then remove the pan from the heat and add the softened gelatine, squeezing it first and reserving the liquid, and begin to whisk the gelatine in until it is completely dissolved. Pour the remaining juice into a large jug, along with the lime juice and the liquid from the squeezed gelatine, add the dissolved gelatine mixture and give it all another good whisk. Then pour the whole lot into the glasses, cover, and chill for at least 3 hours or, preferably, overnight.

Just before serving, halve each passion fruit and scoop out the seeds and juice to spoon on top of the jellies – the fruit will seep down as you eat.

Serves 8
1¾ pints (1 litre) freshly squeezed
tropical fruit juice
9 leaves gelatine
6 large passion fruit
juice 4 limes

You will also need eight serving
glasses with a capacity of about
6 fl oz (175 ml).

Cappuccino Cheesecakes

These are so lovely, no-one will know they're low-fat. You do need to make them the day before as they're much easier to remove from the cases if they've had a chance to become firm.

Serves 8
3½ fl oz (100 ml) freshly made hot espresso (can be made up using instant coffee powder)
6 oz (175 g) Ricotta
6 oz (175 g) cottage cheese
8 biscuits, such as low-fat chocolate-chip cookies or ginger biscuits
½ oz (10 g) powdered gelatine
2 large egg yolks
1 tablespoon granulated sweetener
5 oz (150 g) 5 per cent Greek yoghurt

For the topping:
1 large egg white
2 tablespoons 8 per cent fat fromage frais
2 teaspoons granulated sweetener
½ teaspoon cocoa powder, for dusting

You will also need sixteen muffin cases, and eight 1½ inch (4 cm) deep ramekins with a base diameter of 3 inches (7.5 cm).

First of all, put two of the muffin cases into each ramekin – we find using two gives you firmer sides. Next, put a biscuit into the base of each ramekin. Now make the filling. Sprinkle the gelatine into the espresso and whisk until it has completely dissolved.

Now put the Ricotta, cottage cheese, egg yolks and sweetener into a food processor and process for about a minute, or until smooth. Then pour in the coffee-and-gelatine mixture through a strainer and blend again until everything is thoroughly mixed and absolutely smooth.

After that, transfer the mixture to a bowl and, using a balloon whisk, whisk in the yoghurt until it's all well blended. Now carefully spoon this mixture over the biscuits in the ramekins, cover with clingfilm and chill them overnight.

When you are ready to serve the cheesecakes, remove them from the ramekins and arrange them, in their paper cases, on serving plates. (Because it looks so pretty, I like to serve them like this – the paper can be peeled away before eating.) Then whisk the egg white to soft peaks in a grease-free bowl and fold in the fromage frais and sweetener. Spoon this mixture on top of the cheesecakes and dust each with a little cocoa powder, just like a cappuccino.

Note: This recipe contains raw eggs.

PER SERVING: 130 kcal, FAT 5.8 g, SATURATES 2.9 g, PROTEIN 9.1 g, CARBOHYDRATE 10.9 g

Marmalade Soufflés

You're simply not going to believe this until you taste it – no fat, no sugar, not even any sweetener, and yet you have one of the easiest and most fragrantly lovely soufflés in the world.

First, what you need to do is have the egg whites ready in a grease-free bowl. Then place the marmalade in another, largish bowl and, using a fork, whisk it around to break up any lumps. After that, add a pinch of salt to the egg whites and, using an electric hand whisk, whisk them until they reach the stiff-peak stage. Now take a large kitchen spoon and first fold a spoonful of the egg whites into the marmalade to slacken the mixture, then quickly fold in the rest a spoonful at a time. Next, divide the mixture between the ramekins, piling it up as high as possible – it won't collapse.

Now place them on the baking tray on the centre shelf of the oven and cook them for 10-12 minutes, or until the tops are nicely browned. Serve immediately, but don't worry – they hold up extremely well.

Serves 6

6 oz (175 g) thick-cut, sugar-free orange marmalade
5 large egg whites
½ teaspoon unsalted butter for greasing
salt

You will also need six 2 inch (5 cm) deep ramekins with a base diameter of 2½ inches (6 cm) and a top diameter of 3 inches (7.5 cm), very lightly buttered; and a medium-sized baking tray.

Pre-heat the oven to gas mark 4, 350°F (180°C).

Squidgy Chocolate Cakes with Prunes in Marsala

Serves 4
½ oz (10 g) cocoa powder, plus a
little extra for dusting
3 large eggs
1 tablespoon granulated sweetener
a little groundnut or other flavourless
oil for greasing

For the filling:
12 ready-to-eat vanilla prunes
1½ fl oz (40 ml) Marsala
2 rounded tablespoons 8 per cent
fat fromage frais
1 teaspoon granulated sweetener
1 teaspoon chocolate extract

You will also need four 1½ inch
(4 cm) deep ramekins with a base
measurement of 3 inches (7.5 cm),
very lightly greased; and a small
baking tray.

When I had dinner with a friend from New York recently, he asked me how the low-fat recipes were coming along and gave me a challenge: 'If you can come up with a low-fat, low-sugar chocolate dessert that tastes really good, you'll have broken new ground.' So, here follows what I hope will be a ground-breaking recipe!

First of all, deal with the prunes by placing them in a small saucepan, together with the Marsala, then just bring them up to simmering point and leave to cool. Transfer them to a small, lidded plastic box and leave to soak for as long as possible, turning them now and then. (I always try to let them soak overnight.)

When you're ready to make the cakes, pre-heat the oven to gas mark 4, 350°F (180°C). Then separate the eggs, placing the yolks in a medium-sized bowl and the whites in a large, grease-free one. Next, whisk the yolks and the sweetener together quite briskly for about a minute, then sift the cocoa powder on to the yolks, whisking briefly until it's well blended in.

Now, using an electric hand whisk, whisk the egg whites to the soft-peak stage. (They need to be standing up in peaks that just nod over when you lift the whisk.)

After that, fold a tablespoon of the egg white into the chocolate mixture, then quickly but carefully fold in the rest. Divide the mixture between the ramekins – it will pile up quite high – then place them on the baking tray and bake them for 12-15 minutes, or until they feel springy but still a bit wobbly to the touch. Remove them from the oven, and don't be alarmed to see them shrink because that's quite normal. When they're cool enough to handle, slide a small palette knife around the edges and turn out first on to the palm of your hand, then right-side up on to a cooling rack.

While they're cooling, make the filling. Drain the prunes, reserving the liquid. Next, measure the fromage frais into a bowl, together with the sweetener and chocolate extract, then add the prune-soaking liquid and whisk everything together. Now transfer the prunes to a board, reserving four of them for the tops of the cakes, and roughly chop the rest, before folding them into the fromage-frais mixture.

Finally, slice the chocolate cakes in half horizontally, fill with the prune mixture and sandwich the two halves together again. Pop a whole prune on top of each one and dust lightly with cocoa powder before serving.

Note: If you want to make these in advance, you can cover them loosely with clingfilm and store in the fridge until needed.

PER SERVING: 155 kcal, FAT 6.2 g , SATURATES 1.9 g , PROTEIN 9.5 g, CARBOHYDRATE 14 g

6

Pâtés and starters

In our modern vocabulary, the rather old-fashioned word 'hors d'oeuvre' has been replaced by another – starter. But there is another word for both, and that is appetiser – something that arouses the appetite. I think this is the best description of what a first course should be: something that begins to draw you into the fullest pleasure of eating.

So often, and particularly on holiday, I have groaned about how I'm ever going to face dinner after I've had a rather splendid lunch. Then, when I start to eat the first course, suddenly it's as if the brain has switched back into eating mode, and I end up eating more than anyone!

When I'm cooking, I always choose the first course carefully, and my advice to beginners is to keep it very simple indeed. A rich, over-elaborate starter can have the opposite effect: instead of arousing the appetite, it can kill it completely. I was recently served a first course of quail with a very rich stuffing, sitting on a croûte of fatty bread, with nothing, bland or sharp, to eke out the richness. Although I only ate half of it, I simply didn't want to eat anything after, apart from plain bread!

How to keep it simple

Don't be afraid, is the answer. We can sometimes be dazzled by the grandiose, aspirational cooking we encounter in all areas of the media. But we mustn't be deflected from grasping the virtues of simplicity. If you find some soft, ripe, buttery avocados, make a really good vinaigrette and serve them with some crusty bread and you have a simply beautiful starter.

The same applies to another great first course that's gone missing from most modern menus – in early summer, a plain, boiled globe artichoke (see page 163), from which you strip the leaves and dip the fleshy parts in vinaigrette, savouring all the flavour, until you finally reach the prized part at the end: the heart. Or, at the same time of year, what could possibly be better than English asparagus, simply steamed and served with Foaming Hollandaise (see page 162)?

In the autumn, when tomatoes are ripe and full of fragrance, a plain tomato salad garnished with fresh basil leaves and the fruitiest olive oil you can find, plus bread to soak up all the sweet juices, makes an outstanding start to a meal (and why not serve a few slices of buffalo Mozzarella with them as well?). I know a pub in Norfolk that serves old-fashioned, half-pint tankards filled with fresh-boiled prawns, which you peel yourself, dip into mayonnaise and eat with brown bread and butter. Heaven. And just think of fragrant, juicy melons with slices of Serrano or Parma ham, or, in late autumn, with some fat, squidgy figs…

Smoked fish

Now farmers' markets are springing up all round the country, search them for some good smoked fish, which always makes a fine start to a meal. For me, the best of all are fillets of smoked eel, moist and vivid, served with a sharp horseradish sauce. Smoked wild salmon is a real luxury, but less expensive – and still a treat – are smoked trout and mackerel.

Eggs and salads

I have to confess, my most favourite starter of all is Eggs Mayonnaise (see page 166): boiled eggs with creamy centres and a home-made garlic mayonnaise that stands proud and wobbles, garnished with a few sliced cornichons (baby gherkins) and small black olives. Eggs en Cocotte (see Book One and page 131) taste indulgent but are really simple to prepare. So are salads: in summer, perhaps Salade Niçoise, and in winter, White Bean and Tuna Fish Salad or Tunisian Aubergine Salad (all in Book Two), or Hummus, on page 78.

Soups

'A meal without soup is like a palace without a portico' wrote the famous French chef Carême. I wouldn't go quite that far, but a soup certainly makes a fine entrance to a meal and I have included several of my best-loved ones in this book: Tuscan Bean and Pasta (see page 84), Carrot and Artichoke (see page 50), Ajo Blanco (see page 51) and The London Particular (see page 82). They are all winners, and now that we can buy ready-made stocks and Marigold Swiss vegetable bouillon powder, soupmaking has become so much easier.

Pâtés

In France, pâtés and terrines are a great tradition and regularly served at the beginning of a meal. At one of my favourite restaurants, the Auberge de la Mole in Provence, their splendid meals invariably begin with four lovely, lived-in earthenware or porcelain terrines, each filled with a different variation, a tall jar of cornichons and pickles, complete with tongs to help yourself, and chunks of char-grilled country bread.

Provided the main course is not too heavy, pâtés are perfect for a first course; they're a real blessing when you have a house full of people wanting snacks; or they can be served for lunch, with cheese to follow.

While the French have their pâtés and terrines, we in England have our own tradition of potted meats, fish, game and even cheese. I would love to see a revival of these, so have included my special English Potted Crab (see page 156), a very popular starter in our restaurant at Norwich City Football Club, where we are sometimes having to make enough for 400!

Friends come first

Just to sum up: what I'm offering here is a selection of first courses that are easy to prepare ahead. In fact, the most important aspect of a meal is the relaxed sharing of time with family or friends, and if the food dominates and distracts the host all the time, it's not going to be half as pleasurable. Everything here will taste really good, but will involve you in the minimum amount of last-minute fuss and bother.

Coarse Country Pâté

If you long to eat some of the rough country pâté available all over France but in short supply here, why not make some? You won't believe how blissfully easy it is, and using a food processor instead of buying the meat ready-minced makes it coarser and chunkier. Serve it for lunch with a side salad or watercress, some crisp cornichons (baby gherkins) and char-grilled or toasted country bread, and, if you close your eyes, you're in France!

Serves 10-12

12 oz (350 g) boned shoulder of British veal

1 lb (450 g) streaky pork slices, with as much fat as possible

10 oz (275 g) dry-cured, smoked streaky bacon

8 oz (225 g) pork liver

20 juniper berries, plus a few extra to garnish

20 black peppercorns

¼ rounded teaspoon ground mace

2 fat cloves garlic, crushed

1 heaped teaspoon chopped fresh thyme

4 fl oz (120 ml) dry white wine

1 fl oz (25 ml) brandy

a few fresh bay leaves, to garnish

1 heaped teaspoon salt

You will also need an oval or rectangular terrine with a capacity of 1.75 litres/3 pints (or a 900 g/2 lb loaf tin).

You'll find it's best to process the meat one type at a time (finishing with the pork liver, as it is the messiest). Begin by cutting the meat into rough pieces, then place them in the food processor and process until quite finely chopped.

Next, tip each meat in turn into a large mixing bowl and mix them together very thoroughly. Then coarsely crush first the juniper berries and then the peppercorns with a pestle and mortar and add these to the meat, along with the salt, mace, garlic and thyme. Now you need to mix again even more thoroughly to distribute all the flavours evenly. After that, add the wine and brandy and give it a final mix, then cover the bowl with a clean tea cloth and leave it in a cool place for a couple of hours to allow the flavours to be absorbed.

Now pre-heat the oven to gas mark 2, 300°F (150°C). Then pack the mixture into the terrine (or loaf tin) and decorate the top with the bay leaves and the extra juniper berries. Place the terrine (or tin) in a roasting tin, half filled with hot water, on the centre shelf of the oven and leave it there for about 1¾ hours.

By the time it has cooked, the pâté will have shrunk quite a bit. Remove it from the oven and allow it to cool without draining off any of the surrounding juices; once the pâté has cooled, the surrounding fat and jelly will keep it beautifully moist.

When the pâté is cold, place a double strip of kitchen foil across the top and put a few scale weights on to press it down for at least a few hours – this pressing isn't essential, but it helps to make the pâté less crumbly if you want to serve it in slices. If you don't have weights, use any heavy object: a brick, a tin of food, or any other innovation you can think of. If you don't weight it, you can serve it in chunks rather than slices. Place the pâté, weights and all, into the fridge overnight.

To serve the pâté, you need to take it out of the fridge at least 30 minutes ahead to return it to room temperature, then turn it out of the terrine (or tin), remove the surrounding jelly and any fat and cut into slices.

Note: You can use raw, minced pork or veal, if this is available, but don't be tempted to buy lean meat – the presence of fat is essential.

What happens is that as it cooks it dissolves and surrounds the pâté, and although you won't be eating it, its presence is essential for keeping the pâté moist.

To char-grill bread, pre-heat a cast-iron ridged griddle for about 10 minutes so it is really hot. Cut the bread into fairly thick slices, then lay them on the griddle. Turn them over when they have dark stripes (after about 40 seconds, if the pan is really hot) and repeat on the other side.

Coarse Country Pâté baked in a terrine, left; to make the pâté, it is best to buy the meat in a piece, to chop in a food processor, above.

English Potted Crab

It's sometimes a real treat to take a break from modern, global cooking and return to something purely and simply British or, in this case, English. For centuries in this country there has been a great tradition of potting meat, fish, game and even cheese, and the results could hold their own among any collection of Continental pâtés and terrines. This particular recipe for potted Cromer crab is adapted from one given to me by one of my favourite chefs of all time, Michael Quinn. It's brilliant as a first course for a summer meal for six people, but two or three could easily polish off the whole lot for lunch. Either way, I like to serve it with toasted Irish soda bread, and mustard and cress.

Serves 6 as a starter or 2-3 for lunch
5 oz (150 g) each white crab meat and brown crab meat (or you can use 2 dressed Cromer crabs instead)
1 oz (25 g) shallots (about 1 medium shallot), peeled and finely chopped
2 tablespoons manzanilla sherry
a good pinch each cayenne pepper, ground mace, freshly grated nutmeg
5 oz (150 g) unsalted butter, cut into small cubes
1½ teaspoons anchovy essence
1 teaspoon lemon juice, plus extra if needed
1 large lemon, cut into wedges, to serve
salt and freshly milled black pepper

You will also need six 1¼ inch (3 cm) deep ramekins with a base diameter of 2¼ inches (5.5 cm), or one larger dish.

Begin by placing the shallots, sherry and spices in a small saucepan. Bring the whole lot up to simmering point, then boil quite briskly until the liquid has reduced to about a generous dessertspoon – it should only take 1-2 minutes.

Next, stir in the cubes of butter and, when they are melted, turn the heat down to very low and let it all simmer as gently as possible for 15 minutes, giving it a stir from time to time. After that, remove it from the heat and leave it to cool for about half an hour.

Towards the end of that time, you'll need to assemble a nylon sieve over a bowl, and another, larger bowl filled with ice cubes and a little cold water. Then pour the spicy butter through the sieve and press well to extract all the juice from the shallots. Now set the bowl over the iced water and, using an electric hand whisk, whisk until the butter becomes thick and creamy without becoming hard.

Next, mix in the crab meat, anchovy essence, teaspoon of lemon juice and a really good seasoning of salt and freshly milled black pepper. Taste and check the seasoning – you might like to add a little extra lemon juice. Then spoon the mixture into the ramekins or the larger dish. Cover with clingfilm and chill for 3 hours.

Remove the potted crab from the fridge about half an hour before serving and serve with the lemon wedges.

Note: If you want to make this a day or so ahead, cover the surface with melted butter to seal off the air. To do this, melt 2 oz (50 g) of butter and divide it between the ramekins, pouring a bit over the potted crab in each one, or pour it all over the potted crab in the larger dish.

Smoked Mackerel Pâté with Ricotta and Capers

This is quite simply the easiest pâté I've ever made. All the ingredients are placed together in the food processor and, with one little whiz, it's made! It also has an utterly sublime flavour – brilliant! Serve it with hot, toasted wholemeal bread.

First you need to skin the mackerel fillets, which is no trouble, as the flesh can be lifted away very easily. Next, place the fish into the bowl of a food processor, then add the Ricotta, soured cream, lemon juice, some freshly grated nutmeg and a good seasoning of salt and freshly milled black pepper. Then switch on and blend until completely smooth, stopping the motor to scrape the mixture down the sides of the bowl halfway through. Now taste and add a spot more lemon juice or seasoning, if you think it needs it, then pack the mixture into the ramekins or the larger dish, cover with clingfilm and chill for several hours before serving.

Lastly, place about half a teaspoon of the capers in the centre of each ramekin (or the whole tablespoonful in the middle of the larger dish), sprinkle with a pinch of cayenne pepper and serve with the lemon wedges.

Serves 8 as a starter or 3-4 for lunch
3-4 smoked mackerel fillets (weighing about 10 oz/275 g in total)
4 oz (110 g) Ricotta
5 fl oz (150 ml) soured cream
juice ½ large lemon, plus extra if needed
whole nutmeg
salt and freshly milled black pepper

To garnish:
1 heaped tablespoon miniature capers (nonpareilles)
cayenne pepper
1 large lemon, cut into wedges

You will also need eight 1¼ inch (3 cm) deep ramekins with a base diameter of 2¼ inches (5.5 cm), or one larger dish.

Chicken Liver Pâté with Cognac, with Sweet-and-Sour Red Onion Salad

This is smooth and velvety and also works well with duck livers, if you can get them. The salad helps to cut through the richness. I like to serve this with toasted multi-grain bread.

To make the pâté, take a medium-sized, heavy-based frying pan, melt about 1 oz (25 g) of the butter in it and fry the chicken livers over a medium heat for about 5 minutes. Keep them on the move, turning them over quite frequently. Then remove them from the pan using a draining spoon and transfer them to a blender or food processor.

Now, in the same pan, gently melt 5 oz (150 g) of the remaining butter and add this to the blender or food processor. Then pour the Cognac on to the juices left in the frying pan (to capture all the lovely flavours), and pour that over the livers. Now add the mustard, mace, thyme and garlic, season well with salt and freshly milled black pepper, and blend until you have a smooth, velvety purée.

Next, divide the mixture between the ramekins (or pots). Then melt the remaining 2 oz (50 g) of butter, pour a little over each one to seal, press in a sprig of thyme, and leave them to get quite cold. Cover with clingfilm and leave them in the fridge till needed.

To make the red-onion salad, all you do is heat the oil in a medium-sized saucepan, add the onions, turn the heat down to low and let them cook gently for 5 minutes, stirring now and then. Next, add the sugar and water, stir well, then pop a lid on and let it continue cooking gently for another 10 minutes. After that, add the vinegar, mustard and some salt and freshly milled black pepper, and give everything another really good stir. Then spoon the onions into a serving bowl and cool until needed.

Don't forget to remove the chicken liver pâtés from the fridge about an hour before serving, as both the pâté and the salad need to be served at room temperature.

Serves 6

8 oz (225 g) chicken livers, rinsed and trimmed
2 tablespoons Cognac
8 oz (225 g) butter
2 teaspoons dry mustard powder
¼ teaspoon ground mace
1 teaspoon chopped fresh thyme, plus 6 small sprigs to garnish
2 cloves garlic, crushed
salt and freshly milled black pepper

For the red-onion salad:

3 medium red onions, peeled and cut into 8 wedges through the root
3 tablespoons olive oil
1 heaped teaspoon light soft brown sugar
3 tablespoons water
3 tablespoons red wine vinegar
¾ tablespoon wholegrain mustard
salt and freshly milled black pepper

You will also need six 1¼ inch (3 cm) deep ramekins with a base diameter of 2¼ inches (5.5 cm) (or six similar-sized pots).

Souffléd Sole Creams with Champagne Sauce and Salmon Caviar

This recipe is blissfully easy and all of it can be prepared in advance. In fact, I find it works best if you prepare the purée the day before. Dry white wine can be used instead of Champagne, but if you place an upturned teaspoon in the bottle of Champagne, it will keep its fizz stored in the fridge till your guests arrive.

Serves 6
8 oz (225 g) boneless, skinless lemon sole fillets
2 oz (50 g) jar salmon caviar
whole nutmeg
2 large eggs, lightly beaten
10 fl oz (275 ml) double cream
a little butter for greasing
salt and freshly milled black pepper

For the sauce:
6 fl oz (175 ml) Champagne
¾ oz (20 g) butter
1 large shallot, peeled and finely chopped
¾ oz (20 g) plain flour
5 fl oz (150 ml) double cream
6 sprigs fresh chervil, to garnish
salt and freshly milled black pepper

You will also need six 1½ inch (4 cm) deep ramekins with a base diameter of 3 inches (7.5 cm), well buttered; and a shallow roasting tin measuring 10 x 14 inches (25.5 x 35 cm).

Begin by cutting the lemon sole into pieces about 1½ inches (4 cm) square and placing them in a blender or food processor, along with the lightly beaten eggs, some freshly grated nutmeg and a little salt and freshly milled black pepper. Now blend until the mixture has turned to a smooth, even purée. Then transfer it to a bowl, cover with clingfilm and leave it in the fridge for at least 6 hours or, preferably, overnight.

When you're ready to cook the fish creams, pre-heat the oven to gas mark 5, 375°F (190°C). Fill the roasting tin with about an inch (2.5 cm) of boiling water and place it on the centre shelf of the oven.

Next, make up the sauce. Melt the butter in a medium-sized saucepan and cook the shallot in it over a gentle heat for 5-6 minutes, until softened and golden, but not browned. After that, add the flour to the buttery shallot juices, stir it in and cook for 1-2 minutes more. Now gradually add the Champagne to the pan, a little at a time, then blend in the double cream, whisking until the sauce is smooth. Let it come up to simmering point and cook for a further 1-2 minutes, then taste and add some seasoning. (The shallot can be strained out, if you like.) Now transfer the sauce to a heatproof bowl set over a pan of barely simmering water to keep warm, without letting the bottom of the bowl touch the water.

About 40 minutes before your guests sit down to eat, return the fish mixture to the blender or food processor, together with the cream, and blend them together thoroughly. Then fill each ramekin three-quarters full with the mixture, place all the ramekins in the tin containing the hot water and cook for exactly 30 minutes.

When the time is up, you need to turn out the creams on to warmed serving plates. Do this by holding each ramekin with a cloth, sliding a small palette knife round the edge and tipping the creams very briefly upside down on to the palm of your hand (they will very hot), then straight on to a plate, the right way up.

Serve as soon as possible, with a little of the sauce spooned over, a teaspoon of salmon caviar on top and garnish with chervil. Hand the rest of the sauce around separately in a warmed jug.

Souffléd Arbroath Smokies in Smoked Salmon with Foaming Hollandaise

This is another version of Sole Creams on page 160 – a very old favourite that never fails to delight. It's easy, can be prepared in advance and fulfils all the criteria of a really good first course.

Serves 8

12 oz (350 g) Arbroath smokies, skin and bone intact
8 oz (225 g) sliced smoked salmon
¼ whole nutmeg
2 large eggs, lightly beaten
10 fl oz (275 ml) double cream
8 sprigs watercress, to garnish
salt and freshly milled black pepper

For the foaming hollandaise:

2 large eggs, separated
1 dessertspoon lemon juice
1 dessertspoon white wine vinegar
4 oz (110 g) butter
salt and freshly milled black pepper

You will also need eight 1½ inch (4 cm) deep ramekins with a base diameter of 3 inches (7.5 cm), well buttered, and a large roasting tin.

Begin by carefully skinning the Arbroath smokies – you'll find the flesh will part very easily from the bones. (You should have about 8-10 oz/ 225-275 g of flesh after this.) Flake the fish and place it in a blender or food processor, along with a little salt, freshly milled black pepper and a good grating of nutmeg. Blend until the fish has turned to a smooth, even pulp, then blend in the lightly beaten eggs. Transfer the mixture to a bowl, cover it with clingfilm and leave it in the fridge for at least 6 hours or, preferably, overnight.

After that, pre-heat the oven to gas mark 5, 375°F (190°C). Fill the roasting tin with about an inch (2.5 cm) of boiling water and put this on to the centre shelf of the oven.

Next, return the fish mixture to the blender or food processor, together with the cream, and blend them together thoroughly. Now line the base and sides of each ramekin with smoked salmon – don't worry that you're doing this in pieces and patches as it won't show when they're finally turned out. Fill each ramekin three-quarters full with the fish mixture, then place them in the roasting tin. Cook for exactly 30 minutes.

Meanwhile, make the Foaming Hollandaise. Place the egg yolks into a food processor or blender and season with salt and freshly milled black pepper. Blend together for one minute. Now heat the lemon juice and vinegar in a small saucepan until they start to bubble and simmer. With the food processor or blender running, slowly pour the hot liquid on to the egg yolks in a steady stream, then switch off the machine.

Next, gently melt the butter in the same saucepan and when foaming, with the food processor or blender running again, pour in the butter in a thin, steady, slow trickle. When it is all blended, use a spatula to scrape down any that remains on the sides. Give the sauce one more quick pulse before transferring to a roomy bowl. In another, grease-free bowl, whisk the egg whites to soft peaks and fold them into the sauce. The sauce can be kept warm over a saucepan of simmering water, but make sure the base of the bowl does not touch the water.

Serve the fish creams as soon as possible, either in the ramekins or turned out on to plates, which looks attractive. Do this by holding each ramekin with a cloth, sliding a small palette knife round the edge and tipping the creams upside down very briefly on to the palm of your hand (they will be very hot) then straight on to a plate the right way up. Pour over the sauce and garnish with a sprig of watercress.

Note: This recipe contains raw eggs.

Globe Artichokes with Shallot Vinaigrette

An artichoke is, without doubt, a work of art – dark and pale green leaves with purple edges forming a perfectly shaped bud. There's something extremely satisfying about leisurely peeling off the leaves, dipping them into vinaigrette and biting into the fleshy part at the base of each leaf. Then, of course, the prize – the heart at the very centre, providing a kind of grand finale to the whole affair.

First prepare the artichokes. Remove about four of the toughest outer leaves, then place the artichoke at the edge of a table so that the stalk overhangs the edge. Grasp the artichoke and snap away the stalk, removing some of the tough fibres running up into the base. Now with a large serrated knife, carefully slice off the top quarter of each artichoke and discard. Then, with a pair of scissors, trim away the tips of all the leaves.

Don't boil artichokes in iron or aluminium pans as this can discolour them. Have your chosen large pan ready filled with salted, boiling water, with the tablespoon of lemon juice (or white wine vinegar) added. Simmer the artichokes, uncovered, for 30-40 minutes, or until one of the outer leaves pulls away easily and the bases feel tender when tested with a skewer. Then drain upside down, shaking them to get rid of excess water.

Now remove the hairy 'choke': carefully spread the leaves until you come to the central cone of thinner, lightly-coloured leaves – pull these out and underneath you'll find the choke. Pull it out in clumps – it will come away very easily.

Finally, make up the vinaigrette. Begin by crushing the salt quite coarsely in a mortar, then add the garlic. As it comes into contact with the salt, it will break down into a purée. Next, add the mustard powder and work it in with circular movements. After that, add some freshly milled black pepper. Now work in the vinegar in the same way. Then add the shallot and the oil, switch to a small whisk and whisk thoroughly.

Serve the vinaigrette in a bowl to dip the artichoke leaves into, and on the table, have a finger bowl, napkins, a separate plate for the discarded leaves, and a knife and fork each to eat the heart – wonderful!

Serves 2
2 large globe artichokes (each weighing about 14 oz/400 g)
1 tablespoon lemon juice (or white wine vinegar)

For the vinaigrette:
1 shallot, peeled and finely chopped
1 clove garlic
1 rounded teaspoon mustard powder
1 tablespoon good quality red wine vinegar
5 tablespoons extra virgin olive oil
1 rounded teaspoon sea salt

Roasted Red Pepper and Tomato Tart

In the summer, one of my favourite starters is Piedmont Roasted Peppers (from the Summer Collection*). What I have done here is try to capture all those brilliant flavours and make them into a warm tart more suitable for a winter starter.*

Serves 8

For the pastry:
4 oz (110 g) plain flour
1½ oz (40 g) softened butter, cut into smallish lumps
½ oz (10 g) softened lard, cut into smallish lumps
½ oz (10 g) Parmesan (Parmigiano Reggiano), finely grated
1 teaspoon chopped fresh thyme
a little cold water
a pinch of salt

For the filling:
4 medium red peppers
12 oz (350 g) ripe, red tomatoes
2 tablespoons olive oil
1 large clove garlic, chopped
2 oz (50 g) anchovy fillets in oil
1 tablespoon tomato purée
1 teaspoon finely chopped fresh thyme
2 large eggs and 2 large egg yolks
1 teaspoon sweet, mild pimentón (smoked paprika)
salt and freshly milled black pepper

You will also need a 9 inch (23 cm) loose-bottomed, fluted tart tin, 1 inch (2.5 cm) deep; and two baking trays measuring 11 x 16 inches (28 x 40 cm).

Pre-heat the oven to gas mark 4, 350°F (180°C).

Begin by preparing the filling. First skin the tomatoes. To do this, place them in a heatproof bowl and pour boiling water on to them. Leave them for exactly a minute (or 15-30 seconds, if the tomatoes are small), then remove them, slip off their skins (protecting your hands with a cloth if they are hot) and cut them in half.

Next, prepare the peppers. Halve them, then remove the seeds and slice each half into three strips. Place the peppers and tomato halves in a bowl and add a tablespoon of the oil, the garlic and some seasoning (going easy on the salt because of the anchovies). Give it all a good mix, then spread everything out on one of the baking trays and roast in the top part of the oven for about 50 minutes.

Now make the pastry. Sift the flour and salt into a large mixing bowl, first cutting in the fats with a palette knife and then rubbing lightly with your fingertips, lifting everything up and letting it fall back into the bowl to give it a good airing. When the mixture reaches the crumb stage, sprinkle in the Parmesan and thyme. Then sprinkle in a tablespoon of cold water to bring it together to a smooth dough that leaves the side of the bowl absolutely clean, with no crumbs left, adding a few more drops, if needed. Place the pastry in a plastic food bag in the fridge to rest for 30 minutes. Meanwhile, pre-heat the second baking tray.

Next, transfer the pastry to a flat, lightly floured surface, roll it out to a circle and line the tin with it. Now prick the base with a fork (to prevent it rising) and brush it with a little of the egg for the filling. Bake the tart base on the pre-heated baking tray, at the same temperature as the peppers and tomatoes, for about 20 minutes, or until lightly golden.

Allow the peppers and tomatoes to cool before placing them in a food processor or blender, along with the anchovy fillets and all their oil. Next, add the tomato purée and thyme and blend until everything is reduced to a thick, smooth mixture. Then, in a large bowl, whisk the eggs and yolks together, along with the pimentón, then stir in the pepper-and-tomato mixture and the other tablespoon of olive oil.

When the tart base is cooked, turn the oven temperature up to gas mark 5, 375°F (190°C), then spoon the mixture into it and bake in the oven on the centre shelf for 35 minutes, or until it is firm and set in the centre. Leave the tart to rest for about 10 minutes before serving.

Eggs Mayonnaise

Serves 6
9 large eggs
18 medium cornichons (baby gherkins),
sliced lengthways
about 18 small black olives

For the mayonnaise:
2 large egg yolks
1 clove garlic, crushed
1 heaped teaspoon mustard powder
10 fl oz (275 ml) groundnut or other
flavourless oil
1 teaspoon white wine vinegar
freshly milled black pepper
1 teaspoon salt

Not the kind you get in help-yourself salad bars and cafés – this is the real thing. Eggs, boiled – not hard, but with a bit of squidge at the centre – anointed with a shimmering, golden emulsion laced with a little garlic. I have to admit, this is probably my most favourite starter. I like to serve it with sliced cornichons or pickled cucumbers and tiny black Provençal olives.

First, place a medium-sized mixing bowl on a damp tea cloth so it will remain steady and leave you both hands free to make the mayonnaise – one to drip the oil, the other to hold an electric hand whisk.

Next, measure out the oil into a jug. Now put the egg yolks into the bowl, adding the garlic, mustard powder, salt and a little freshly milled black pepper and mix all of these together well. Then, holding the jug of oil in one hand and the whisk in the other, add just a drop of oil to the egg mixture and whisk this in. However stupid it may sound, the key to a successful mayonnaise is making sure each drop of oil is thoroughly whisked in before adding the next drop. It won't take all day, because after a few minutes – once you've added several drops of oil – the mixture will begin to thicken and go very stiff and lumpy. When it gets to this stage, you need to add the vinegar, which will thin it.

Now the critical point has passed, you can begin pouring in the oil in large drops, keeping the whisk going all the time. When all the oil has been added, taste and add more salt and freshly milled black pepper, if it needs it. If you'd like the mayonnaise to be a bit lighter, add 2 tablespoons of boiling water and whisk it in.

Mayonnaise only curdles when you add the oil too quickly at the beginning. If that happens, don't despair. All you need to do is put a fresh egg yolk into a clean basin, add the curdled mixture to it drop by drop, then continue adding the rest of the oil as though nothing had happened.

Now place the eggs in a pan in cold water. Bring them up to the boil and boil for 6 minutes, then cool them rapidly under cold, running water and leave them in the cold water for about 2 minutes. Next, remove them from the water, peel off the shells, cover the eggs with clingfilm, and leave them in a cool place until needed.

Now cut the eggs in half, arranging three halves on each plate, top with a heaped tablespoon of the mayonnaise and garnish with the cornichons and olives.

Any leftover mayonnaise should be stored in a screw-top jar in the fridge, but for no longer than a week.

Note: You could also serve this with a couple of anchovies per person draped over the mayonnaise in a criss-cross pattern.

Grilled Polenta with Ham, Cheese and Sage

As well as being a brilliant starter, this can also be made into bite-sized canapés to serve with drinks, if you stamp out small rounds and distribute the toppings in small portions.

First of all, make the polenta. To do this, pour 1 pint (570 ml) boiling water from the kettle into a large saucepan and allow it to come back to simmering point. Then add the polenta in a long, steady stream, along with half a teaspoon of salt, stirring all the time with a wooden spoon. Place the pan on a low heat and allow the polenta to cook for 5 minutes, continuing to stir, until thickened – it should look like yellow porridge.

As soon as the polenta is ready, season it generously with freshly milled black pepper, then stir in the Parmesan and butter. Taste to check the seasoning and add more salt and pepper, if necessary. Then, as quickly as you can, spoon the polenta into the lined baking tin, smooth the top with a palette knife and allow it to get quite cold.

When the polenta is cold, lift it out of the tin, cut it out into six circles with the cutter and place these on the baking tray. Next, pre-heat the grill to its highest setting for 10 minutes. Measure the olive oil into a saucer and brush each piece of polenta with some of it, then season generously again with salt and freshly milled black pepper. Now place the baking tray under the grill, about 4 inches (10 cm) below the heat source. Grill the polenta for 3 minutes on each side until it becomes golden and toasted at the edges, then remove it from the grill.

Next, loosely fold the pieces of ham and place one on top of each polenta round. Then arrange a slice of cheese on top of the ham and, finally, dip the sage leaves into the remaining olive oil and lay two on top of the cheese on each one. All this can be done in advance if you allow the grilled polenta to get cold before you put the topping on.

When you are ready to serve the polenta, put them back under a hot grill for another 3-4 minutes, or until the cheese has melted and the sage leaves are crisp. Serve with warm ciabatta bread and extra virgin olive oil to dip the bread into.

Serves 6
4 fl oz (120 ml) easy-cook polenta
1 oz (25 g) Parmesan (Parmigiano Reggiano), finely grated
1 oz (25 g) softened butter
salt and freshly milled black pepper

For the topping:
3¼ oz (85 g) Parma ham (about 6 slices)
3 oz (75 g) Fontina (or Gruyère), cut into 6 slices
12 small fresh sage leaves
2 tablespoons olive oil
salt and freshly milled black pepper

You will also need a baking tin measuring 6 x 10 inches (15 x 25.5 cm), 1 inch (2.5 cm) deep, lined with silicone paper (parchment); a 3 inch (7.5 cm) pastry cutter; and a small baking tray, lightly oiled.

Char-grilled Squid with Chilli Jam

We have a tradition with some close friends that involves always having Easter Sunday lunch at Yetman's restaurant, in Holt in Norfolk where Alison and Peter Yetman cook and serve my absolute favourite kind of food. Last year, we had this brilliant starter, for which Alison has kindly given me the recipe.

Serves 4
1 lb (450 g) small squid (cleaned weight)
1 dessertspoon groundnut or other flavourless oil
salt and freshly milled black pepper
rocket leaves, to serve

For the chilli jam:
1½ medium-sized red chillies, deseeded and roughly chopped
1 lb (450 g) very ripe tomatoes
2 cloves garlic, roughly chopped
1 inch (2.5 cm) piece fresh root ginger, peeled and roughly chopped
1 tablespoon Thai fish sauce
8 oz (225 g) demerara sugar
2 fl oz (55 ml) red wine vinegar
1 tablespoon balsamic vinegar

You will also need a cast-iron ridged griddle; and a 1 lb (350 ml capacity) jar, sterilised (see page 97).

Firstly, make the chilli jam. This can be done well in advance. First of all, you need to roughly chop the tomatoes. (You can leave on their skins.) Then put half of them into a blender, along with the chillies, garlic, ginger and fish sauce, whiz everything to a fine purée and pour the mixture into a large saucepan. Now pulse the remaining tomatoes in the blender until just chopped, but this time not puréed. Add these to the purée in a medium-sized saucepan, along with the sugar and vinegars, and slowly bring the mixture up to boiling point, stirring all the time.

When the mixture reaches the boil, turn the heat down to a gentle simmer. Skim off any foam from the surface and cook gently, uncovered, for 30-40 minutes, stirring every 5 minutes to prevent the chopped tomato settling at the bottom. You will also need to scrape down the sides of the pan during the cooking so that everything cooks evenly. The mixture should reduce to half its volume. Now pour it into the hot, sterilised jar, allow it to cool and then cover and store it in the fridge. (You will need about a third of the chilli jam for this recipe.)

Next, pre-heat the griddle over a high heat. Meanwhile, prepare the squid. Slit it on one side and open it out to give two flaps (retaining the tentacles). Pat dry with kitchen paper. (It's important that you dry the squid properly, otherwise it will stew in the pan, rather than fry.) Now, using a small sharp knife, lightly score it on the inside – if you score it on the outside, it won't curl properly. Score diagonally in one direction, then do the same in the other direction, to give little diamond shapes, taking great care not to cut right through the squid.

When the pan is searing hot, lightly brush the squid and the tentacles on both sides with the oil, then season with salt and freshly milled black pepper. Only season the squid the moment it goes into the pan – if you do it in advance, the salt will draw out all the moisture. Now add the squid and tentacles in batches to the hot pan and cook for 1-2 minutes, turning halfway through, until lightly charred. (Be warned – the tentacles will look as though they're coming alive!) Use tongs to transfer the first batch to a warmed plate while you cook the rest. Serve warm or cold on a bed of rocket leaves, with the chilli jam drizzled over.

Note: The chilli jam will keep in the fridge for up to 3 months, and is also wonderful with sausages.

7

Hot puddings

Young cooks of Britain, I have a question to ask you. Are you aware of our unmatched reputation – dating back to the 17th century – for making and serving a multitude of baked, boiled and steamed puddings? Our history of pudding-making is a joyous tradition of marrying and blending simple ingredients into a unique miscellany of tastes, textures and sweetness. But what will happen to our glorious puddings now we are in the grip of an obsession with so-called healthy eating? Do we really want to write off this wonderful tradition that we have excelled at for centuries?

Long live puddings, is my message – a voice crying in the low-fat wilderness of the 21st century saying, please don't stop making and eating them! The pleasure we derive from our food is a gift and we mustn't turn our backs on what is superior in favour of the vastly inferior – I'd swap you a ton of over-sweet, short-on-cocoa-solids chocolate bars and a lorry-load of artificially flavoured supermarket yoghurts for one glorious, home-made British pudding.

Puddings are not wicked. My lifelong friend, chef John Tovey, wrote a wonderful book called *Wicked Puddings*, a title that serves to remind us of our modern mind-set: puddings are naughty, puddings mean guilt. But it's all a big deception. The truth is, my grandfather never ate a supper in his entire life that did not include a pudding, and he died at the age of 87, a little but not greatly overweight. Such a scenario would be unheard of now. The reason for his long good health is he never owned a car – he walked everywhere – and his work was far from sedentary either.

Today we drive everywhere, have mostly static jobs and lack exercise, so we couldn't possibly live like my grandfather (who also invariably had bacon and eggs for breakfast, too). But what I am saying is, instead of pudding every day, why not treat yourself once a week? I'm always being ticked off by people who say, oh Delia, all that butter and cream! What I have failed to communicate is that recipes containing butter and cream are not for every day, but for *special* occasions. So, by all means, don't eat *too* much pudding but, please, have one now and then.

The health issue. Fat is fat is fat. Butter, margarine, vegetable fat, lard, suet, olive and other oils are all fats, and if you eat too much fat, you get fat. Animal fats (as I said in the dairy chapter in Book Two) also came under fire because it was thought they increased cholesterol in the blood, which, in turn, blocked arteries and caused strokes and heart disease. But the evidence is by no means conclusive and some scientists believe that stress and other factors are the real culprits. Be that as it may, eating large amounts of fat, animal or otherwise, is not wise. What *is* wise is balance, and in a balanced diet, a pudding once a week is absolutely *not* unhealthy, and let's not be duped into thinking it is.

A final word before we embark on our recipes – a wonderful quote from a French visitor to London at the beginning of the 18th century, M. Misson: 'Blessed be he that invented pudding, for it is a manna that hits the palates of all sorts of people.' So say I.

A note on puddings. Suet puddings have a somewhat undeserved reputation for heaviness, but they can always be lightened up by replacing some of the flour with breadcrumbs, as in the recipes in this chapter.

Steamers are described on page 20, but there are two important points to remember: (i) Don't let the water under the steamer ever come off the boil – this *can* make a pudding heavy. (ii) You must make sure the water is topped up out of a boiling kettle. The advantage of the old-fashioned, double-pan, deep, lidded steamer is that the saucepan can be filled almost to the brim, and may not need to be topped up as frequently.

Pudding basins have caused something of a problem with regard to their size – a bit of confusion that needs to be unravelled. If you pour water right up to the brim of a so-called 40 oz (2 pint) basin, it actually takes 2½ pints! The measurements for this standard size are as follows: 3½ inches (9 cm) base diameter, 6½ inches (16 cm) top diameter and 4½ inches (11.5 cm) deep. This is the one you need for our Old English Apple Hat on page 182 and Steamed Panettone Pudding in Book One.

Canary Lemon Sponge Puddings with Lemon Curd Cream

Canary Pudding is an old English steamed sponge pudding with jam. Because our football team is called the Canaries, I have adapted it to become a lemony version, so as to add a little canary colour. It's very popular at our restaurant in Norwich City Football Club. If you haven't got time to make the Lemon Curd (see page 103), you can now buy some quite good ones – or use jam and serve with custard.

Serves 6

For the sponge pudding:
4 oz (110 g) self-raising flour
4 oz (110 g) softened unsalted butter, at room temperature, cut into small cubes, plus a little extra for greasing
2 large eggs
4 oz (110 g) golden caster sugar
1 teaspoon baking powder
grated zest 1 lemon and 1 tablespoon lemon juice

For the lemon curd:
a half quantity of lemon curd
(see page 103)

For the lemon curd cream:
the remainder of the lemon curd
5 fl oz (150 ml) hot water
5 fl oz (150 ml) double cream

You will also need six mini pudding basins with a capacity of 6 fl oz (175 ml); some kitchen foil and silicone paper (parchment); and a steamer.

Begin by making the lemon curd for the puddings. After that, butter the basins well and place a round piece of well-buttered silicone paper (parchment) in the bottom of each one. Then take a large mixing bowl and sift the flour and baking powder into it, holding the sieve high to give the flour a good airing. Next, add the butter, eggs, sugar, lemon zest and juice. Then, using an electric hand whisk, beat the mixture for about a minute until it is thoroughly blended.

After that, fill the base of each basin with a dessertspoon of lemon curd and then spoon in the sponge mixture, dividing it equally between the basins and levelling the tops. Then place a piece of kitchen foil over each one, making a pleat in the centre and twisting the edges all round.

Now place a saucepan over the heat and add boiling water from the kettle. When it comes back to the boil, arrange the puddings in the steamer (you'll have to stack them on top of each other) and fit it over a saucepan. Pop a lid on and steam them for about 25 minutes, keeping the water at a steady simmer. They are ready when the centres spring back when pressed lightly.

While the puddings are cooking, you can make the lemon sauce. All you do is place the remaining lemon curd in a saucepan, add the water and the cream, and then heat very gently, stirring all the time, until hot but not bubbling. Then pour it into a warmed serving jug and keep warm. When the puddings are cooked, remove the kitchen foil and loosen them all round with a small palette knife. Then turn them out on to warmed serving plates, remove the paper discs and hand the sauce round separately, or pour a little over each one.

Spiced Bread Pudding with Brandy Cream

Sometimes this gets confused with bread-and-butter pudding, but it's quite different. It was invented, I think, to use up stale bread, which is still a good reason for making it – however, it has developed into something so wonderful, it's worth letting the bread go stale on purpose.

Serves 6

For the bread pudding:
8 oz (225 g) white or brown bread, crusts removed
2 teaspoons mixed spice
whole nutmeg
4 oz (110 g) sultanas
1 oz (25 g) currants
1 oz (25 g) raisins
2 oz (50 g) whole candied lemon or orange peel, chopped
3 tablespoons brandy
10 fl oz (275 ml) milk
2 oz (50 g) butter, melted, plus a little extra for greasing
3 oz (75 g) dark soft brown sugar
1 large egg, beaten
grated zest ½ orange
grated zest 1 lemon
1 tablespoon demerara sugar

For the brandy cream:
1 dessertspoon brandy
5 fl oz (150 ml) double cream
1 oz (25 g) golden caster sugar

You will also need a baking dish with a base measurement of 6¼ x 8 inches (15.5 x 20 cm), 1¾ inches (4.5 cm) deep, buttered.

Begin by placing the sultanas, currants, raisins and candied peel in a bowl. Pour over the brandy and leave aside to marinate. Then, in a large bowl, break the bread into ½ inch (1 cm) pieces. Add the milk, then give the mixture a good stir and leave it for about 30 minutes so the bread becomes well soaked. Pre-heat the oven to gas mark 4, 350°F (180°C).

Next, mix the melted butter, sugar, mixed spice and beaten egg together and then add to the second bowl. Now, using a fork, beat the mixture well, making sure there are no lumps, then stir in the marinated fruits, with any brandy remaining, and also the orange and lemon zest.

After that, spread the mixture in the baking dish and sprinkle the sugar over it, along with some freshly grated nutmeg. Bake on the centre shelf of the oven for about 1¼ hours. Meanwhile, whisk together the ingredients for the brandy cream and serve it with the pudding warm from the oven.

Individual Queen of Puddings with Morello Cherry Conserve

This is another great English classic, yet when you look at the recipe, you can hardly believe such simple ingredients could be transformed into such wonderfully light lusciousness. It is a moveable feast because the conserve can be whichever you prefer. Our home-made Dark Apricot and Almond Preserve on page 102 would be a star choice. It works divinely with marmalade, cranberry jelly, or even lemon curd. Definitely one of my top puddings of all time.

First, pour the milk into a saucepan and bring to the boil. Remove from the heat and stir in the butter, breadcrumbs, 2½ oz (60 g) sugar and the lemon zest, and leave for 20 minutes to allow the breadcrumbs to swell.

Now separate the eggs. Put the whites into a large, grease-free bowl and the yolks into a small bowl. Then beat the yolks and whisk them into the breadcrumb mixture. After that, divide the mixture between the ramekins, smoothing the tops with a palette knife. Now place on the baking tray in the centre of the oven and bake for about 25 minutes until set.

Meanwhile, in a small saucepan, melt the conserve over a low heat and, when the puddings are ready, remove them from the oven and spread it carefully and evenly all over the tops.

Next, use an electric hand whisk with clean, dry beaters to beat the egg whites to the stiff-peak stage, then whisk in 1½ oz (40 g) sugar. Now divide this meringue mixture between each ramekin, piling it up into high peaks. Finally, sprinkle the teaspoon of sugar over the tops of the puddings and bake them on the baking tray on the centre shelf for a further 10-15 minutes, until the tops are golden brown.

Don't worry if the puddings are ready before you've finished the main course – they won't mind waiting in a warm place.

Note: If it's easier, you can make one large pudding, using an oval baking dish measuring 10 x 7 inches (25.5 x 18 cm), 2 inches (5 cm) deep, generously buttered. The initial baking time will be 30-35 minutes and the meringue will take the same time as above: 10-15 minutes.

Serves 6

6 dessertspoons (about 5 oz/150 g) Morello cherry conserve
1 pint (570 ml) milk
½ oz (10 g) butter, plus a little extra for greasing
4 oz (110 g) fresh white breadcrumbs
4 oz (110 g) golden caster sugar, plus 1 extra teaspoon
grated zest 1 small lemon
3 large eggs

You will also need six 2 inch (5 cm) deep ramekins, with a base diameter of 2½ inches (6 cm) and a top diameter of 3 inches (7.5 cm) (or six similar-sized heatproof glass dishes), generously buttered; and a medium-sized baking tray.

Pre-heat the oven to gas mark 4, 350°F (180°C).

Warm Chocolate Rum Soufflés with Chocolate Sauce

These are very light and chocolatey, and made even more wonderful by the addition of chocolate sauce and cream. They're also reasonably well-behaved and though they may shrink a little, they won't collapse.

Serves 6
For the soufflés:
4 oz (110 g) dark chocolate
(75 per cent cocoa solids)
2 tablespoons rum
2 tablespoons double cream
4 large egg yolks
6 large egg whites
a little melted butter for greasing
a little golden caster sugar for dusting

For the sauce:
3 oz (75 g) dark chocolate
(75 per cent cocoa solids)
2 tablespoons double cream

To serve:
10 fl oz (275 ml) double or single cream
a little icing sugar for dusting

You will also need a medium-sized baking tray; six 3 inch (7.5 cm) deep ramekins, with a base diameter of 2½ inches (6 cm) and a top diameter of 3 inches (7.5 cm) (or six similar-sized heatproof dishes).

Pre-heat the oven to gas mark 6, 400°F (200°C).

First of all, pop the baking tray into the oven to pre-heat. Now break the chocolate into a heatproof mixing bowl, add the rum and cream, and place the bowl over a pan of barely simmering water, making sure the base of the bowl doesn't touch the water. Leave it until the chocolate is just soft, which will take about 6 minutes, then remove it from the heat and beat with a wooden spoon until it's smooth and glossy. Allow it to cool. In the meantime, brush the ramekins with melted butter and dust with golden caster sugar.

Now, in a small bowl, whisk the egg yolks thoroughly and stir them into the chocolate mixture. Then, in another, large, grease-free bowl – and making sure the beaters of your electric hand whisk are clean and dry – whisk the egg whites until they form stiff peaks. Then, using a metal spoon, fold a quarter of the egg white into the chocolate mixture to loosen it and then fold in the rest gently and carefully.

Next, pour the whole lot into the ramekins and bake on the baking tray for about 10 minutes, or until the soufflés are puffy and springy to the touch.

Meanwhile, make the chocolate sauce. Break the chocolate into another heatproof mixing bowl and add the cream. Place it over a pan of barely simmering water, once again making sure the base of the bowl doesn't touch the water. After about 6 minutes, remove it from the heat and beat it with a wooden spoon until smooth. Pour the sauce into a warmed jug and keep warm.

Serve the soufflés straight from the oven, dusted with the icing sugar. Hand around the chocolate sauce and the cream in jugs – then the surface of the soufflés can be gently divided using a teaspoon, and the sauce and cream poured into the space.

Spotted Dick Rides Again

This was once a very famous pudding, but it's now sadly forgotten – except by a certain supermarket that has a problem with its name! Just the thing to serve for Sunday lunch after a freezing cold, wintry walk. The ultimate comfort pudding.

Serves 4-6
For the suet pastry:
4 oz (110 g) self-raising flour, plus a little extra for dusting
2 oz (50 g) fresh white breadcrumbs
3 oz (75 g) shredded suet
2 fl oz (55 ml) water
2 fl oz (55 ml) milk
salt

For the filling:
6 oz (175 g) raisins
1 medium cooking apple (weighing about 6 oz/175 g), washed, cored and roughly chopped (no need to peel)
3 oz (75 g) dark soft brown sugar
grated zest ½ lemon

You will also need a sheet of kitchen foil measuring 10 x 14 inches (25.5 x 35 cm), and a steamer.

First of all, mix the filling ingredients together in a bowl. After that, make the suet pastry: sift the flour into a bowl, add the breadcrumbs, suet and a pinch of salt, and mix to combine. Mix the water and milk together and add a little to the dry ingredients, sprinkling it here and there. Now, using a flat-bladed knife, begin to mix, adding a little more liquid until the mixture looks as it is coming together. Finish off using your hands, adding drops of liquid until you end up with a smooth, elastic dough that feels moist.

Next, transfer the dough to a flat, lightly floured surface and roll it out to a rectangle roughly measuring 8 x 12 inches (20 x 30 cm). Then spread the filling evenly over it and roll it up gently and carefully from the narrow end. Now wrap the pudding in the kitchen foil, twisting it at each end to form a seal.

After that, fit a steamer over a saucepan filled with boiling water from a kettle and as soon as it comes back to the boil, pop the pudding in, put a lid on and steam for 2 hours, keeping the water at a steady simmer, and making sure it is topped up if it needs it. Serve the pudding in warmed bowls, cut in thick slices, with Traditional English Custard (see Book One) – an absolutely essential accompaniment.

Old English Apple Hat

If it's true there's 'a time for everything under Heaven', then midwinter is quite definitely the most appropriate time to make an old-fashioned steamed pudding. There's nothing wrong with a cold, grey month in the calendar when it can justify such wonderful culinary indulgence. Here, I am offering you the real thing – a soft, steamy suet crust encasing fragrant and luscious apples, with a hint of cloves. It's no trouble at all to make, and you can leave it gently steaming away while you go for a brisk walk in the wintry chill, knowing all that soothing, comforting pleasure is awaiting you on your return.

Serves 6-8
For the suet pastry:
8 oz (225 g) self-raising flour, plus a little extra for dusting
4 oz (110 g) shredded suet
cold water
a little butter for greasing
salt

For the filling:
1 lb (450 g) Bramley apples (weight after coring), washed (no need to peel)
8 oz (225 g) Cox's apples (weight after coring), washed (no need to peel)
2 oz (50 g) golden caster sugar
6 cloves

You will also need a large pudding basin (see page 173), very well buttered; some kitchen foil and string; and a steamer.

To make the suet pastry, all you do is sift the flour into a bowl, add the suet and a pinch of salt and mix them together. Now start to add a little cold water, sprinkling it here and there. Then take a flat-bladed knife and begin to mix with it, still adding water, until the mixture looks like it is coming together. Finish off using your hands, adding drops of water until you get a smooth, elastic dough. There's no need to rest the dough, so you can straightaway reserve a quarter of the pastry (for the lid) and then roll the rest out on a flat, lightly floured surface to a 10 inch (25.5 cm) round, giving it quarter turns as you roll to keep the round shape.

Now transfer the pastry to the pudding basin and arrange it to form a lining, using your hands to press it round as evenly as possible. If you have some pastry above the rim, just squeeze it down to form a neat edge.

Next, cut the apples into quarters. Now slice them into ½ inch (1 cm) chunks and, as you add them to the basin, sprinkle in the sugar and tuck in a clove here and there. Pack the apples down as you go and don't worry if they rise a bit above the top, as they will shrink in the cooking.

Now roll out the reserved pastry to form the lid, dampen the edge all round with water, then place it over the apples. Press the edge all round to weld it to the edge of the pastry lining the basin.

After that, take a double sheet of kitchen foil, about 10 inches (25.5 cm) square, make a pleat in the centre and cover the top of the pudding with it. Then tie it securely with string around the top of the basin, and make a string handle (to help you lift it into the steamer) by attaching a length of string to both sides. Now boil a kettle and pour the boiling water into a saucepan to about halfway, place it over a medium heat and when it comes back to the boil, fit the steamer over the top.

Pop the pudding in, put the lid on and steam the pudding for exactly 2 hours, keeping the water at a steady simmer. After an hour, check the water level in the saucepan and, if necessary, top up with boiling water.

To serve the pudding, remove the string and kitchen foil, loosen the pudding all round with a palette knife, then turn it out on to a warmed plate. Serve cut into slices, with the apples strewn around the pastry and – it has to be said – lots of proper custard.

Bread-and-Butter Pudding

This traditional English recipe, which I have made for years, has, I'm afraid, suffered from foreign chefs who have adapted it into 'modern' concoctions. This version is fragrant, soft, moist, wobbly beneath and toasted and crunchy on top. I would go the whole hog and serve it with some chilled, untreated Jersey cream.

First of all, cut each slice of buttered bread in half and then into quarters, leaving the crusts on. Now arrange one layer of bread over the base of the dish, sprinkle over the candied peel and half the currants, then cover with another layer of bread and the remainder of the currants.

Next, in a measuring jug, measure out the milk and add the double cream. Stir in the sugar and lemon zest, then whisk the eggs, first on their own in a small bowl and then into the milk mixture.

Now pour the whole lot over the bread, grate some nutmeg over the surface, then bake on the centre shelf of the oven for 30-40 minutes, or until the top is golden brown and crusty. Remove it and leave for 5 minutes before serving.

Serves 4-6
8 slices bread (from a small loaf), buttered
½ oz (10 g) whole candied lemon or orange peel, finely chopped
2 oz (50 g) currants
10 fl oz (275 ml) milk
2½ fl oz (60 ml) double cream
2 oz (50 g) golden caster sugar
grated zest ½ small lemon
3 large eggs
whole nutmeg
butter for greasing

Pre-heat the oven to gas mark 4, 350°F (180°C).

You will also need a rectangular baking dish with a base measurement of 7 x 9 inches (18 x 23 cm), well-buttered.

Individual Sussex Pond Puddings with Lemon Butter Sauce

Serves 6

For the suet pastry:
4 oz (110 g) self-raising flour, plus a little extra for dusting
2 oz (50 g) fresh white breadcrumbs
grated zest 1 lemon
3 oz (75 g) shredded suet
2 fl oz (55 ml) water
2 fl oz (55 ml) milk
a little butter for greasing

For the filling:
1 lemon
6 oz (175 g) butter
6 oz (175 g) demerara sugar

You will also need six mini pudding basins with a capacity of 6 fl oz (175 ml), very well buttered; some kitchen foil; and a steamer.

This is one of the truly great English puddings, which has, sadly, fallen victim to the health lobby. Originally, a whole lemon was placed inside, along with butter, and when the pudding was opened, all the buttery juices spilled out, creating a 'pond' all around it. I have converted it to small individual puddings and it's still truly wonderful.

First of all, sift the flour into a bowl, then sprinkle in the breadcrumbs, lemon zest and suet and just mix everything lightly with your hands to distribute it evenly. Next, mix the water and milk together and sprinkle about 3 fl oz (75 ml) of this liquid into the flour. Begin mixing with a round-bladed knife, and then use your hands at the end to bring it all together to a smooth, elastic dough that leaves the bowl clean. If the mixture seems a little dry, add more of the liquid.

Next, transfer the dough to a flat, lightly floured surface, give it a light kneading and then divide it into six equal portions, slicing off a small piece from each for a lid. After that, roll out the large pieces into rounds big enough to line each basin. Now transfer the pastry to the basins and arrange it to form the lining, using your hands to press it round as evenly as possible. If you have some pastry above the rim, just squeeze it down to form a neat edge.

After that, cut the lemon into thin slices and divide the slices equally between the basins. Next, put 1 oz (25 g) butter and 1 oz (25 g) sugar into each basin. Finally, roll out the extra pieces of pastry into rounds and use these as lids, dampening the edges with a little water and pressing to seal them firmly all round. Now cover each basin with a double sheet of kitchen foil, pleated in the centre and twisted at the edges, and place in a steamer fitted over a saucepan filled with boiling water. Pop the lid on and steam for 2 hours, keeping the water at a steady simmer, and making sure it is topped up if it needs it.

When the puddings are ready, turn them out into warmed bowls, sliding a small palette knife around the edges to loosen them, and serve with some chilled pouring cream to mingle with the juices.

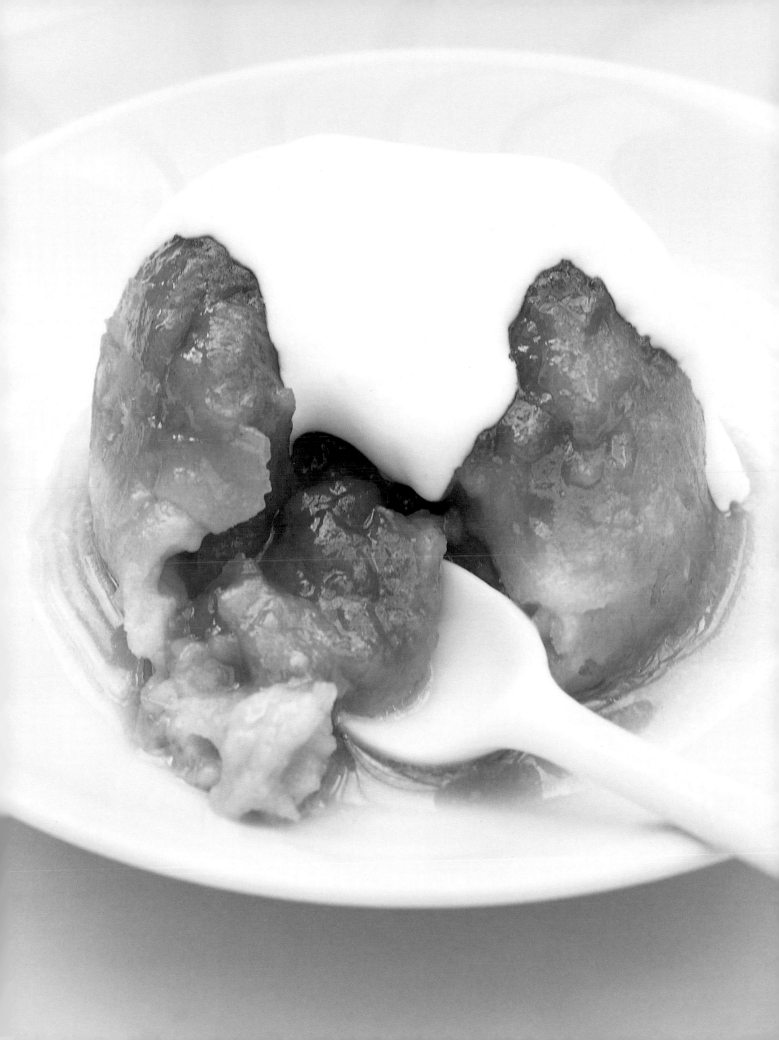

8
Parties and gatherings

Parties and gatherings so often present problems, beginning with where you are going to hold the event. You look for a venue, find one at the right price and then – what do you know? – you can't find a free date because the venue has been booked up months ahead. So, this is where I come in, hoping to encourage you to throw open your own doors, welcome your family and friends, and have a go yourself.

Although there will be a certain amount of hard work involved, it's not going to be difficult and it can also be enormous fun – and I'm sure you can rope in a few friends to help. The huge plus is going to be the quality of the food because, however inexperienced you are, proper home-made food is usually streets ahead of what's on offer from caterers – with the exception of Norwich City Football Club, of course!

Here, I've planned two types of buffet party: one hot and one cold. Both serve twelve people but can be increased to serve eighteen or twenty-four by making one-and-a-half times or twice the amounts specified in the recipes. Before embarking on the recipes themselves, I thought it would be helpful to give you a running order to show what can be prepared ahead, what on the day itself and what should be left until the time of serving.

The other two menus – one perfect at any time of the year, the other especially good in summer – are for eight people, but can likewise be increased to serve sixteen or twenty-four.

Finally, I have included some recipes for pre-dinner nibbles suitable for absolutely any occasion.

A Hot Middle Eastern Buffet

Why Middle Eastern, you're thinking? Let me explain. I sometimes think buffet food can be rather bland – a quiche served straight from the oven may be an absolute delight, but cold or re-heated, it loses much of its charm. The combination of lively flavours and contrasting textures in Middle Eastern cooking, though, makes for perfect buffet fare. A nice addition to this would be to include some warm Pitta Bread (see page 54) and a double quantity of Hummus (see page 78). Serves 12.

Menu
Spiced Lamb Koftas Braised in Tomato Sauce
Stuffed Yellow Peppers with Pilau Rice, Currants
and Toasted Pine Nuts
Courgette and Potato Cakes with Mint and Feta Cheese
Mixed Vegetable Salad à la Grècque
Greek Orange and Honey Syrup Cake with Yoghurt and Pistachios
Pistachio Ice Cream with Pistachio Wafers

Two days before

Vegetable Salad à la Grècque   Make the salad and store in a lidded container in the fridge.
Pistachio Ice Cream   Make the ice cream and freeze in a lidded plastic container.
Greek Orange Cake   Make the cake, drizzle with the syrup and store in a cool place in an airtight tin.

The day before

Make the koftas, simmering them in a covered saucepan for 30 minutes only, then cool, transfer them to a lidded plastic container and store in the fridge.

Roast the peppers for the rice, then cool and store them in a lidded container in the fridge.

Make the courgette cakes so they are ready to bake, arrange in layers on a tray, separated by silicone paper (parchment), cover well with clingfilm and then refrigerate.

Make the wafers and store in an airtight container in a cool place.

On the morning of your party

Weigh out the pilau rice ingredients. Chop and cook the onions in the oil, add the garlic and cook for a few minutes more. Remove the pan from the heat, cover and leave on one side until later. Chop the mint to garnish the rice, cover and store in the fridge until needed.

Chop the parsley and spring onions for garnishing the salad, cover and refrigerate until needed.

Transfer the ice cream from the freezer to a cool place to stand, then put a baking tray lined with silicone paper (parchment) into the freezer. After about 30 minutes, shape the ice cream into balls using a scoop, put them on to the chilled baking tray and return them, uncovered, to the freezer.

Arrange the pistachio wafers on a plate and cover with clingfilm.

Two hours before your guests arrive

Put the butter and oil for the courgette cakes into a small saucepan ready to melt.

Put the salad into two serving dishes, drizzle with the oil and sprinkle with the prepared parsley-and-spring-onion garnish, and cover with clingfilm.

Place the cake on a serving plate, spread with the yoghurt and sprinkle with the pistachios. Then push five cocktail sticks into the cake to stop the cover touching the topping. Cover loosely with clingfilm and refrigerate.

When your guests begin to arrive

Pre-heat the oven to gas mark 7, 425°F (220°C), with a baking tray on the top and middle shelf.

50 minutes before serving the buffet

Put the koftas into a large saucepan, cover and bring to a simmer over a medium heat, then remove the lid and allow to simmer for 30 minutes to reduce the sauce and heat the koftas thoroughly. Transfer to one or two warmed serving bowls and cover with kitchen foil.

Lamb Koftas

Stuffed Peppers

Courgette Cakes

Pistachio Wafers

Stuffed Peppers

Vegetable Salad à la Grècque

Pistachio Ice Cream

Pistachio Wafers

Courgette Cakes

Vegetable Salad à la Grècque

Greek Orange Cake

Lamb Koftas

	40 minutes before serving the buffet
Courgette Cakes	Melt the butter-and-oil mixture and brush the courgette cakes, then arrange them on the pre-heated baking trays and bake for 25-30 minutes (turning them over once after 15 minutes, and at the same time, swapping over the baking trays). Transfer to a warmed serving dish once heated through and cover with kitchen foil.
	30 minutes before serving the buffet
Stuffed Peppers	Warm the cooked onions and garlic for the rice, stir in the pine nuts, currants and cinnamon, then the rice, add the boiling stock, stir once and then cover. Cook on the lowest setting for 15 minutes. Remove the lid and cover with a clean tea cloth.
	20 minutes before serving the buffet
Stuffed Peppers	Place the cooked peppers on a baking tray and warm through in the oven for 10 minutes. Then fill them with the cooked rice and serve the remaining rice in a warmed serving bowl. Cover with kitchen foil and keep warm.
	Before calling your guests to the buffet
Vegetable Salad à la Grècque, Courgette Cakes, Lamb Koftas and Stuffed Peppers	Uncover the vegetable salad, courgette cakes, koftas and rice. Garnish the stuffed peppers with the prepared mint.
	When you're ready for dessert
Pistachio Ice Cream	Remove the ice cream from the freezer.
Pistachio Wafers	Uncover the wafers.
Greek Orange Cake	Remove the clingfilm and cocktail sticks from the cake and drizzle with the honey.

Clockwise, from top right: Spiced Lamb Koftas Braised in Tomato Sauce; Mixed Vegetable Salad à la Grècque; Courgette and Potato Cakes with Mint and Feta Cheese; Stuffed Yellow Peppers with Pilau Rice, Currants and Toasted Pine Nuts; and extra Pilau Rice

Spiced Lamb Koftas Braised in Tomato Sauce

This is a great buffet recipe, but it's also extremely good for smaller numbers – cut all the ingredients by a third and it will serve four.

Serves 12 (makes 48)
For the koftas:
3 lb (1.35 kg) minced lamb
3 teaspoons coriander seeds
3 teaspoons cumin seeds
3 small onions, peeled and cut into chunks
3 tablespoons fresh mint leaves
3 tablespoons fresh coriander leaves
5-6 tablespoons olive oil
salt and freshly milled black pepper

For the sauce:
3 lb (1.35 kg) tomatoes
12 oz (350 g) onions (about 2 medium onions), finely chopped
3 cloves garlic, crushed
1½ sticks cinnamon
salt and freshly milled black pepper

You will also need a lidded, flameproof casserole with a capacity of 7 pints (4 litres).

First of all, you need to dry-roast the coriander and cumin seeds to draw out their flavour: place them in a small frying pan over a medium heat and toss them around for 2 minutes until they begin to jump and pop, then crush them as finely as possible with a pestle and mortar.

Next, place the lamb in a large mixing bowl. Put the onions in a food processor, along with the mint and coriander leaves, then pulse everything until the onion is finely chopped. Transfer all this to join the meat in the bowl, add the spices and a good seasoning of salt and freshly milled black pepper, then mix everything thoroughly and evenly together with your hands (easiest) or a large fork (takes longer). Then take small amounts of the mixture and roll them with your palms into little rounds slightly larger than a walnut.

Now heat about a tablespoon of the oil in a large frying pan over a medium to high heat and when it's hot, begin to brown the koftas, about six at a time, turning them to get brown on all sides. As they cook, transfer them to a plate and add more oil when needed as you continue browning all the others.

Meanwhile, skin the tomatoes for the sauce. Place them in a heatproof bowl and pour boiling water on to them. After exactly a minute (or, if the tomatoes are small, 15-30 seconds), remove them from the water, slip off their skins (protecting your hands with a cloth if they are hot) and chop them into small pieces.

After that, place the casserole over a high heat, add another tablespoon of oil and when it's hot, soften the onions, stirring them around now and then and keeping the heat highish so they turn golden brown, which should take about 6 minutes. Next, add the garlic to the onions and cook for about a minute more. Now add the tomatoes and cinnamon, stir well, then add the koftas, stir once more, turn the heat down to low and let them simmer slowly for about 30 minutes with the lid on. Then remove the lid to allow the sauce to reduce, continuing to simmer for a further 30 minutes before serving.

Stuffed Yellow Peppers with Pilau Rice, Currants and Toasted Pine Nuts

The beauty of these peppers is that they can be made well in advance, then warmed through and filled with the pilau rice just before serving.

All you do is cut the peppers in half lengthways through the stalk, then scrape out the seeds and place the halves on the baking tray. Now sprinkle a little of the garlic into each one and follow that with a teaspoon of oil. Brush a little more oil around the edges of the peppers, add a seasoning of salt and freshly milled black pepper, then bake them on a high shelf in the oven for 50-60 minutes, or until they are well browned at the edges.

Meanwhile, prepare the rice. Heat the oil in the frying pan over a medium heat. Add the onions and pine nuts and fry for 10 minutes, or until everything is golden. Then add the currants, cinnamon and garlic. When you are ready to cook the rice, stir it into the pan and turn the grains over until they are thoroughly coated in the oil. Then pour in the hot stock and season with salt. Stir once only, then put the lid on, turn the heat down to its lowest setting and let the rice cook for exactly 15 minutes. After that, take the pan off the heat, remove the lid and cover the pan with a clean tea cloth until the rice is needed.

When the peppers are cooked, transfer them to a warmed dish and fill each one with the rice, adding the mint at the last moment. Serve the remaining rice in a warmed bowl to accompany the peppers.

Serves 12
For the roasted peppers:
6 large yellow peppers
2 cloves garlic, chopped
4-5 tablespoons olive oil, including a little for greasing
salt and freshly milled black pepper

For the pilau rice:
1 pint (570 ml) basmati rice (use a measuring jug)
4 oz (110 g) currants
4 oz (110 g) pine nuts
3 tablespoons olive oil
2 medium onions, peeled and finely chopped
3 cinnamon sticks, halved
2 cloves garlic, crushed
2 pints of hot stock made with Marigold Swiss vegetable bouillon powder
12 sprigs fresh mint, to garnish
salt and freshly milled black pepper

You will also need a baking tray measuring 11 x 16 inches (28 x 40 cm), greased, and a large, lidded frying pan.

Pre-heat the oven to gas mark 4, 350°F (180°C).

Courgette and Potato Cakes with Mint and Feta Cheese

These quite brilliant little courgette cakes used to have to be fried, which is tiresome when you have much to prepare for a party. However, we have tried baking them in the oven, which works a treat.

Serves 12 (makes 16 cakes – one per person, plus a few extra)

6 medium courgettes (weighing about 1 lb 8 oz/700 g in total)
4 medium Desirée potatoes (weighing about 1 lb 8 oz/700 g in total)
4 tablespoons chopped fresh mint
1 lb (450 g) Feta, crumbled
4 spring onions, finely chopped
2 large eggs, beaten
2 tablespoons plain flour
2 oz (50 g) butter
1½ tablespoons olive oil
salt and freshly milled black pepper

You will also need two baking trays, each measuring 10 x 14 inches (25.5 x 35 cm).

First you need to coarsely grate the courgettes – a food processor is good for this – and put them into a colander. Then sprinkle them with 2 teaspoons of salt to draw out some of their excess moisture and leave them to drain for about an hour, with a plate or bowl underneath to catch the juices.

Meanwhile, scrub the potatoes and place them in a very large saucepan, with a little salt. Pour just enough boiling water over them to cover them, then simmer gently with a lid on for 8 minutes to parboil them. After that, drain them and leave them aside until they're cool enough to handle. Then peel them and, using the coarse side of a grater, grate them into a large bowl and season with more salt and some freshly milled black pepper.

When the hour is up, rinse the courgettes under cold, running water, squeeze out as much moisture as possible with your hands, then spread them out on a clean tea cloth and roll it up to wring out every last drop – this is very important, so the cakes are not wet.

Now, add the courgettes to the grated potatoes, along with the spring onions, mint, Feta and beaten eggs, and using two forks, lightly toss it all together. Next, divide the mixture into 16 and shape into rounds about ½ inch (1 cm) thick, pressing them firmly together to form little cakes. They don't have to be very neat – it's nice to have a few jagged edges. Then lightly dust the cakes with the flour.

To cook them, first pre-heat the oven to gas mark 7, 425°F (220°C) and also pre-heat the baking trays. Meanwhile, melt the butter and oil in a small saucepan, then brush the cakes on both sides with it. When the oven is up to heat, place the cakes on the trays, returning one to the top shelf and the other to the middle shelf for 15 minutes. After that, carefully turn the cakes over using a palette knife and a fork, swap the positions of the trays in the oven and cook them for a further 10-15 minutes. Serve hot.

Mixed Vegetable Salad à la Grècque

This is not a new recipe, but one I've always loved to serve at buffet parties. It has lots of gutsy flavours, can be made well in advance and doesn't need any last-minute attention.

First of all, you need to dry-roast the coriander seeds. To do this, place them in a small frying pan over a medium heat and stir and toss them around for 1-2 minutes, or until they begin to look toasted and start to jump in the pan. Now crush them quite coarsely with a pestle and mortar, along with the peppercorns.

Next, finely chop the onions, heat the oil in the saucepan and soften the onion in it for 10 minutes. Meanwhile, skin the fresh tomatoes, if using. Place them in a heatproof bowl and pour boiling water on to them. Leave them for exactly a minute (or 15-30 seconds, if they are small), then remove them and slip off their skins (protecting your hands with a cloth if they are hot). Now quarter them and add them (or the tinned tomatoes) to the pan. Then add the crushed coriander seeds and peppercorns, garlic, vinegar, oregano, lemon juice, water and tomato purée, and a teaspoon of salt. Bring everything up to the boil, stir in the shallots, cover the pan and simmer for 20 minutes.

Next, break the cauliflower into 1 inch (2.5 cm) florets, halve the mushrooms and add them both, along with the beans, to the pan. Cover it again and simmer for a further 20 minutes, stirring the vegetables around once or twice during the cooking time. After 20 minutes, test them with a skewer – they should be tender but still firm. Now taste to check the seasoning. Then pour the contents of the pan into the serving dishes and leave to cool. I think this is best left covered in the fridge overnight to allow the flavours to develop, so it can be made up to two days ahead.

To serve, remove the dishes from the fridge an hour in advance, drizzle the vegetables in each serving dish with half the oil, then scatter over the chopped parsley and spring onions.

Serves 12
3 medium onions, peeled
3 lb (1.35 kg) ripe, red tomatoes, (or 3 x 400 g tins Italian chopped tomatoes)
18 shallots, peeled
12 oz (350 g) cauliflower
12 oz (350 g) small to medium open-cap mushrooms, wiped
2 tablespoons coriander seeds
24 black peppercorns
5 fl oz (150 ml) olive oil
3 fat cloves garlic, crushed
7 fl oz (200 ml) red wine vinegar
1 tablespoon chopped fresh oregano (or 2 teaspoons dried oregano)
juice 3 medium lemons (about 4 fl oz/120 ml)
6 fl oz (175 ml) water, mixed with 1½ tablespoons tomato purée
6 oz (175 g) dried butter beans (or judion beans), pre-soaked (see page 72), cooked and drained
salt and freshly milled black pepper

To serve:
5 fl oz (150 ml) olive oil
1½ oz (40 g) chopped fresh flat-leaf parsley
6 spring onions, finely chopped, including the green parts

You will also need a saucepan with a capacity of 7 pints (4 litres), and two large, shallow serving dishes.

Pistachio Ice Cream

This is so many people's favourite ice cream — pale green and fragrant, with lovely bits of frozen pistachio to bite into. Lovely on its own or served with the Pistachio Wafers (see opposite), the ice cream is also delicious with the Greek Orange and Honey Syrup Cake (see page 198).

Serves 12
8 oz (225 g) unsalted, shelled pistachio nuts
1 pint (570 ml) each double and single cream
4 oz (110g) golden caster sugar
8 large egg yolks
1½ tablespoons custard powder

You will also need an ice-cream maker (pre-frozen according to the manufacturer's instructions); and two lidded plastic boxes measuring 6 x 8 x 3 inches (15 x 20 x 7.5 cm).

First of all, whip the double cream until it reaches the 'floppy' stage but isn't too thick, then pop it into the fridge to chill. Then take 4 oz (110 g) of the pistachio nuts, place them in a food processor with the sugar and process until very fine. After that, roughly chop the remaining nuts.

Next, pour the single cream into a medium-sized saucepan, along with the finely ground pistachios, and gently heat to just below boiling point. While that is happening, in a large bowl, beat together the egg yolks and custard powder until smooth. Now pour the hot cream on to this mixture, whisking as you go. After that, return the pistachio custard to the pan and continue to whisk it over a medium heat until it has thickened and just come up to boiling point again. (Ignore any curdled appearance, which may come about if you don't keep whisking and have the heat too high; the custard powder will stabilise it, provided you beat it off the heat, and poured into a bowl, it will become quite smooth again.) Now pour the custard into a bowl and place it in a larger bowl of chilled water, stirring it now and then until cold.

Meanwhile, fold the double cream into the ice cream mixture. Now place half the mixture into the ice-cream maker, add half the remaining nuts and freeze-churn for about 30 minutes, until it has the consistency of soft-scoop ice cream. Then transfer it to one of the plastic boxes and place in the freezer. Repeat with the other half of the mixture.

Note: If you make a smaller quantity, not for a party, remember to remove the ice cream from the freezer 20 minutes before serving.

If you don't have an ice-cream maker, instructions for making ice cream without one are on page 63.

Pistachio Wafers

These pretty little triangular wafers are the perfect accompaniment to the Pistachio Ice Cream (see opposite). Their irregular shape is part of their charm.

First mix together the pistachios, icing sugar and cinnamon. Next, take a sheet of filo, covering the others with a clean tea cloth, and butter it generously, using a brush. Then sprinkle it with a sixth of the nut-and-sugar mixture. Now place another sheet on top, butter it and sprinkle with the same amount. Repeat with a third sheet and more of the mixture, pressing down the layers. Now begin again, so you end up with two stacks. Next, take each stack, cut it into four equal-sized rectangles, then take each rectangle and cut it into three haphazard triangles. Place half the triangles on the baking tray and bake them on the middle shelf for 10-12 minutes, or until they are crisp and golden brown. Then transfer the first batch to a wire rack and allow the tray to cool before baking the second. Allow this batch to cool, too. When the wafers are cold, store them in an airtight plastic box and sprinkle with a little icing sugar just before serving.

Serves 12

4 oz (110 g) unsalted, shelled pistachio nuts, finely chopped
3 oz (75 g) unrefined icing sugar, sifted, plus a little extra for dusting
½ teaspoon ground cinnamon
4 oz (110 g) fresh filo pastry (6 sheets)
4 oz (110 g) unsalted butter, melted, plus a little extra for greasing

You will also need an 11 x 16 inch (28 x 40.5 cm) baking tray, buttered.

Pre-heat the oven to gas mark 4, 350°F (180°C).

Greek Orange and Honey Syrup Cake with Yoghurt and Pistachios

The sharp acidity of the orange in this cake combines beautifully with the sweetness of the Greek mountain honey. Because the cake is soaked in syrup, you can make it well ahead and just whip it out when you're ready to serve.

Serves 12
For the cake:
2 small oranges (weighing about 9 oz/250 g)
4½ oz (125 g) ground almonds
6 oz (175 g) well-softened butter, plus a little extra for greasing
6 oz (175 g) golden caster sugar
3 large eggs, beaten
9oz (250 g) semolina
4½ teaspoons baking powder

For the syrup:
8 fl oz (225 ml) Greek mountain honey
5 tablespoons water
5 tablespoons orange juice
1½ tablespoons lemon juice
1½ inch (4 cm) cinnamon stick

For the topping:
7 oz (200 g) Greek yoghurt
1½ oz (40 g) unsalted, shelled pistachio nuts
2 tablespoons Greek mountain honey

You will also need a 10 inch (25.5 cm) springform cake tin, lightly greased and the base lined with greased silicone paper (parchment).

Pre-heat the oven to gas mark 6, 400°F (200°C).

First, cut the oranges into chunks, removing the pips. Then tip the whole lot – flesh, pith and zest – into a food processor and whiz it to a thick purée. Now all you do is simply put all the other cake ingredients into a large bowl and, provided the butter is really soft, just go in with an electric hand whisk and whisk everything together until you have a smooth, well-combined mixture. After that, fold in the orange purée, spoon the mixture into the prepared tin and smooth the top with the back of the spoon.

Now place the cake on the centre shelf of the oven and bake it for an initial 10 minutes. Then lower the temperature to gas mark 4, 350°F (180°C) and bake for a further 40-45 minutes, or until it is golden brown, springy in the centre and has shrunk slightly from the sides of the tin.

Meanwhile, make the syrup. To do this, simply combine the honey and water with the cinnamon stick in a small saucepan, place it over a gentle heat, bring it up to simmering point and let it simmer gently for about 5 minutes. After that, take the pan off the heat, remove the cinnamon stick and stir in the orange and lemon juices.

Leave the cake aside to cool for 5 minutes, then remove it from the tin to a wire rack to cool, with a large plate underneath. Make a few holes all over it with a skewer before pouring the syrup over it. (It will look like there is far too much, but don't worry, the cake will absorb more than you think, and any that is not absorbed can be poured from the plate back over the cake.) Then, when the cake is absolutely cold, place it on a serving plate, cover it and leave it in a cool place overnight.

Just before serving, spread the top of the cake with the Greek yoghurt, sprinkle over the pistachios, drizzle with the honey and serve cut into chunky slices.

Note: This cake can also be made to serve 8-10, in an 8 inch (20 cm) tin, using 1 orange, 3 oz (75 g) ground almonds, 4 oz (110 g) each softened butter and sugar, 2 large eggs, 6 oz (175 g) semolina and 3 teaspoons baking powder. For the syrup, use 5 fl oz (150 ml) honey, 3 tablespoons each water and orange juice, 1 tablespoon lemon juice and 1 inch (2.5 cm) cinnamon stick. For the topping, use 7 oz (200g) Greek yoghurt, 1 oz (25 g) pistachios and 1½ tablespoons honey. Bake the cake for 10 minutes at the higher temperature and 25-30 minutes at the lower temperature.

A Cold Buffet

What I've done here is devise a cold buffet menu that can all be prepared in advance – but I do think that in winter, particularly, it's essential to have just one hot item, so I've included some crunchy jacket potatoes. It's a truly delightful feast of flavours and textures that is bound to please – and still leave you blissfully free to join in the party yourself without ending up a nervous wreck. Serves 12.

Menu
Curried Turkey Salad with Dried Fruits
Mini Yorkshire Puddings with Rare Beef and Horseradish-and-
Mustard Crème Fraîche
Caramelised Onion Tartlets with Goats' Cheese and Thyme
Brown and Wild Rice Salad with Dried Cranberries
Gruyère Potato Halves with Chives
Thai Pork Satays with Thai Peanut Sauce
Lemon Roulades
Chocolate Ricotta Cheesecake

Up to a week ahead

Mini Yorkshire Puddings — Bake the Yorkshires, cool and freeze in a lidded container.

The day before

Curried Turkey Salad — Prepare all of the ingredients for the salad, then put the spring onions into a small plastic food bag and store in the fridge. Put the toasted almonds into a small lidded container and store in a cool place. Mix together the turkey, apricots, raisins and dressing and refrigerate. Prepare the coriander leaf garnishes, put them into a small plastic food bag with a wet piece of kitchen paper and pop in the fridge.

Mini Yorkshire Puddings — Seal and roast the beef for the Yorkshires, cool and refrigerate on a plate, covered. Prepare the watercress garnishes, put them into a plastic food bag with a piece of wet kitchen paper and chill. Mix together the sauce ingredients and store in the fridge, too.

Caramelised Onion Tartlets — Make the pastry for the tartlets and allow it to rest. Pre-heat the oven, then line the patty tins, prick the bases and brush with beaten egg. Bake, then cool, cover with a clean tea cloth and store in a cool place overnight. Prepare and cook the onions, then cool and refrigerate. Whisk together the egg, cream, mustard and some seasoning and chill in a small plastic box. Prepare the 24 thyme sprigs, mix them with the oil and chill in a plastic food bag.

200

Make the rice salad, mix with the dressing and dried cranberries only, then cool, cover and refrigerate. Prepare the cucumber, tomatoes and pepper and refrigerate. Put the spring onions into a small plastic food bag and pop in the fridge, too (separated from those for the turkey salad). Toast the walnuts, put into a lidded container and store in a cool place.

Brown and Wild Rice Salad

Wash the potatoes and leave in a cool place to dry. Grate the Gruyère, snip the chives and refrigerate separately from each other.

Gruyère Potato Halves

Make the marinade/sauce for the satays. Pour half into a large bowl for the pork, then add the peanuts to the remainder in the food processor and pulse the mixture once. Transfer the sauce to a lidded box and chill. Refrigerate the reserved coriander in a small plastic food bag. Cut the pork, add it to the marinade in the bowl and stir well, before transferring to a suitable container in the fridge.

Thai Pork Satays

Make the sponge bases and roll them up in silicone paper (parchment), as in the recipe. Then, when cool, wrap them in clingfilm and keep them in a cool place. Make the Mascarpone cream filling and the lemon curd and chill separately in lidded containers in the fridge.

Lemon Roulades

Make the cheesecake, cover and chill overnight. Make the chocolate curls and store in a box in the fridge.

Chocolate Ricotta Cheesecake

On the morning of your party

Assemble the turkey salad, arrange on the salad leaves, cover and keep in the fridge.

Curried Turkey Salad

Prick the potatoes and rub with sea salt.

Gruyère Potato Halves

Mix the salad with the prepared cucumber, tomatoes and pepper, add two-thirds each of the spring onions and walnuts, cover and refrigerate.

Brown and Wild Rice Salad

Soak the skewers for the satays. Chop the reserved coriander, add to the sauce and refrigerate until later. Pre-heat the grill and line the grill pan with kitchen foil, then thread the pork on to the dried and oiled skewers. Place the pork skewers on the grill rack and brush with some of the marinade. Grill for 15-20 minutes, turning the skewers over and brushing them with some more marinade halfway through cooking. Cool the satays, then arrange them on a serving dish, cover and store in the fridge until later.

Thai Pork Satays

Spread a third of the Mascarpone and a third of the lemon curd on to each of the sponges, then roll them. Arrange them on serving dishes.

Lemon Roulades

Make the icing and decorate the roulades. Push 5 cocktail sticks into each of the roulades to stop the clingfilm touching the topping. Cover and refrigerate. Mix together the remaining Mascarpone and lemon curd, put into a serving bowl and chill this, too.

Chocolate Ricotta Cheesecake — Unmould and plate the cheesecake, decorated with the curls, then cover with clingfilm and keep in a cool place.

Two hours before your guests arrive
Pre-heat the oven to gas mark 4, 350°F (180°C).

Mini Yorkshire Puddings — Crisp the Yorkshires in the oven (from frozen) for a couple of minutes, or until heated through. Slice the beef ready to top the Yorkshires, cover and store in the fridge.

Caramelised Onion Tartlets — Slice each of the goats' cheeses into 12 slices for the tartlets. Divide the cooked onion between the pastry cases, then the egg mixture and then the cheese slices. Top each one with the prepared sprig of thyme, sprinkle with cayenne pepper, then bake, then cool. As soon as the tartlets are ready, increase the oven temperature to gas mark 5, 375°F (190°C), ready to bake the potatoes. When the tartlets are cool, arrange them on a serving plate and cover.

While guests are having drinks on arrival
Gruyère Potato Halves — Put the potatoes in the oven and bake for 1-1¼ hours.

Before calling your guests to the buffet, finally garnish and arrange the food on the buffet table:

Mini Yorkshire Puddings — Top the Yorkshires with the sauce, beef and watercress.
Thai Pork Satays — Garnish the satays with the lime wedges and put the sauce into a bowl.
Curried Turkey Salad — Uncover the turkey salad. Sprinkle with the remaining spring onions, almonds and coriander.
Brown and Wild Rice Salad — Mix in the apple and garnish with the spring onions and walnuts.
Lemon Roulades — Allow the roulades to return to room temperature.
Gruyère Potato Halves — Split the potatoes, top with the Gruyère and return them to the oven 15 minutes before serving, then sprinkle with chives.

When you're ready for dessert
Lemon Roulades — Remove the clingfilm and cocktail sticks from the roulades and serve with the lemon curd/Mascarpone cream from the fridge.

Chocolate Ricotta Cheesecake — Dust the cheesecake with a little of the cocoa powder and pour the cream to accompany it into a jug.

From top to bottom: Mini Yorkshire Puddings with Rare Beef and Horseradish-and-Mustard Crème Fraîche; Curried Turkey Salad with Dried Fruits; Caramelised Onion Tartlets with Goats' Cheese and Thyme; and Brown and Wild Rice Salad with Dried Cranberries

Curried Turkey Salad with Dried Fruits

This is also a great recipe for leftover turkey on Boxing Day and if you're short of time, you can make it with ready-cooked chicken.

Serves 12 as part of the buffet
2 lb (900 g) cooked turkey (or chicken or 2 medium ready-to-eat chickens)
1 tablespoon Madras curry paste
3 oz (75 g) each raisins; ready-to-eat dried apricots, quartered; and whole blanched almonds
5 fl oz (150 ml) mayonnaise
3 fl oz (75 ml) natural yoghurt
2 tablespoons mango chutney
1 bunch spring onions, chopped, including the green parts
5 oz (150 g) baby leaf salad
1 tablespoon fresh coriander leaves
salt and freshly milled black pepper

You will also need a small baking tray.

Begin by pre-heating the oven to gas mark 4, 350°F (180°C). Next, spread the almonds out on the baking tray and toast them in the oven for 8 minutes, using a timer so they do not burn. Let them cool for a couple of minutes, then roughly chop them.

Next, cut the turkey (or chicken) into bite-sized pieces and place it in a large bowl. (If using ready-to-eat chickens, strip all the meat from the carcasses, discarding the skin and bones.)

Then, in a small bowl, mix the mayonnaise and yoghurt with the curry paste and chutney (finely chop any bits of mango), and pour this sauce over the meat. Now add the raisins, apricots, three-quarters of the spring onions and two-thirds of the almonds. Mix everything together thoroughly, taste and season, then cover and chill until needed.

When you are ready to serve, place the salad leaves in the base of one or two serving dishes and spoon the turkey (or chicken) over the top, heaping it up to give it some height. Then scatter the reserved spring onions and almonds and the coriander leaves over the top.

Gruyère Jacket Potato Halves with Chives

I always like to serve one hot dish with a cold buffet, and jacket potatoes are great in winter. In summer, I would serve hot new potatoes with butter and chives.

Serves 12 (makes 12 halves)
6 medium-sized Desirée potatoes (each weighing about 4 oz/110 g)
3 oz (75 g) Gruyère, finely grated
a little olive oil
2 tablespoons freshly snipped chives, to garnish
sea salt, crushed

You will also need a medium-sized baking tray.

Pre-heat the oven to gas mark 5, 375°F (190°C)

First scrub the potatoes, dry them with a clean tea cloth, then leave them aside to dry thoroughly for as long as possible. If they are already washed, all you need do is wipe them with damp kitchen paper. Next, prick their skins a few times with a fork, then put a few drops of oil on to each potato and rub it all over the skin. After that, rub on some crushed sea salt.

Place the potatoes straight on to the centre shelf of the oven and let them bake for 1-1¼ hours, until the skins are really very crisp.

Now cut each potato in half lengthways and score the flesh in a diamond pattern to break it up a bit. Then place the potatoes on the baking tray, and while still hot, divide the grated Gruyère between them. Return them to the oven for 15 minutes, until the cheese is melted and golden. Sprinkle with the chives just before serving.

This recipe is from Lindsey Greensted-Benech, our Catering Director at Norwich City Football Club. I found it hard to believe at first: could a cold Yorkshire taste good? All I can say is, as you live, you learn – it is one of the most ingenious buffet-party recipes I've ever come across, and disappears like lightning.

You need to start this by making the batter, so sift the flour into a bowl, make a well in the centre, break the eggs into it and add salt and freshly milled black pepper. Begin to whisk the eggs with an electric hand whisk and as you beat them, the flour around the edges will slowly be incorporated. When the mixture becomes stiff, simply add the milk-and-water mixture gradually, keeping the whisk going. Stop and scrape the sides of the bowl with a spatula so that any lumps can be pushed down into the batter, then whisk again until all is smooth. Now the batter is ready to use.

Next, place the muffin tin on the baking tray and brush the cups generously with the dripping. Now pop the tin on the tray into the oven to pre-heat for 10-15 minutes. After that, use a thick oven glove and remove them from the oven, placing the baking tray over direct heat, and quickly spoon a tablespoon of batter into each cup. Immediately return them to the middle shelf of the oven and bake for 15-20 minutes, until well risen and very crispy. Then remove the Yorkshires to a wire rack to cool. Now repeat the whole process with the remaining batter.

For the beef, turn the oven up to gas mark 8, 450°F (230°C). In the meantime, pre-heat a large, heavy-based frying pan on the hob, brush it with a little dripping and, when that's hot, seal the beef on all sides, but don't move it around until each side has sealed properly. Remove the meat to a roasting tin, season with freshly milled black pepper and roast in the oven for 18 minutes for rare beef, or up to 25 minutes, if you like it less rare. After that, allow it to cool, then cover and chill thoroughly in the fridge to make it easier to slice.

When you are ready to serve the Yorkshire puddings, thinly slice the beef into 24 slices and arrange a fold of beef in each one. Mix together all the sauce ingredients, then add a teaspoon of the sauce and a sprig of watercress to each Yorkshire.

Makes 24
1 lb 8 oz (700 g) piece trimmed fillet of British beef
6 oz (175 g) plain flour
2 large eggs
6 fl oz (175 ml) milk mixed with 4 fl oz (120 ml) water
about 2 tablespoons beef dripping, melted
salt and freshly milled black pepper

For the sauce:
2 rounded tablespoons hot horseradish sauce
2 teaspoons wholegrain mustard
1 heaped tablespoon crème fraîche
salt and freshly milled black pepper

To garnish:
24 sprigs watercress

You will also need a 12-hole muffin tin with cups measuring 2 inches (5 cm) at the base and 3 inches (7.5 cm) at the top, 1¼ inches (3 cm) deep; and a large baking tray.

Pre-heat the oven to gas mark 7, 425°F (220°C).

Caramelised Onion Tartlets with Goats' Cheese and Thyme

When we made these tartlets for the photography, we couldn't stop eating them! Crisp, light pastry with such a luscious filling – and also lovely as a first course at a supper party.

Makes 24
For the pastry:
6 oz (175 g) plain flour
3 oz (75 g) butter, at room
temperature, cut into smallish lumps,
and a little extra for greasing
1½ oz (40 g) Parmesan (Parmigiano
Reggiano), finely grated
½ teaspoon mustard powder
cayenne pepper
about 1½ tablespoons cold water
1 large egg, beaten

For the filling:
2 large Spanish onions, peeled and
finely chopped
2 x 4 oz (110 g) Welsh goats' cheese logs
24 small sprigs fresh thyme,
dipped in olive oil
1 oz (25 g) butter
1 large egg
4 fl oz (120 ml) single cream
¼ teaspoon mustard powder
cayenne pepper
salt and freshly milled black pepper

You will also need a 3¼ inch (8 cm)
pastry cutter; and two 12-hole patty
tins with cups measuring 1¾ inches
(4.5 cm) at the base, 2½ inches (6 cm)
at the top, ¾ inch (2 cm) deep, well
greased.

First make the pastry. Sift the flour into a large bowl, then add the butter. Take a knife and begin to cut it into the flour until it looks fairly evenly blended, then add the Parmesan, mustard and a pinch of cayenne pepper, plus just enough cold water to make a smooth dough, before discarding the knife and bringing it together with your fingertips. Then place the dough in a plastic food bag and put it into the fridge to rest for 30 minutes. In the meantime, pre-heat the oven to gas mark 4, 350°F (180°C).

After that, roll it out as thinly as possible, use the cutter to stamp out twenty-four rounds and line the tins with them. (The pastry will stand proud of the rim of the cups to allow for shrinkage.) Then prick the bases and brush with the beaten egg. Now bake on the middle and top shelves of the oven (swapping them over halfway through to ensure even browning) for about 10 minutes, or until the pastry is just cooked through, then cool them on a wire rack.

Meanwhile, for the filling, melt the butter in a large frying pan and cook the onions very gently, uncovered and stirring often, for about 30 minutes, or until they have turned a lovely golden brown caramel colour. Then leave them to cool and set aside until needed.

Now whisk the egg with the cream and mustard in a jug and add some seasoning. Next, spoon a little of the onion mixture into each pastry case, spread it out evenly and pour the egg mixture over. Cut each cheese log into 12 thin slices (wiping the knife between slices to cut more cleanly; the cheese is quite soft, so you may have to reshape a few slices into rounds). Place a slice on the top of each tartlet, then top with a sprig of thyme and a sprinkling of cayenne pepper. Bake for 20 minutes, or until puffy and golden, swapping the tins again halfway through cooking.

Brown and Wild Rice Salad with Dried Cranberries

Good old rice salad is an absolute must at a buffet party. This one, made with wild rice, looks very pretty with the jewelled colours of the dried cranberries and nuts.

Begin by heating half the groundnut oil in the smaller frying pan, then add the wild rice and toss it around to coat the grains. Now pour over 8 fl oz (225 ml) of boiling water and add a little salt. Give it one stir, put the lid on and cook over a gentle heat for 50 minutes. Meanwhile, repeat the process with the brown rice, this time adding 16 fl oz (450 ml) of boiling water – it will take 40-45 minutes for the water to be absorbed and the rice to become tender.

While the rice is cooking, you can make the dressing. Pound the garlic and salt to a creamy paste with a pestle and mortar. Next, work in the mustard powder, then switch to a small whisk and add the vinegar and olive oil. Season with plenty of freshly milled black pepper.

Now you'll need to toast the walnuts, so spread them out on a baking tray and place them in the oven for 8 minutes, putting a timer on so you don't forget them. Meanwhile, place the tomatoes in a heatproof bowl and pour boiling water on to them. After exactly a minute, remove them from the water and slip off their skins (protecting your hands with a cloth if the tomatoes are hot), then halve them, squeeze out the seeds and chop them into small pieces.

When both amounts of rice are cooked, mix them together in a serving bowl and add 3-4 tablespoons of the dressing. Toss the rice around in the dressing and then leave it to cool.

When it's cool, mix in the cucumber, tomatoes, diced pepper, apple, cranberries, two-thirds of the spring onions and two-thirds of the walnuts. Drizzle with the remaining dressing and mix again so that everything is thoroughly combined and coated in dressing. Finally, just scatter the remaining spring onions and walnuts over the surface of the salad.

Note: I have tried to make this salad by cooking the two sorts of rice together, but I've found I can't get the timing right, as the wild rice takes a little longer, so you do need to cook them separately.

Serves 12 as part of the buffet
8 fl oz (225 ml) brown basmati rice
(use a measuring jug)
4 fl oz (120 ml) wild rice
(use a measuring jug)
2 oz (50 g) dried cranberries
1 dessertspoon groundnut or other
flavourless oil
2 oz (50 g) walnuts, roughly chopped
3 medium-sized ripe, red tomatoes
3 inch (7.5 cm) piece cucumber, cut
into small dice (no need to peel)
1 small red (or yellow) pepper,
deseeded and diced
1 red-skinned dessert apple, washed,
cored and finely chopped (no need
to peel)
3 spring onions, finely chopped,
including the green parts
salt and freshly milled black pepper

For the dressing:
1 clove garlic
1 teaspoon mustard powder
3 tablespoons Champagne vinegar
(or good-quality white wine vinegar)
6 tablespoons extra virgin olive oil
freshly milled black pepper
1 teaspoon sea salt

You will also need one small and
one large heavy-based frying pan
with tight-fitting lids.

Pre-heat the oven to gas mark 4,
350°F (180°C).

Thai Pork Satays with Thai Peanut Sauce

My thanks to John Curtis, formerly Head Chef at Norwich City Football Club, for this brilliant recipe. It has all the exotic fragrances and flavours of the East, yet it's very simple to make.

Makes 12

1 lb 4 oz (570 g) British pork
tenderloin, trimmed
6 oz (175 g) smooth peanut butter
2 oz (50 g) salted, roasted peanuts
3 freeze-dried kaffir lime leaves
1 stem lemon grass, ends trimmed
and tough outer layer discarded,
roughly chopped
1 medium-sized red chilli, deseeded
1 clove garlic, crushed
½ tablespoon peeled, chopped fresh
root ginger
grated zest 1 lime
juice 2 limes
1 tablespoon Thai fish sauce
¾ oz (20 g) fresh coriander
7 fl oz (200 ml) tinned coconut milk
1 oz (25 g) light soft brown sugar
a little groundnut or other flavourless
oil, for brushing
lime wedges, to garnish

You will also need twelve wooden
skewers.

You need to start by making the sauce, half of which is used as a marinade for the pork, the other half as a dipping sauce. Start off by placing the lime leaves in a small bowl, cover with boiling water and leave to soak for 5 minutes. Then, remove them, roll them up very tightly and shred finely.

Place the lime leaves in a food processor with the lemon grass. Now add the chilli, garlic, ginger, lime zest and juice, and fish sauce. Next, separate the leaves from the coriander stalks, and reserve them until later. Pop the stalks into the food processor and process until everything is very finely chopped. Now add the peanut butter, coconut milk and sugar and whiz again until everything is thoroughly blended. Then pour half the sauce (about 8 fl oz/225 ml) into a large bowl for the pork marinade.

Next, add the peanuts and reserved coriander leaves to the remaining sauce in the processor and pulse once again until coarsely chopped. (The chopped peanuts add a bit more texture.) Now pour the sauce into another bowl, cover and keep stored in the fridge until about an hour before you are ready to serve for the buffet.

Next, to prepare the satays, cut the pork into bite-sized cubes measuring about ¾ inch (2 cm). (You're aiming for 36 pieces.) Now add them to the marinade in the large bowl and mix well, then cover and leave aside for a minimum of an hour. Meanwhile, put the wooden skewers in a shallow dish, cover with hot water and leave to soak for a minimum of 30 minutes. (This helps to prevent them from burning under the grill.)

When you are ready to cook the satays, pre-heat the grill to its highest setting for at least 10 minutes and line the grill pan with kitchen foil. Remove the skewers from their water bath, dry them in a clean tea cloth, then brush them with the oil to prevent the pork from sticking. Thread three cubes of pork on to each skewer, keeping the pieces slightly spaced apart, and arrange the kebabs on the grill rack. Brush liberally with some of the remaining marinade and place under the grill, about 3 inches (7.5 cm) from the heat source. They will take 15-20 minutes to cook, and during that time, you need to turn them and brush them with the remaining marinade as they cook.

When the satays have cooled, cover and refrigerate until needed. Then serve with the sauce, garnished with the wedges of lime.

Lemon Roulade

This is very light, fresh and lemony, with a lovely squidgy centre and it always looks very pretty. And rolling up a roulade is much easier than you think!

Serves 12-16 (makes 2 roulades)
grated zest 2 lemons (juice reserved for the lemon curd)
4 oz (110 g) softened butter, plus a little extra for greasing
8 oz (225 g) golden caster sugar
4 large eggs
8 oz (225 g) self-raising flour, sifted
2 tablespoons hot water
a little icing sugar, sifted, for dusting

For the lemon curd:
grated zest 2 lemons
juice 4 lemons (half from the cake base)
4 large eggs
6 oz (175 g) golden caster sugar
4 oz (110 g) softened unsalted butter, cut into small cubes
1 dessertspoon cornflour

For the Mascarpone cream:
1 lb 2 oz (500 g) Mascarpone, chilled
14 oz (400 g) fromage frais, chilled
1½ tablespoons golden caster sugar

For the icing:
juice and zest 2 lemons
2 oz (50 g) icing sugar, sifted

You will also need two shallow baking tins measuring 9 x 13 inches (23 x 32.5 cm) and ½ inch (1 cm) deep, lightly greased and lined with silicone paper (parchment); and two 18 inch (45 cm) long sheets of silicone paper (parchment).

Begin by making the lemon curd ahead of time, as it needs to be well chilled (for method, see page 103). When the curd is ready, allow it to cool, then cover it with clingfilm pressed over the surface and chill it in the fridge. Meanwhile, pre-heat the oven to gas mark 6, 400°F (200°C).

When you're ready to make the sponge base, place all the ingredients except the icing sugar and hot water in a large mixing bowl and whisk, preferably with an electric hand whisk, for about a minute, then add the hot water and whisk briefly again. Next, divide the mixture between the two prepared baking tins, smooth it out and bake in the oven on the middle shelf for 8-10 minutes. (Don't be tempted to open the oven door until 8 minutes have elapsed, or the sponges may sink.) When the sponges are ready, they should feel springy in the centre when lightly touched with your little finger. Remove them from the oven and let them cool in the tins for 5 minutes.

Meanwhile, lay the sheet of silicone paper for each sponge on a flat surface and dust it all over with the icing sugar. Then, taking each sponge in turn, carefully turn them out on to the silicone paper and gently strip away the paper lining the bases. Cover them with a clean, damp tea cloth and leave for another 5 minutes (but no longer, as they should still be warm, to make the rolling easy).

Now, don't panic – this next part really is quite easy: just lift the paper along the shorter edge and fold it over, then gently roll each sponge up with the paper tucked inside as a lining. If cracks appear, don't worry – they can look very attractive. Now leave the sponges to get cold.

When you're ready to fill them, carefully unroll them and spread each with a third of the lemon curd all over. Now whisk the Mascarpone, fromage frais and sugar together and spread a third of that over each roulade. Then roll each roulade up carefully, but much more loosely.

For the finishing touch, place the zest of the two lemons (removed with a zester, so you get nice curly strands) in a saucer and mix with about a tablespoon of the lemon juice. Next, in a bowl, mix the icing sugar with 2 tablespoons of the lemon juice to make a thin glaze. Drizzle this with a spoon, using sweeping movements back and forth across the top of each roulade. Then drain the lemon zest and scatter half over the icing on each cake.

Combine the leftover Mascarpone mixture with the lemon curd and serve the roulades cut into slices, with the extra lemon Mascarpone cream handed round separately.

Chocolate Ricotta Cheesecake

This cheesecake is not intensely 'in-your-face' chocolatey, but more subtle. The texture and the slight acidity in the Ricotta gives it an unusual edge and this, combined with the pure chocolate on top, is what makes it a very classy dessert. One thing is essential, though, and that's lots of chilled pouring cream to go with it.

Serves 12 as part of the buffet
For the base:
2 oz (50 g) unblanched whole almonds
6 oz (175 g) dark chocolate
oatmeal biscuits
1 oz (25 g) Grape-Nuts cereal
2 oz (50 g) butter, melted
a little groundnut or other flavourless
oil for greasing

For the cheesecake:
5 oz (150 g) dark chocolate
(75 per cent cocoa solids), broken
into small pieces
12 oz (350 g) Ricotta, at
room temperature
7 fl oz (200 ml) half-fat crème
fraîche, at room temperature
2 large eggs, separated
2 oz (50 g) golden caster sugar
3 leaves gelatine
2 tablespoons milk

For the chocolate curls:
4 oz (110 g) dark chocolate
(75 per cent cocoa solids), broken
into small pieces
a little cocoa powder, sifted, for dusting

You will also need an 8 inch (20 cm)
springform cake tin, the sides and
base lightly oiled; and a plate with a
diameter of about 4 inches (10 cm)
not including the rim.

Pre-heat the oven to gas mark 6,
400°F (200°C).

First of all, spread the almonds out on a small baking tray and toast them in the oven for 7 minutes, using a timer. After that, chop them quite finely. Next, place the biscuits in a plastic food bag and crush them, using a rolling pin. Then tip the crumbs into a mixing bowl and add the nuts and Grape-Nuts. Now add the butter to bind it all together, then press the mixture into the base of the tin, pop it into the oven and bake for 10 minutes. After that, remove it and leave it to cool.

Meanwhile, melt the chocolate for the cheesecake in a heatproof bowl over a pan of barely simmering water, making sure the bowl doesn't touch the water, then remove it from the heat and let it cool as well. Next, in a large mixing bowl, whisk together the Ricotta, crème fraîche, egg yolks and sugar until smooth and well blended.

Now soak the leaves of gelatine in a small bowl of cold water for about 5 minutes, and while that's happening, heat the milk in a small saucepan up to simmering point before taking it off the heat. Squeeze the excess water from the gelatine, then add it to the milk and whisk until it has dissolved. Now stir the gelatine and milk, along with the cooled chocolate, into the Ricotta mixture, until it's all thoroughly blended.

Now, in another, grease-free bowl and using clean beaters, whisk the egg whites to the soft-peak stage. Then, first fold a tablespoon of egg white into the cheesecake mixture to loosen it, and after that, carefully but thoroughly fold in the rest of the egg white. Next, pour the mixture on to the cheesecake base, cover with clingfilm and chill in the fridge for at least 4 hours or, preferably, overnight – the longer the better.

To make the chocolate curls, melt the chocolate as before, then pour it on to the base of the plate to form an even layer about ¼ inch (5 mm) thick. Place the plate into the fridge for 45 minutes to chill and set. (The chocolate should be hard enough so that, if you press the surface, it doesn't leave an indentation, but not rock hard.) Then, using a large-bladed knife held carefully at either end with both hands (or a cheese slice), pull the blade across the chocolate, pressing down slightly. As the blade comes towards you, the chocolate will form curls. (If it is too hard, it will be brittle and will break rather than forming curls, in which case, leave it at room temperature for 5 minutes before trying again.) Store the curls in a sealed container in the fridge until you are ready to use them. You probably won't need all this chocolate to make enough curls to top the cake, but as the layer of chocolate gets thinner, it will be harder to form nice curls, so the remaining chocolate can be lifted off the plate and melted again for another recipe (or simply eaten!).

To unmould the cheesecake, first run a palette knife around the edge of the tin, then release the spring-clip and remove it. After that, carefully lift it off the base of the tin and transfer it to a serving plate. Decorate it with the chocolate curls and give them a light dusting of sifted cocoa powder.

Note: This recipe contains raw eggs.

An Italian Lunch or Supper

Once again, this menu leaves you perfectly free to enjoy your guests' company, as absolutely everything can be prepared ahead and be ready to go when you want. All you will have to do is pre-heat the oven and pop in the lasagne 45-50 minutes before you want to serve it, and dress the salad just before you eat. Serves 8.

Menu
Antipasti
Traditional Lasagne al Forno
Zabaglione Torta

Antipasti

Serves 8
16 slices Mortadella (12 oz/350 g)
16 slices Parma ham (6 oz/175 g)
24 slices salami (10 oz/275 g)
1 lb (450 g) Mozzarella
16 each olives, cornichons and radishes
4 tablespoons olive oil
freshly milled black pepper

This is my favourite Italian first course. If you can buy the meats and cheese from a specialist Italian deli, so much the better; alternatively, counters at supermarkets will cut you the correct quantities. You could serve it with some of the sharp Giardiniere Pickles on page 110. Then all it needs is some warm Italian bread and good, creamy butter.

All you need to do is divide the meats and cheese equally between eight plates, garnish with the olives, cornichons and radishes, and just before serving, drizzle the cheese with the olive oil and season it with freshly milled black pepper.

Traditional Lasagne al Forno

My first lasagne recipe is clearly in need of an update and that's simply because we are now able to buy more authentic ingredients. I have also discovered from an Italian friend that the long, slow cooking of the ragù really does develop all the flavours in a wonderful way. Lasagne has suffered greatly from being anglicised, factory made and served as cheap nosh, its authenticity obliterated – all the more reason to reinvent this great classic dish in all its original glory.

First of all, begin by making the ragù. Heat a tablespoon of the oil in your largest frying pan over a medium heat and gently fry the onion for about 10 minutes, moving it around from time to time. While it is softening, chop the pancetta: the best way to do this is to roll it into a sausage shape, then, using a sharp knife, slice it lengthways into four, then slice the lengths across as finely as possible. After the 10 minutes is up, add this to the pan, along with the garlic, and continue cooking the whole lot for about 5 minutes. Now transfer this mixture to the casserole.

Next, add another tablespoon of oil to the pan, turn up the heat to its highest, then add the minced beef and brown it, breaking it up and moving it around in the pan. (A wooden fork is really helpful here.) When the beef is browned, tip it into the casserole to join the onion mixture, then heat another tablespoon of oil and do exactly the same with the minced pork.

While the pork is browning, trim the chicken livers, rinse them under cold, running water and dry them thoroughly with kitchen paper. Pull off any skin and snip out any tubes or odd bits of fat with kitchen scissors, then chop the livers minutely small. When the pork is browned, transfer it to the casserole, too. Finally, heat the remaining tablespoon of oil and cook the pieces of chicken liver, adding these to the casserole as soon as they have browned nicely.

After that, you need to remove the pan and place the casserole over the direct heat, and give everything a really good stir. Then add the contents of both tins of tomatoes, the tomato purée, red wine, a really good seasoning of salt and freshly milled black pepper and about a quarter of a nutmeg, grated. More stirring now, then allow this to come up to simmering point. While that happens, strip the leaves from half the basil, tear them into small pieces and add them to the casserole. Then, as soon as everything is simmering, place the casserole on the centre shelf of the oven and leave it to cook slowly, without a lid, for exactly 4 hours. It's a good idea to have a look after 3 hours to make sure all is well and to have a good stir, but what you should end up with is a thick, reduced, concentrated sauce, with only a trace of liquid left in it. When that happens, remove the casserole from the oven, taste to check the seasoning, then strip the remaining leaves off the basil, tear them into small pieces and stir them in.

Serves 8
1 lb (450 g) green no-cook dried lasagne sheets (about 24 sheets)
14 oz (400 g) Mozzarella, diced
4 oz (110 g) Parmesan (Parmigiano Reggiano), freshly grated or shaved

For the ragù:
4 tablespoons extra virgin olive oil
1 large onion, peeled and finely chopped
7 oz (200 g) sliced pancetta
2 fat cloves garlic, chopped
12 oz (350 g) minced British beef
12 oz (350 g) minced British pork
6 oz (175 g) chicken livers
1 x 400 g tin Italian chopped tomatoes
1 x 230 g tin chopped tomatoes
6 tablespoons tomato purée
6 fl oz (175 ml) red wine
¼ whole nutmeg
⅓ oz (15 g) fresh basil
salt and freshly milled black pepper

For the cream sauce:
6 fl oz (175 ml) double cream
2½ pints (1.5 litres) milk
6 oz (175 g) butter, plus a little extra for greasing
4 oz (110 g) plain flour
¼ whole nutmeg
salt and freshly milled black pepper

You will also need a flameproof casserole with a capacity of 4½ pints (2.6 litres); and a roasting tin (or ovenproof dish) measuring about 10 x 12 x 3 inches (25.5 x 30 x 7.5 cm), well buttered.

Pre-heat the oven to gas mark 1, 275°F (140°C).

Now, to make the cream sauce, place the milk, butter, flour and some seasoning in a large, thick-based saucepan. Place this over a gentle heat and whisk continuously with a balloon whisk until the sauce comes to simmering point and thickens. Then, with the heat as low as possible, continue to cook the sauce for about 10 minutes.

After that, sieve the sauce into a bowl, beat in the cream, taste and season if it needs it, and grate in another quarter of the whole nutmeg. Now spread about a quarter of the ragù over the base of the roasting tin (or dish). Cover this with one fifth of the sauce, followed by a quarter of the Mozzarella, then arrange a single layer (about six sheets) of the lasagne. (I find you need four placed side by side lengthways and the other two halved and spread along the gap that's left.) Repeat this process three more times, finishing with a final layer of sauce, then cover the whole lot with the grated Parmesan and the lasagne is ready for the oven. All this can be done well in advance. Then, when you're ready to bake the lasagne, pop it on to the top shelf of the oven, pre-heated to gas mark 4, 350°F (180°C) for 45-50 minutes, or until it's bubbling and turning slightly golden on top.

Zabaglione Torta

This is my version of a truly wonderful dessert cake, which I first ate in Harry's Dolci, my favourite Venetian restaurant. The original recipe is in Harry's Bar Cookbook.

Serves 8
For the cake:
4 oz (110 g) self-raising flour
½ teaspoon baking powder
2 large eggs, at room temperature
4 oz (110 g) well-softened butter,
plus a little extra for greasing
4 oz (110 g) golden caster sugar
¼ teaspoon pure vanilla extract
a little icing sugar, sifted, to decorate

For the filling:
3 large egg yolks
3 oz (75 g) golden caster sugar
1½ oz (40 g) plain flour, sifted
9 fl oz (250 ml) Marsala
12 fl oz (340 ml) double cream

You will also need an 8 inch (20 cm) sponge tin, 1½ inch (4 cm) deep, lightly greased and the base lined with silicone paper (parchment).

First of all, make the zabaglione filling. Using an electric hand whisk, beat the egg yolks for a minute in a medium bowl, then add the sugar and beat again until the mixture is thick and pale yellow – about 3 minutes.

Next, whisk in the flour a tablespoon at a time, mixing it in really well, then gradually whisk in the Marsala. Now tip the mixture into a medium-sized heavy-based saucepan and place it over a medium heat. Stir constantly until it has thickened and is just about to boil – this will take about 5 minutes. (Don't worry if it looks lumpy, just tip it into a clean bowl, then whisk until smooth again.) Now let it cool, whisking it from time to time to stop a skin forming. When it is cold, cover with clingfilm and pop it into the fridge for at least 2 hours.

Now pre-heat the oven to gas mark 3, 325°F (170°C). Meanwhile, make the cake. First sift the flour and baking powder into a large mixing bowl, holding the sieve high to give them a good airing as they go down. All you do next is simply add the other ingredients and just go in with the electric hand whisk. Whisk for about a minute, until you have a smooth, well-combined mixture that drops off a spoon when you give it a tap on the side of the bowl. If it seems a bit stiff, add a little water and mix again.

Now spoon the mixture into the tin, level it out with the back of the spoon and bake on the centre shelf for 30-35 minutes – don't open the oven door before 30 minutes have elapsed. To test, touch the centre lightly: if it leaves no impression and the sponge springs back, it is ready. Remove it from the oven, but wait about 5 minutes before turning it out on to a cooling rack. Carefully peel off the base paper by making a fold in it first, then pull it gently away without trying to lift it off too quickly. Now leave the sponge to cool completely.

To assemble the torta, whip the cream in a large bowl until stiff, then add the zabaglione and whisk again until thoroughly mixed. Now place the cake flat on a board and, holding a serrated palette knife horizontally, carefully slice it into two thin halves. Next, reserving 2-3 heaped tablespoons of the zabaglione to decorate the sides, spread the rest of it over the bottom half, easing it to the edges. Place the other half on top and press down very gently. Before you spread the zabaglione on the sides, brush away any loose crumbs, so they don't get mixed up in it. Now, using a small palette knife, spread the sides evenly with the reserved mixture. Finally, dust the top with the icing sugar before serving. If the cake is made and decorated ahead of time, store it, covered, in the fridge (to keep it firm), but remove it half an hour before serving.

Note: This recipe contains partially cooked eggs.

A Summer Lunch or Supper

Because of the vagaries of the British summer, this menu has been designed with sun *or* rain in mind. If you find the weather's not that good, it helps to serve a hot watercress soup and, as the main course is served cold, you could also serve the potato salad warm, if you prefer. On the other hand, if it's a lovely, hot, sunny day, then the soup can be served cold, in chilled bowls with ice cubes. There is nothing, but nothing quite like serving a whole salmon on a summer's day. Because the salmon is cooked slowly in kitchen foil, with bone, skin and head intact, the flavour will be far superior to cooking it any other way. Serves 8.

Menu
Watercress Soup
Baked Whole Salmon with Sauce Verte
Anya Potato Salad with Shallots and Vinaigrette
Chunky Green Salad
Gooseberry Crème Fraîche Tart

Watercress Soup

Serves 8
9 oz (250 g) watercress, destalked and chopped, a few leaves reserved for garnishing
4 oz (110 g) butter
the white parts of 5 leeks (weighing about 14 oz/400 g), cleaned and roughly chopped
4 medium potatoes (weighing about 1 lb 8 oz /700 g), peeled and roughly chopped
3 pints (1.75 litres) hot stock made with Marigold Swiss vegetable bouillon powder
4 heaped tablespoons crème fraîche
salt and freshly milled black pepper

Watercress is a star performer in so many ways. I love the fat, green leaves in salads, sprinkled with rock salt in sandwiches, in a sauce and perhaps most of all, in this soup, which is always a joy to make and eat.

First of all, melt the butter in a large, heavy-based saucepan, then add the leeks, potato and watercress and stir them around so they are coated with the melted butter.

Next, sprinkle in some salt, then cover with a lid and let the vegetables sweat over a very gentle heat for about 20 minutes, giving the mixture a good stir about halfway through.

After that, add the stock, bring everything up to simmering point and simmer, covered, for 10-15 minutes, or until the vegetables are quite tender. Then remove the pan from the heat and when the soup has cooled a little, liquidise it in batches, then return it to the saucepan.

Now stir in 3 tablespoons of crème fraîche, season to taste and re-heat the soup very gently, without letting it boil. Serve it in hot bowls and garnish each one with the reserved watercress leaves and an extra swirl of crème fraîche. Alternatively, cool the soup and serve chilled, garnished in the same way.

Baked Whole Salmon with Sauce Verte

With summer in mind, when, if the weather allows, there can be all kinds of outdoor celebrations, nothing is nicer on a buffet table than a whole salmon. I wouldn't say I was the last of the big spenders foodwise, but I am very happy to fork out once a year and buy a wild salmon – the king of fish – and cook it to perfection to enjoy one of the best feasts of summer. The best accompaniment is a sweet Sauce Verte, flavoured with summer herbs, which I think is best made the day before, if possible, to allow the flavours to develop.

The way I cook a salmon is extremely slowly, wrapped in kitchen foil in the oven. I cannot recommend this method highly enough. Unfortunately, the gas equivalent of 250°F (130°C), which used to be gas mark ½, no longer exists. So, if you use a modern gas cooker that begins at gas mark 1, give the fish 25 minutes less cooking time.

Serves 8

4 lb (1.8 kg) fresh whole salmon, cleaned and gutted
2 oz (50 g) butter, plus a little extra for greasing
1 small onion, peeled and thinly sliced
3 bay leaves
4 sprigs chopped fresh tarragon
salt and freshly milled black pepper

For the sauce:
2 large eggs
2 teaspoons mustard powder
1 fat clove garlic
½ pint (275 ml) groundnut or other flavourless oil
2 dessertspoons white wine vinegar
3 oz (75 g) spinach
1½ oz (40 g) watercress, tough stalks removed
1½ oz (40 g) fresh flat-leaf parsley
2 tablespoons chopped fresh tarragon
1 tablespoon freshly snipped chives
1 tablespoon (or more) lemon juice, to taste
salt and freshly milled black pepper

You will also need a baking tray measuring 11 x 16 inches (28 x 40 cm), and some kitchen foil.

First make the sauce. Break the eggs straight into your blender or food processor, then sprinkle in the mustard powder and add the garlic clove and a teaspoon of salt. Next, measure the oil into a jug, switch the machine on and pour in the oil in a thin, steady trickle with the motor running. (You must be very careful here: too much oil too quickly and the sauce will curdle.) When all the oil is in, blend in the vinegar.

Now rinse the spinach, watercress and parsley under a little cold, running water and put them into a saucepan. Then, with the heat turned to medium, stir them around until everything has just wilted. Next, tip them into a colander and rinse them again under cold, running water to keep their colour. Squeeze out the excess moisture very carefully, thoroughly pressing with a wooden spoon. Then transfer the leaves to the blender or food processor, along with the tarragon and chives, and whiz until the sauce is smooth and green. (There will be some fine specks, but that's okay.) Now taste and season with the lemon juice and freshly milled black pepper, and some more salt, if it needs it.

When you are ready to cook the salmon, pre-heat the oven to 250°F (130°C). (For the gas mark, see introduction). Start by wiping the fish with some damp kitchen paper, then place it in the centre of a large, double sheet of kitchen foil that you've generously buttered. Put 1 oz (25 g) butter, the onion slices, bay leaves and tarragon into the centre cavity, along with a seasoning of salt and freshly milled black pepper. The rest of the butter should be smeared over the top of the fish. Now wrap the kitchen foil over the fish to make a loose but well-sealed parcel and place it diagonally on the baking tray, so that it fits in the oven. If it's still too long, bend the tail end upwards. Bake in the centre of the oven for 2½ hours.

After that, remove the salmon from the oven and allow it to completely cool in the kitchen foil before serving. The skin will peel off very easily now the salmon is cooked. Slit the fish down the middle, following the backbone, and ease the fillets away. Serve with the sauce, crisp, dressed salad leaves (such as Cos lettuce), cucumber, and some hot, buttered new potatoes, or potato salad.

Note: For other weights of salmon, the cooking times are as follows: for 2 lb (900 g), 1½ hours; for 3 lbs (1.35 kg), 2 hours; for 5 lb (2.25 kg), 3 hours.

This recipe contains raw eggs.

Anya Potato Salad with Shallots and Vinaigrette

I love the consistently good flavour of Anya potatoes, which we use all the time at our catering functions at Norwich City Football Club, buying them direct from the grower. If you can't get them, try to buy other good-flavoured salad potatoes for this.

Serves 8
2 lb (900 g) Anya or other new
potatoes, washed
6 shallots, peeled and finely chopped
4 tablespoons freshly snipped chives

For the vinaigrette:
2 cloves garlic
1 rounded dessertspoon
mustard powder
1 tablespoon balsamic vinegar
1 tablespoon sherry vinegar
10 tablespoons extra virgin olive oil
freshly milled black pepper
1 rounded dessertspoon sea salt

You will also need a steamer.

Steam the potatoes over a pan of boiling water, sprinkled with salt and covered with a lid, for about 20 minutes until they are tender.

Meanwhile, make up the dressing. Begin by crushing the salt quite coarsely with a pestle and mortar, and then add the garlic. As you begin to crush it and it comes into contact with the salt, it will quickly break down into a purée. Next, add the mustard powder and really work it in, giving it about 20 seconds of circular movements to get it thoroughly blended. After that, add some freshly milled black pepper. Now add the vinegars and work these in in the same way. Then add the oil, switch to a small whisk and give everything a really good whisking.

As soon as the potatoes are cooked, cool them in a mixing bowl for 10 minutes, then stir in the vinaigrette and the shallots while they are still just warm. Now add the chives and give everything a good toss to distribute any dressing that has collected in the base of the bowl and transfer the salad to a serving bowl.

Chunky Green Salad

This is a simple salad of leaves with a bit of bite to them.

Serves 8
1 round lettuce and 1 head chicory,
outer leaves removed
2 oz (50 g) rocket and watercress,
stalks removed
½ cucumber, peeled and sliced thinly
3 spring onions, finely chopped

For the vinaigrette:
As above

First of all, tear the lettuce and chicory leaves and place them in a large serving bowl, along with the rocket and watercress. Now scatter in the cucumber and spring onions and toss well.

Next, make the vinaigrette as for the potato salad, above. Just before serving, whisk the dressing again, add half of it to the salad leaves and toss them, then add the remaining dressing and toss again, so that everything gets a good coating. Serve immediately.

Gooseberry Crème Fraîche Tart

This one disappeared in seconds when we were photographing the book. It's simple – just thin, crispy pastry and a layer of gooseberries set in custard. Delicious with or without some thick, yellow Jersey cream.

Serves 8
For the pastry:
5 oz (150 g) plain flour
1¼ oz (30 g) softened butter, cut into smallish lumps, plus a little extra for greasing
1¼ oz (30 g) softened lard, cut into smallish lumps
about 1½ tablespoons cold water
salt

For the filling:
1 lb (450 g) gooseberries, topped and tailed
3½ fl oz (100 ml) crème fraîche
2 large egg yolks
1½ oz (40 g) golden caster sugar
1 teaspoon balsamic vinegar

You will also need a 9 inch (23 cm) loose-based fluted tart tin, 1 inch (2.5 cm) deep, lightly greased; and a medium-sized baking tray.

First of all, make the pastry. Sift the flour and a pinch of salt into a bowl from a height to ensure it gets a good airing. Then take a knife and begin to cut the fat into the flour. Go on doing this until it looks fairly evenly blended, then rub in the fat using your fingertips only and with as light a touch as possible. As you do so, lift it up high and let it fall back into the bowl, which means that, all the time, air is being incorporated – and air is what makes pastry light. Speed is what's needed here, so don't go on rubbing all day – just long enough to make the mixture crumbly, with a few odd lumps here and there.

Next sprinkle a tablespoon of the water over the mixture, then start bringing the dough together, using the knife to make it cling. Now discard the knife and finally bring it together with your fingertips. When enough liquid is added, the pastry should leave the bowl completely clean. If this hasn't happened, then keep adding a spot more. (Sometimes it only needs your fingers dipped into water.) Place the pastry in a plastic food bag and rest it in the fridge for about 20 minutes. Meanwhile, pre-heat the oven to gas mark 5, 375°F (190°C) and pre-heat the baking tray at the same time.

Next, transfer the pastry to a flat, lightly floured surface and roll it out to a circle the diameter of the tin. Line the tin with the pastry, press it up about ¼ inch (5 mm) above the rim of the tin all round, then prick the base all over with a fork. Now brush the base and sides with some of the egg white left over from the eggs for the filling.

After that, place the pastry-lined tin on the hot baking tray and bake for 20 minutes until the pastry is just beginning to turn golden. Then remove it and reduce the heat to gas mark 4, 350°F (180°C).

Next, whisk the crème fraîche, yolks, sugar and vinegar together for the filling. Arrange the gooseberries in the pastry case, pour the crème fraîche mixture over them and return the tart to the oven for 40-45 minutes, or until it is a light golden brown. Then remove it from the oven and allow it to settle for about 20 minutes before serving. It also tastes extremely good served cold.

Savoury Mini Muffins with Two Flavourings

Makes 24
For the muffins:
10 oz (275 g) plain flour
1 tablespoon baking powder
2 large eggs
8 fl oz (225 ml) milk
a little butter for greasing
1 teaspoon salt

For the goats' cheese, red onion and rosemary flavouring:
2 oz (50 g) goats' cheese, cut into
¼ inch (5 mm) cubes
2 oz (50 g) red onion, peeled and finely chopped
2 teaspoons chopped fresh rosemary, plus 12 small sprigs for garnishing
½ oz (10 g) butter

For the Gruyère, sage and onion flavouring:
2 oz (50 g) Gruyère, grated
2 teaspoons chopped fresh sage, plus 12 small leaves for garnishing
2 oz (50 g) spring onions, finely sliced
2 teaspoons Parmesan (Parmigiano Reggiano), grated

You will also need two 12-hole mini-muffin tins, lightly greased; or two 12-hole mini-muffin tins, and 24 mini-muffin cases that have been lightly greased.

For a fresh approach to party nibbles, I offer you these magic little savouries that can be served warm from the oven or, if made in advance, frozen, defrosted and re-heated. First some simple muffin mathematics: the basic muffin recipe makes 24, and after that there are two flavourings – each for half that quantity – which should be prepared first. They can be made with or without muffin cases.

First, you need to prepare the two muffin flavourings. To make the goats' cheese, red onion and rosemary muffins, begin by melting the butter in a small saucepan and softening the onion in it for about 5 minutes. Then allow it to cool. Next, prepare and set aside the ingredients for the Gruyère, sage and onion muffins. Now pre-heat the oven to gas mark 6, 400°F (200°C) while you make the basic muffin mixture.

First of all, sift the flour, baking powder and salt on to a large plate, then take a large mixing bowl and sift the mixture again, this time into the bowl, holding the sieve up high to give the flour a good airing.

Now, in a jug, beat one egg, then whisk it together with the milk. Next, fold all this into the flour, using the minimum number of folding movements. (Ignore the unpromising look of the mixture at this stage and don't overmix.) Divide the mixture equally between two bowls in order to add the two different flavourings.

Now return to the first flavouring and gently mix the onion into the muffin mixture in one bowl, along with the goats' cheese and chopped rosemary, folding in, as before, with as few strokes as possible. Next, add the prepared ingredients for the second flavouring to the muffin mixture in the other bowl and fold them in in the same gentle way.

After that, if you are using muffin cases, arrange them in the tins and spoon the mixture into them; alternatively, spoon the mixture straight into the greased tins. You can pile the mixture quite high. Beat the second egg and brush the surfaces with it, then top the goats' cheese muffins with a sprig of rosemary, and the Gruyère muffins with the Parmesan and a sage leaf. Then bake them for about 20 minutes, or until well risen and golden. Remove the muffins from the tins to a rack and eat as warm as possible.

Bloody Mary Tomatoes

Serves 6
9 oz (250 g) baby plum tomatoes
(or cherry tomatoes), stalks removed
7 fl oz (200 ml) vodka
1 tablespoon sherry
1 tablespoon Worcestershire sauce
a few drops Tabasco sauce
½ teaspoon celery salt

To serve:
1 teaspoon celery salt, ¼ teaspoon
cayenne pepper, 2 tablespoons sea salt,
all mixed together

You will also need a small lidded
plastic box.

These look quite deceptive – I mean, what harm is there in a bowl of little tomatoes? But once swallowed, never forgotten! All the kick of a bloody Mary in one bite. Don't forget you need to start this two days in advance.

All you do is score a little cross on the base of each tomato, then place them in the plastic box cross-side up. Then whisk together the vodka, sherry, Worcestershire sauce, Tabasco and celery salt, and spoon it over them. Put the lid on the box and leave it in the fridge to allow the tomatoes to marinate for two days.

Before serving, drain the tomatoes and let them come back to room temperature. (You can keep any leftover marinade to use as a base for future batches.) Then arrange them on a plate with a bowl containing the salt mixture and invite your guests to dip in a tomato before eating.

Quails' Eggs with Cracked Pepper and Salt

Peeling boiled quails' eggs is not my favourite job so I usually rope in some help, but it's worth it because they look so pretty and taste wonderful dipped in cracked pepper and salt.

Serves 6
24 quails' eggs
1 tablespoon mixed peppercorns,
crushed in a mortar
1 tablespoon sea salt

To cook the eggs, put them into plenty of boiling water, bring them quickly back to the boil and using a timer, give them one minute and 45 seconds.

Next, run cold water over them to stop them cooking and peel them while they are still slightly warm, reserving a few with the shell on, to garnish. Then, to serve, arrange them on a platter with the unpeeled eggs and a little dipping pot containing the pepper and salt, which have been mixed together.

David's Chocolate Fudge with Roasted Nuts and Raisins

Makes 60 squares

14 oz (400 g) dark chocolate (75 per cent cocoa solids), chopped quite finely

3 oz (75 g) mixed nuts, such as hazelnuts and almonds

3 oz (75 g) raisins

1½ oz (40 g) unsalted butter

3½ fl oz (100 ml) liquid glucose

12 fl oz (340 ml) whipping cream

9 oz (250 g) golden caster sugar

For the top:

4 oz (110 g) milk chocolate

You will also need a small baking tray; a wide, heavy-based saucepan with a capacity of 6 pints (3.5 litres); a sugar thermometer; and a baking tin measuring 6 x 10 inches (15 x 25.5 cm), lined with silicone paper (parchment).

Pre-heat the oven to gas mark 4, 350°F (180°C).

At the football club, we always serve home-made chocolates with coffee, and when we served 450 readers of BBC Good Food Magazine *this chocolate fruit-and-nut fudge last year, it was widely appreciated and we had lots of pleas for the recipe. David Baker, our pastry chef, who makes the best confectionery I've ever tasted, has given me his recipe – which makes not only a very suitable finale to our party chapter, but a sublime and sweet end to* How To Cook.

Begin by roasting the nuts. Spread them out on the small baking tray and roast them for 8 minutes, using a timer so you don't forget them. Then remove them from the oven to a chopping board, let them cool a bit and chop them roughly. Now place them, along with the dark chocolate, raisins and butter in a large, heatproof bowl.

Next, measure out the glucose. (A hot spoon will be useful here – just dip it in boiled water for a few seconds, then wipe it dry.) Place the glucose, cream and sugar in the saucepan over a high heat. (It does need to be a large, wide pan as the mixture will come to a really fast, rolling boil.) Stir everything together until it gets really hot, and then stop stirring because the mixture does tend to catch on the bottom of the pan and you'll stir scorched bits into the fudge.

What you need to do now is insert the sugar thermometer (protecting your hands with thick oven gloves and being really careful not to splash yourself). When the temperature of the mixture reaches 225°F (110°C) – after about 5 minutes – the mixture will look like dark condensed milk. Now remove it from the heat and pour it over the nuts, dark chocolate, raisins and butter, and stir with a wooden spoon until the mixture is well blended, smooth and glossy. (Don't be tempted to add the chocolate to the hot pan – it will simply burn.) Now all you do is pour the whole lot into the lined tin. Then soak the saucepan in hot water immediately.

When the fudge is absolutely cold, cover it with more clingfilm and chill it in the fridge for at least 6 hours or, preferably, overnight.

The next day, melt the milk chocolate in a heatproof bowl over a saucepan of simmering water, making sure the base of the bowl doesn't touch the water. Then turn the fudge out on to a chopping board, discarding the silicone paper, and use a palette knife to spread the melted chocolate over the top. Use a serrated palette knife or a fork to make a ridged pattern across the topping and allow it to set before cutting the fudge into 1 inch (2.5 cm) cubes.

Party Checklist

Item	Notes
In advance	
Plastic boxes and food bags; kitchen paper and foil; and clingfilm	Assemble the equipment you'll need to store party food cooked in advance. Lidded plastic boxes of varying sizes are invaluable for keeping prepared ingredients separate in the fridge to prevent flavour tainting, and plastic food bags are useful when space is limited. A piece of wet kitchen paper popped into a box or bag helps keep herbs and salad leaves damp and fresh. Kitchen foil and clingfilm are handy for covering both ingredients and made-up dishes
Ice	If you need to chill your bottles with ice, you will need about 1 lb (450 g) per person. Make it in batches and store it in bags in the freezer, or, if space is tight, ask your supermarket or off-licence to reserve you some bags of ice and collect it a few hours in advance (taking a cooler box with you)
Flowers	Order and collect
Menus, seating plan and place settings (if required)	Write, or design them on the computer, if you're lucky enough to have one
Music	Plan your choice of CDs or tapes
On the morning of your party	
Napkins	Tie or fold. Assemble cocktail napkins, if required
Table	Lay a cloth and assemble main, starter, side, cheese and dessert plates; cutlery; salt and pepper mills; a bread basket; butter dishes; napkins; and menus, a seating plan and place settings, as required
Glasses	Polish and set out on trays, ready to be filled
Flowers	Arrange around the room and on the table
Candles or nightlights (if required)	Put in place around the room and on the table
Ashtrays (if required)	Put in place around the room
Tea cloths	Make sure you have plenty of clean cloths for kitchen tasks
Serving dishes and cutlery	Assemble in the kitchen
Coats	Clear coats from coat hooks, or decide on a bedroom where they can go
Guest cloakroom	Assemble toilet paper, hand towels, tissues, a scented candle and flowers
Before your guests arrive	
Drinks	Chill bottles in the fridge, if you have space, or on ice, if not – put them into a large plastic container (or a couple of washing-up bowls) an hour before the party, pour over the ice and add some cold water
Wine buckets or coolers	Assemble or chill, as appropriate
Rubbish bins	Empty all bins for the final time
Dishwasher	Empty and put away the contents
Music	Put on a CD or tape
Lighting and heating (if appropriate)	Adjust to suit
Candles or nightlights	Light
Cushions	Plump up
Shower, dress, pour yourself a cool drink or a glass of wine and relax!	Enjoy!

Clockwise, from top left: four of our chefs at Norwich City Football Club: David Baker, Lucy Crabb, Alain Benech and Lindsey Greensted-Benech

Suppliers and stockists

www.deliaonline.com
Includes recommended food shops
and equipment suppliers, Delia's
recipes, culinary advice and
techniques, and live on-line
chats with Delia

Ingredients
Italian
Fratelli Camisa Ltd
www.camisa.co.uk
Telephone 01992 763076
Mail order available

Esperya
www.esperya.com
info@esperya.com
Mail order available

Japanese
Clearspring Ltd
www.clearspring.co.uk
Telephone 020 8746 0152
Mail order available

Spanish
PataNegra
www.patanegra.net
Telephone 020 7736 1959
info@patanegra.net
Mail order available

Cheese
La Fromagerie
www.lafromagerie.co.uk
30 Highbury Park
London N5 2AA
Telephone 020 7359 7440
info@lafromagerie.co.uk
European cheeses by mail order

Neal's Yard Dairy
17 Short's Gardens
London WC2H 9UP
Telephone 020 7645 3555
mailorder@nealsyarddairy.co.uk
British and Irish cheeses by
mail order

Fish
Martin's Seafresh
www.martins-seafresh.co.uk
Telephone 0800 027 2066
sales@martins-seafresh.co.uk
Mail order available

Alex Spink & Sons
24 Seagate
Arbroath DD1 1BJ
Telephone 01241 879056
aspink@fastfish.co.uk
Arbroath smokies by mail order

Flour for bread machines
Carrs Flour Mills Ltd
www.breadflour.co.uk
Telephone 01697 331661
sales@breadflour.co.uk
Mail order available

Smoked gammon, bacon and pork
Lane Farm Country Foods
www.lanefarm.co.uk
Telephone 01379 384593
ian@lanefarm.co.uk
Mail order available

Spices
The Spice Shop
www.thespiceshop.co.uk
1 Blenheim Crescent
London W11 2EE
Telephone 020 7221 4448
Mail order available

Kitchen equipment
Cucina Direct
www.cucinadirect.co.uk
Telephone 020 8246 4311
sales@cucinadirect.co.uk
Mail order available

David Mellor
www.davidmellordesign.com
4 Sloane Square
London SW1W 8EE
Telephone 020 7730 4259
Mail order available

Divertimenti
www.divertimenti.co.uk
45-47 Wigmore Street
London W1H 9LE
Telephone 020 7935 0689
sales@divertimenti.co.uk
Mail order available

Lakeland Limited
www.lakelandlimited.co.uk
Telephone 015394 88100
net.shop@lakelandlimited.co.uk
Mail order available and outlets
nationwide

For more information on Delia's
restaurant and Canary Catering:
Norwich City Football Club
Carrow Road
Norwich NR1 1JE
Telephone 01603 218704
reception@ncfc-canaries.co.uk

For more information on
equipment or ingredients in
this book, send an A4 SAE to:
How To Cook Book Three
20 Upper Ground
London SE1 9PD

Index

Page numbers in *italic* refer to the illustrations

Adzuki beans *73*
  sesame blancmange with sweetened compote of adzuki beans 93, *93*
Ajo blanco – chilled almond soup 51, *51*
Alain's passion fruit brûlée 59, *59*
Almonds
  ajo blanco – chilled almond soup 51, *51*
  dark apricot and almond conserve 102, *102*
  Easter simnel cake 34-5, *35*
Almost mayonnaise 126, *127*
Almost vinaigrette 125, *125*
Antipasti 214, *214*
Anya potato salad with shallots and vinaigrette 224, *225*
Apple corers 21, *21*
Apples
  baked apple meringues with orange-soaked raisins 144, *144*
  Lucy's tarte Tatin 32, *33*
  old English apple hat 182, *182*
  spiced damson chutney 105, *105*
  Spike's apple sorbet 65, *65*
  spotted Dick rides again 180, *181*
Apricots
  dark apricot and almond conserve 102, *102*
Arbroath smokies
  souffléd Arbroath smokies in smoked salmon with foaming hollandaise 162, *162*
Armagnac, spiced pickled Agen prunes in 106, *107*
Artichokes *see* Globe artichokes; Jerusalem artichokes
Asparagus steamers 21

Bacon
  coarse country pâté 154-5, *155*
  the London Particular – green split pea soup 82, *82*
  smoked collar of bacon with pease pudding and creamy onion mustard sauce 80, *81*
Baked apple meringues with orange-soaked raisins 144, *144*
Baked whole salmon with sauce verte 222-3
Baker, David 232, *234*
Baking beans, ceramic 21
Baking equipment 18-19
Baking trays 19
Balance scales 17, *17*
Bean slicers 21
Beans 71-3, *73*
  braised sausages with borlotti beans, rosemary and sage 92, *92*

Mexican chicken chilli with yellow tomato salsa 87, *87*
old-fashioned shin of beef stew with butter beans and crusted onion dumplings 88, *89*
sesame blancmange with sweetened compote of adzuki beans 93, *93*
Tuscan bean and pasta soup with rosemary 84, *85*
vegetarian shepherd's pie with goats' cheese mash 83, *83*
Beef
  braised beef goulash with smoked pimentón 24, *24*
  mini Yorkshire puddings with rare beef and horseradish-and-mustard crème fraîche 203, 205
  old-fashioned shin of beef stew with butter beans and crusted onion dumplings 88, *89*
  pepper-crusted fillet of beef with roasted balsamic onions and thyme 22, *23*
  traditional lasagne al forno 215-16, *216-17*
Belarussian carrot salad 44, *45*
Benech, Alain 59
Biscotti, zabaglione ice cream with 64, *64*
Black beans *73*
Black-eyed beans *73*
  vegetarian shepherd's pie with goats' cheese mash 83, *83*
Blackiston, Galton 65
Blancmange
  sesame blancmange with sweetened compote of adzuki beans 93, *93*
Blenders 46, *47*
Bloody Mary soup with vodka tomato salsa 121, *121*
Bloody Mary tomatoes 230, *230*
Blowtorches 58, *58*
Blue-cheese dressing 125, *125*
Borlotti beans *73*, 74
  braised sausages with borlotti beans, rosemary and sage 92, *92*
  Tuscan bean and pasta soup with rosemary 84, *85*
Braised beef goulash with smoked pimentón 24, *24*
Braised lamb shanks with cannellini beans 76, *77*
Braised sausages with borlotti beans, rosemary and sage 92, *92*
Brandy
  molasses brandy snap baskets 67, *67*
  spiced bread pudding with brandy cream 176, *176*
Bread
  celeriac and Lancashire cheese bread 49, *49*

filled focaccia with ham and melted Fontina 56, *56*
pitta bread 54, *55*
poppy and sesame seed rolls 57, *57*
Bread puddings
  bread-and-butter pudding 183, *183*
  spiced bread pudding with brandy cream 176, *176*
Breadmakers 52-3, *53*
Broad beans, dried 75
Brochettes
  marinated chicken brochettes with green couscous 122, *123*
  Thai pork satays with Thai peanut sauce 208, *209*
Brown and wild rice salad with dried cranberries *203*, 207
Brown beans 75
Brushes 18, *18*
Buffets
  cold buffet 200-13
  Middle Eastern buffet 188-99
Butter 120
Butter beans *73*, 74
  old-fashioned shin of beef stew with butter beans and crusted onion dumplings 88, *89*
Buttermilk 120
  buttermilk scones with Cheshire cheese and chives 30, *30*
  marinated chicken brochettes with green couscous 122, *123*

Cake tins 18, *19*
Cakes
  Easter simnel cake 34-5, *35*
  Greek orange and honey syrup cake with yoghurt and pistachios 198, *199*
  squidgy chocolate cakes with prunes in Marsala 148, *149*
  very sticky prune and date cake 26, *27*
  zabaglione torta 218, *218-19*
Canary lemon sponge puddings with lemon curd cream 174, *175*
Canelle knives 21
Cannellini beans *73*, 74
  braised lamb shanks with cannellini beans 76, *77*
Capers, smoked mackerel pâté with Ricotta and 157, *157*
Cappuccino cheesecakes 146, *146*
Caramel
  Alain's passion fruit brûlée 59, *59*
  caramelised onion tartlets with goats' cheese and thyme *203*, 206
  summer-fruit brûlée 60, *60-1*
Carrots
  Belarussian carrot salad 44, *45*
  carrot and artichoke soup 50, *50*
Casseroles and stews 20

braised beef goulash with smoked pimentón 24, *24*
braised sausages with borlotti beans, rosemary and sage 92, *92*
Mexican chicken chilli with yellow tomato salsa 87, *87*
old-fashioned shin of beef stew with butter beans and crusted onion dumplings 88, *89*
Cast-iron griddles 20
Caviar
  souffléd sole creams with Champagne sauce and salmon caviar 160, *161*
Celeriac
  celeriac and Lancashire cheese bread 49, *49*
  slow-cooked celery and celeriac soup 48
Celery
  slow-cooked celery and celeriac soup 48
Ceviche, swordfish 124, *124*
Champagne
  souffléd sole creams with Champagne sauce and salmon caviar 160, *161*
Char-grilled squid with chilli jam 168, *169*
Cheese 120
  antipasti 214, *214*
  blue-cheese dressing 125, *125*
  buttermilk scones with Cheshire cheese and chives 30, *30*
  caramelised onion tartlets with goats' cheese and thyme *203*, 206
  celeriac and Lancashire cheese bread 49, *49*
  courgette and potato cakes with mint and Feta cheese *191*, 194
  filled focaccia with ham and melted Fontina 56, *56*
  grilled polenta with ham, cheese and sage 167, *167*
  Gruyère jacket potato halves with chives 204
  Mexican chicken chilli with yellow tomato salsa 87, *87*
  savoury mini muffins with two flavourings 228, *229*
  smoked mackerel pâté with Ricotta and capers 157, *157*
  traditional lasagne al forno 215-16, *216-17*
  vegetarian shepherd's pie with goats' cheese mash 83, *83*
Cheesecakes
  cappuccino cheesecakes 146, *146*
  chocolate Ricotta cheesecake 212-13, *213*
Cherries

individual queen of puddings with Morello cherry conserve 177, *177*

Chicken
marinated chicken brochettes with green couscous 122, *123*
Mexican chicken chilli with yellow tomato salsa 87, *87*
Oriental chicken 134, *134*
Chicken liver pâté with Cognac, with sweet-and-sour red onion salad 158, *159*

Chickpeas *73, 74*
hummus bi tahina 78, *78*
spiced chickpea cakes with red onion and coriander salad 86, *86*
spiced lamb curry with chickpeas, green coconut sambal and tomato-and-red-onion pickle 90-1, *91*

Chillies
char-grilled squid with chilli jam 168, *169*
Mexican chicken chilli with yellow tomato salsa 87, *87*
oriental green beans with red chillies and toasted sesame seeds 135, *135*
pasta with pepper relish 141, *141*
spiced lamb curry with chickpeas, green coconut sambal and tomato-and-red-onion pickle 90-1, *91*
Thai crab salad with mango 140, *140*

Chinese steamed trout with ginger and spring onions 130, *130*

Chives
buttermilk scones with Cheshire cheese and chives 30, *30*
Gruyère jacket potato halves with chives 204

Chocolate
chocolate Ricotta cheesecake 212-13, *213*
David's chocolate fudge with roasted nuts and raisins 232, *232*
squidgy chocolate cakes with prunes in Marsala 148, *149*
warm chocolate rum soufflés with chocolate sauce 178, *179*

Chopping boards 14
Chunky green salad 224
Chutneys 99, *99*
smoky tomato chutney *107*, 108
spiced damson chutney 105, *105*
Citrus reamers 15
Claret
spiced cranberry and claret jelly 104
Coarse country pâté 154-5, *155*
Coconut
spiced lamb curry with chickpeas, green coconut sambal and tomato-and-red-onion pickle 90-1, *91*
Coconut milk
Thai pork satays with Thai peanut sauce 208, *209*
Cod
steamed cod with nori and soba noodle salad 136, *137*
Coffee
cappuccino cheesecakes 146, *146*
espresso coffee machines 68, *68*

vanilla bean ice cream with espresso 69, *69*
Cognac
chicken liver pâté with Cognac, with sweet-and-sour red onion salad 158, *159*
Colanders 16, *16*
Cold buffet 200-13
Conserve, dark apricot and almond 102, *102*
Cook's knives 13, *13*
Cooling racks *10*, 19
Coriander leaves
spiced chickpea cakes with red onion and coriander salad 86, *86*
spiced lamb curry with chickpeas, green coconut sambal and tomato-and-red-onion pickle 90-1, *91*
Cornichons
eggs mayonnaise 166, *166*
Cottage cheese 120
Courgettes
courgette and potato cakes with mint and Feta cheese 191, *194*
pickled peppers and courgettes 113, *113*
Couscous
marinated chicken brochettes with green couscous 122, *123*
Crab
English potted crab 156, *156*
Thai crab salad with mango 140, *140*
Crabb, Lucy 32, 110, *234*
Cranberries
brown and wild rice salad with dried cranberries *203*, 207
spiced cranberry and claret jelly 104
Cream
Alain's passion fruit brûlée 59, *59*
brandy cream 176
pistachio ice cream 196, *197*
preserved ginger ice cream 66, *66*
summer-fruit brûlée 60, *60-1*
vanilla bean ice cream with espresso 69, *69*
zabaglione ice cream with biscotti 64, *64*
Crème brûlée
Alain's passion fruit brûlée 59, *59*
summer-fruit brûlée 60, *60-1*
Crème fraîche 120
gooseberry crème fraîche tart 226, *227*
mini Yorkshire puddings with rare beef and horseradish-and-mustard crème fraîche *203*, 205
vanilla bean ice cream with espresso 69, *69*
Cucumber
sour dill pickles 114, *115*
teriyaki grilled marinated salmon with marinated cucumber and sesame salad 142, *142*
Currants
bread-and-butter pudding 183, *183*
stuffed yellow peppers with pilau rice, currants and toasted pine nuts 191, *193, 193*
Curries

curried turkey salad with dried fruits *203*, 204
spiced lamb curry with chickpeas, green coconut sambal and tomato-and-red-onion pickle 90-1, *91*
Curtis, John 208
Cutters 18, *18*

Damsons
spiced damson chutney 105, *105*
Dark apricot and almond conserve 102, *102*
Dates
very sticky prune and date cake 26, 27
David, Elizabeth 58
David's chocolate fudge with roasted nuts and raisins 232, *232*
Deep fat fryers 38
Desserts
Alain's passion fruit brûlée 59, *59*
bread-and-butter pudding 183, *183*
canary lemon sponge puddings with lemon curd cream 174, *175*
chocolate Ricotta cheesecake 212-13, *213*
gooseberry crème fraîche tart 226, *227*
individual queen of puddings with Morello cherry conserve 177, *177*
individual Sussex pond puddings with lemon butter sauce 184, *185*
lemon roulade 210, *211*
Lucy's tarte Tatin 32, *33*
old English apple hat 182, *182*
pistachio ice cream 196, *197*
preserved ginger ice cream 66, *66*
sesame blancmange with sweetened compote of adzuki beans 93, *93*
spiced bread pudding with brandy cream 176, *176*
Spike's apple sorbet 65, *65*
spotted Dick rides again 180, *181*
summer-fruit brûlée 60, *60-1*
traditional lemon meringue pie 28, *29*
vanilla bean ice cream with espresso 69, *69*
warm chocolate rum soufflés with chocolate sauce 178, *179*
zabaglione ice cream with biscotti 64, *64*
zabaglione torta 218, *218-19*
Dhals 75
Dill pickles, sour 114, *115*
Dips
hummus bi tahina 78, *78*
Dredgers 16, *16*
Dressings
almost mayonnaise 126, *127*
almost vinaigrette 125, *125*
blue-cheese dressing 125, *125*
Thousand Island dressing 125, *125*
Dried fruit
curried turkey salad with dried fruits *203*, 204
Easter simnel cake 34-5, *35*
spiced bread pudding with brandy cream 176, *176*
very sticky prune and date cake 26, 27

Dumplings
old-fashioned shin of beef stew with butter beans and crusted onion dumplings 88, *89*
Dwarf beans
oriental green beans with red chillies and toasted sesame seeds 135, *135*

Easter simnel cake 34-5, *35*
Easy omelette Arnold Bennett 25, *25*
Eggs 152-3
almost mayonnaise 126, *127*
easy omelette Arnold Bennett 25, *25*
eggs and leeks en cocotte 131
eggs mayonnaise 166, *166*
marmalade soufflés 147, *147*
quails' eggs with cracked pepper and salt 230, *230*
zabaglione 40, *40-1*
zabaglione ice cream with biscotti 64, *64*
Electric hand whisks 38-9, *39*
English potted crab 156, *156*
Equipment 11-21, 96-7
Espresso coffee machines 68, *68*
Evaporated milk 120
slimmers' wild mushroom risotto *138*, 139
Fat 118-19, 172
Filled focaccia with ham and melted Fontina 56, *56*
Fish
baked whole salmon with sauce verte 222-3
Chinese steamed trout with ginger and spring onions 130, *130*
easy omelette Arnold Bennett 25, *25*
smoked fish 152
smoked mackerel pâté with Ricotta and capers 157, *157*
souffléd Arbroath smokies in smoked salmon with foaming hollandaise 162, *162*
steamed cod with nori and soba noodle salad 136, *137*
teriyaki grilled marinated salmon with marinated cucumber and sesame salad 142, *142*
Fish kettles 21
Flageolet beans *73, 74*
Flour, in breadmakers 52
Food processors 42-3, *42*
Forks 16, *16*
Fromage frais 120
Fruit 119
jam-making 97-8
summer-fruit brûlée 60, *60-1*
tropical fruit jellies 145, *145*
see also Dried fruit *and individual types of fruit*
Fudge
David's chocolate fudge with roasted nuts and raisins 232, *232*
Ful medames 75
Funnels 96, *96*

Gadgets 37-9
Garlic presses 20, *21*
Giardiniere pickles 110, *111*
Ginger
    Chinese steamed trout with ginger
    and spring onions 130, *130*
    preserved ginger ice cream 66, *66*
Globe artichokes with shallot
vinaigrette 163, *163*
Goats' cheese
    caramelised onion tartlets with
    goats' cheese and thyme *203*, 206
    savoury mini muffins with two
    flavourings 228, *229*
    vegetarian shepherd's pie with
    goats' cheese mash 83, *83*
Gooseberry crème fraîche tart
226, *227*
Goulash
    braised beef goulash with smoked
    pimentón 24, *24*
Grapes
    grilled venison steaks with red
    onion, grape and raisin confit
    143, *143*
Graters 14, *15*
Greek orange and honey syrup cake
with yoghurt and pistachios 198, *199*
Greek yoghurt 120
Green beans
    oriental green beans with red
    chillies and toasted sesame seeds
    135, *135*
Greensted-Benech, Lindsey *234*
Griddles 20
Grilled polenta with ham, cheese and
sage 167, *167*
Grilled venison steaks with red onion,
grape and raisin confit 143, *143*
Grinding tools 15
Gruyère jacket potato halves with
chives 204

Haddock *see* Smoked haddock
Ham
    antipasti 214, *214*
    filled focaccia with ham and
    melted Fontina 56, *56*
    turkey saltimbocca 132, *133*
Haricot beans *73*, 74
'Healthy' foods 118
Hill, Shaun 79
Hollandaise sauce, foaming 162
Honey
    Greek orange and honey syrup
    cake with yoghurt and pistachios
    198, *199*
Horseradish
    mini Yorkshire puddings with rare
    beef and horseradish-and-mustard
    crème fraîche *203*, 205
Hummus bi tahina 78, *78*

Ice cream
    pistachio ice cream 196, *197*
    preserved ginger ice cream 66, *66*
    vanilla bean ice cream with
    espresso 69, *69*
    zabaglione ice cream with biscotti
    64, *64*
Ice-cream makers 38, 62-3, *63*

Ice-cream scoops 21, *21*
Individual queen of puddings with
Morello cherry conserve 177, *177*
Individual Sussex pond puddings
with lemon butter sauce 184, *185*
Italian garden pickles 110, *111*
Italian lunch or supper 214-19

Jams 97-9, *98*
    dark apricot and almond conserve
    102, *102*
Jars
    preserving 96-7, *96*
    sterilising 97
Jellies, tropical fruit 145, *145*
Jelly, spiced cranberry and claret 104
Jerusalem artichokes
    carrot and artichoke soup 50, *50*
Judion beans 73
Jugs, measuring 17, *17*

Kidney beans *73*, 75
Knives 12-14, *13*

Labels, for preserves 97
Lamb
    braised lamb shanks with cannellini
    beans 76, *77*
    spiced lamb curry with chickpeas,
    green coconut sambal and tomato-
    and-red-onion pickle 90-1, *91*
    spiced lamb koftas braised in
    tomato sauce *191*, 192
Lasagne al forno 215-16, *216-17*
Lattice cutters 19
Leeks
    eggs and leeks en cocotte 131
    watercress soup, 220, *221*
Lemon
    canary lemon sponge puddings
    with lemon curd cream 174, *175*
    individual Sussex pond puddings
    with lemon butter sauce 184, *185*
    lemon curd 103, *103*
    lemon roulade 210, *211*
    traditional lemon meringue pie
    28, *29*
Lemon squeezers 15, *15*
Lentils 73, *74-5*
    sea bass with Puy lentil salsa
    128, *129*
    Shaun Hill's sautéed scallops with
    lentil sauce 79, *79*
    vegetarian shepherd's pie with
    goats' cheese mash 83, *83*
Limes
    Spike's apple sorbet 65, *65*
    swordfish ceviche 124, *124*
    tropical fruit jellies 145, *145*
Liver
    chicken liver pâté with Cognac,
    with sweet-and-sour red onion
    salad 158, *159*
    coarse country pâté 154-5, *155*
Loaf tins *10*, 18-19
The London Particular – green split
pea soup 82, *82*
Lucy's tarte Tatin 32, *33*

Macaroni
    Tuscan bean and pasta soup with
    rosemary 84, *85*
MacMillan, Deborah 112
Mango, Thai crab salad with 140, *140*
Marinated chicken brochettes with
green couscous 122, *123*
Marmalade
    marmalade soufflés 147, *147*
    traditional Seville orange
    marmalade 100, *101*
Marsala
    squidgy chocolate cakes with prunes
    in Marsala 148, *149*
    turkey saltimbocca 132, *133*
    zabaglione 40, *40-1*
    zabaglione ice cream with biscotti
    64, *64*
Marzipan
    Easter Simnel cake 34-5, *35*
Mascarpone
    lemon roulade 210, *211*
Mayonnaise 126, *127*
    eggs mayonnaise 166, *166*
    tartare sauce 126
Measuring equipment 17-18, *17*
Meat
    antipasti 214, *214*
    see also Beef; Lamb *etc*
Melon ballers 21, *21*
Membrillo (quince paste)
    Spike's apple sorbet 65, 65
Menus
    cold buffet 200-13
    Italian lunch or supper 214-19
    Middle Eastern buffet 188-99
    summer lunch or supper 220-33
Meringues
    baked apple meringues with
    orange-soaked raisins 144, *144*
    individual queen of puddings with
    Morello cherry conserve 177, *177*
    traditional lemon meringue pie
    28, *29*
Mexican chicken chilli with yellow
tomato salsa 87, *87*
Microplane® Graters 14, *15*
Middle Eastern buffet 188-99
Milk 120
    bread-and-butter pudding 183, *183*
    sesame blancmange with sweetened
    compote of adzuki beans 93, *93*
Mincemeat
    Easter simnel cake 34-5, 35
Mini Yorkshire puddings with rare
beef and horseradish-and-mustard
crème fraîche *203*, 205
Mint
    courgette and potato cakes with
    mint and Feta cheese *191*, 194
Mixed vegetable salad à la Grècque
191, 195
Molasses brandy snap baskets 67, *67*
Muffins
    savoury mini muffins with two
    flavourings 228, *229*
Mushrooms
    slimmers' wild mushroom risotto
    138, 139
Muslin 97
Mustard

mini Yorkshire puddings with rare
beef and horseradish-and-mustard
crème fraîche *203*, 205
    smoked collar of bacon with pease
    pudding and creamy onion
    mustard sauce 80, *81*
    spiced mustard pickle (piccalilli)
    107, 109

Noodles
    steamed cod with nori and soba
    noodle salad 136, *137*
Nori seaweed
    steamed cod with nori and soba
    noodle salad 136, *137*
Nutmeg graters 14, 15
Nuts
    David's chocolate fudge with roasted
    nuts and raisins 232, *232*

Oils 120
Okra, pickled 112
Old English apple hat 182, *182*
Old-fashioned shin of beef stew with
butter beans and crusted onion
dumplings 88, *89*
Omelette Arnold Bennett 25, *25*
Onions
    caramelised onion tartlets with
    goats' cheese and thyme *203*, 206
    chicken liver pâté with Cognac,
    with sweet-and-sour red onion
    salad 158, *159*
    grilled venison steaks with red
    onion, grape and raisin confit
    143, *143*
    old-fashioned shin of beef stew
    with butter beans and crusted
    onion dumplings 88, *89*
    pepper-crusted fillet of beef with
    roasted balsamic onions and thyme
    22, *23*
    savoury mini muffins with two
    flavourings 228, *229*
    smoked collar of bacon with pease
    pudding and creamy onion
    mustard sauce 80, *81*
    spiced chickpea cakes with red
    onion and coriander salad 86, *86*
    spiced lamb curry with chickpeas,
    green coconut sambal and tomato-
    and-red-onion pickle 90-1, *91*
    see also Spring onions
Oranges
    baked apple meringues with
    orange-soaked raisins 144, *144*
    Greek orange and honey syrup
    cake with yoghurt and pistachios
    198, *199*
    traditional Seville orange
    marmalade 100, *101*
Oriental chicken 134, *134*
Oriental green beans with red chillies
and toasted sesame seeds 135, *135*
Oriental ingredients 120
Oven thermometers 20

Palette knives 13, *13*
Pancetta
    braised sausages with borlotti
    beans, rosemary and sage 92, *92*

traditional lasagne al forno 215-16, *216-17*
Paprika
  braised beef goulash with smoked pimentón 24, *24*
Paring knives 13, *13*
Parma ham
  antipasti 214, *214*
  turkey saltimbocca 132, *133*
Parsley
  baked whole salmon with sauce verte 222-3
Parties 187-233
Passion fruit
  Alain's passion fruit brûlée 59, *59*
  tropical fruit jellies 145, *145*
Pasta
  pasta with pepper relish 141, *141*
  traditional lasagne al forno 215-16, *216-17*
  Tuscan bean and pasta soup with rosemary 84, *85*
Pasta machines 38
Pasta tongs 20, *21*
Pastries
  pistachio wafers 197, *197*
Pâtés 153
  chicken liver pâté with Cognac, with sweet-and-sour red onion salad 158, *159*
  coarse country pâté 154-5, *155*
  smoked mackerel pâté with Ricotta and capers 157, *157*
Peanuts
  Thai pork satays with Thai peanut sauce 208, *209*
Peas, dried 73, *75*
  the London Particular–green split pea soup 82, *82*
  smoked collar of bacon with pease pudding and creamy onion mustard sauce 80, *81*
  vegetarian shepherd's pie with goats' cheese mash 83, *83*
Pepper mills 15
Peppercorns
  pepper-crusted fillet of beef with roasted balsamic onions and thyme 22, *23*
  quails' eggs with cracked pepper and salt 230, *230*
Peppers
  pasta with pepper relish 141, *141*
  pickled peppers and courgettes 113, *113*
  roasted red pepper and tomato tart 164, *165*
  stuffed yellow peppers with pilau rice, currants and toasted pine nuts 191, 193, *193*
Pestle and mortar 15, *15*
Piccalilli *107*, 109
Pickles 99
  giardiniere pickles 110, *111*
  pickled okra 112
  pickled peppers and courgettes 113, *113*
  sour dill pickles 114, *115*
  spiced mustard pickle (piccalilli) *107*, 109

spiced pickled Agen prunes in Armagnac 106, *107*
  tomato-and-red-onion pickle 90-1, *91*
Pie tins 19
Pies
  traditional lemon meringue pie 28, *29*
Pine nuts
  stuffed yellow peppers with pilau rice, currants and toasted pine nuts 191, 193, *193*
Pinto beans 73, 75
  Mexican chicken chilli with yellow tomato salsa 87, *87*
Piping bags 21
Pistachio nuts
  Greek orange and honey syrup cake with yoghurt and pistachios 198, *199*
  pistachio ice cream 196, *197*
  pistachio wafers 197, *197*
Pitta bread 54, *55*
Polenta
  grilled polenta with ham, cheese and sage 167, *167*
Poppy and sesame seed rolls 57, *57*
Pork
  coarse country pâté 154-5, *155*
  Thai pork satays with Thai peanut sauce 208, *209*
  traditional lasagne al forno 215-16, *216-17*
Potato peelers 13, *13*
Potato ricers 21
Potatoes
  Anya potato salad with shallots and vinaigrette 224, *225*
  courgette and potato cakes with mint and Feta cheese *191*, 194
  Gruyère jacket potato halves with chives 204
  vegetarian shepherd's pie with goats' cheese mash 83, *83*
  watercress soup, 220, *221*
Preserved ginger ice cream 66, *66*
Preserves 95-115
Preserving pans 96
Pressure cookers 38
Prunes
  spiced pickled Agen prunes in Armagnac 106, *107*
  squidgy chocolate cakes with prunes in Marsala 148, *149*
  very sticky prune and date cake 26, *27*
Pudding basins 173, *173*
Puddings 170-85
Pulses 71-3, *73*
  cooking 73
  soaking 72-3

Quails' eggs with cracked pepper and salt 230, *230*
Quark 120
Queen of puddings with Morello cherry conserve 177, *177*
Quiche tins 19
Quinn, Michael 156

Racks 10, 19
Raisins
  baked apple meringues with orange-soaked raisins 144, *144*
  David's chocolate fudge with roasted nuts and raisins 232, *232*
  grilled venison steaks with red onion, grape and raisin confit 143, *143*
  spiced damson chutney 105, *105*
  spotted Dick rides again 180, *181*
Red kidney beans 73, 75
Relish, pepper 141
Rice
  brown and wild rice salad with dried cranberries 203, 207
  slimmers' wild mushroom risotto 138, 139
  stuffed yellow peppers with pilau rice, currants and toasted pine nuts 191, 193, *193*
Ricotta
  cappuccino cheesecakes 146, *146*
  chocolate Ricotta cheesecake 212-13, *213*
Risotto, slimmers' wild mushroom 138, 139
Roasted red pepper and tomato tart 164, *165*
Rocket
  Thai crab salad with mango, 140, *140*
Rolling pins 18
Rolls, poppy and sesame seed 57, *57*
Rosemary
  braised sausages with borlotti beans, rosemary and sage 92, *92*
  Tuscan bean and pasta soup with rosemary 84, *85*
Roulade, lemon 210, *211*
Rum
  warm chocolate rum soufflés with chocolate sauce 178, *179*

Sage
  braised sausages with borlotti beans, rosemary and sage 92, *92*
  grilled polenta with ham, cheese and sage, 167, *167*
  savoury mini muffins with two flavourings 228, *229*
  turkey saltimbocca 132, *133*
Salad spinners 38
Salads 152-3
  Anya potato salad with shallots and vinaigrette 224, *225*
  Belarussian carrot salad 44, *45*
  brown and wild rice salad with dried cranberries 203, 207
  chicken liver pâté with Cognac, with sweet-and-sour red onion salad 158, *159*
  chunky green salad 224
  curried turkey salad with dried fruits *203*, 204
  mixed vegetable salad à la Grècque *191*, 195
  spiced chickpea cakes with red onion and coriander salad 86, *86*
  steamed cod with nori and soba noodle salad 136, *137*

teriyaki grilled marinated salmon with marinated cucumber and sesame salad 142, *142*
  Thai crab salad with mango 140, *140*
Salmon
  baked whole salmon with sauce verte 222-3
  teriyaki grilled marinated salmon with marinated cucumber and sesame salad 142, *142*
Salmon caviar, soufflèd sole creams with Champagne sauce and 160, *161*
Salsas
  Puy lentil salsa 128, *129*
  vodka tomato salsa 121, *121*
  yellow tomato salsa 87, *87*
Salt mills 15
Sambal, green coconut 90-1, *91*
Sandwich toasters 38
Satays, Thai pork 208, *209*
Saucepans 19-20, *20*
Sauces
  chocolate sauce 178
  sauce verte 222-3
  tartare sauce 126
Sausages
  braised sausages with borlotti beans, rosemary and sage 92, *92*
Savoury mini muffins with two flavourings 228, *229*
Scales 17, *17*
Scallops
  Shaun Hill's sautéed scallops with lentil sauce 79, *79*
Scissors 13, *13*
Scones
  buttermilk scones with Cheshire cheese and chives 30, *30*
Scottish semolina shortbread 31, *31*
Sea bass with Puy lentil salsa 128, *129*
Semi-skimmed milk 120
Semolina shortbread, Scottish 31, *31*
Sesame seeds
  oriental green beans with red chillies and toasted sesame seeds 135, *135*
  poppy and sesame seed rolls 57, *57*
  sesame blancmange with sweetened compote of adzuki beans 93, *93*
  teriyaki grilled marinated salmon with marinated cucumber and sesame salad 142, *142*
Seville orange marmalade 100, *101*
Shallots
  Anya potato salad with shallots and vinaigrette 224, *225*
  globe artichokes with shallot vinaigrette 163, *163*
Sharpening knives 14
Shaun Hill's sautéed scallops with lentil sauce 79, *79*
Shepherd's pie, vegetarian 83, *83*
Shidlovskaya, Irina 44
Shidlovskaya, Sasha 44
Shortbread, Scottish semolina 31, *31*
Sieves 16, *16*
Simnel cake 34-5, *35*
Skewers 21, *21*
Slices 16-17, *16*
Slimmers' wild mushroom risotto 138, 139

Slimming 117-20
Slow-cooked celery and celeriac soup 48
Slow cookers 38
Smoked collar of bacon with pease pudding and creamy onion mustard sauce 80, *81*
Smoked fish 152
Smoked haddock
  easy omelette Arnold Bennett 25, *25*
  souffléd Arbroath smokies in smoked salmon with foaming hollandaise 162, *162*
Smoked mackerel pâté with Ricotta and capers 157, *157*
Smoked salmon
  souffléd Arbroath smokies in smoked salmon with foaming hollandaise 162, *162*
Smoky tomato chutney *107*, 108
Sole
  souffléd sole creams with Champagne sauce and salmon caviar 160, *161*
Sorbet, Spike's apple 65, *65*
Souffléd Arbroath smokies in smoked salmon with foaming hollandaise 162, *162*
Souffléd sole creams with Champagne sauce and salmon caviar 160, *161*
Soufflés
  marmalade soufflés 147, *147*
  warm chocolate rum soufflés with chocolate sauce 178, *179*
Soups 153
  ajo blanco – chilled almond soup 51, *51*
  Bloody Mary soup with vodka tomato salsa 121, *121*
  carrot and artichoke soup 50, *50*
  the London Particular–green split pea soup 82, *82*
  slow-cooked celery and celeriac soup 48
  Tuscan bean and pasta soup with rosemary 84, *85*
  watercress soup 220, *221*
Sour dill pickles 114, *115*
Soy beans 75
Soy sauce
  Oriental chicken, 134, *134*
  teriyaki grilled marinated salmon with marinated cucumber and sesame salad, 142, *142*
Spatulas 16, *16*
Spiced bread pudding with brandy cream 176, *176*
Spiced chickpea cakes with red onion and coriander salad 86, *86*
Spiced cranberry and claret jelly 104
Spiced damson chutney 105, *105*
Spiced lamb curry with chickpeas, green coconut sambal and tomato-and-red-onion pickle 90-1, *91*
Spiced lamb koftas braised in tomato sauce *191*, 192
Spiced mustard pickle (piccalilli) *107*, 109

Spiced pickled Agen prunes in Armagnac 106, *107*
Spike's apple sorbet 65, *65*
Sponge puddings
  canary lemon sponge puddings with lemon curd cream 174, *175*
Spoons 16, *16*
  measuring spoons 18, *18*
Spotted Dick rides again 180, *181*
Spring onions
  Chinese steamed trout with ginger and spring onions, 130, *130*
Squid
  char-grilled squid with chilli jam 168, *169*
Squidgy chocolate cakes with prunes in Marsala 148, *149*
Starters 151-69
Steamed cod with nori and soba noodle salad 136, *137*
Steamed puddings 173
  canary lemon sponge puddings with lemon curd cream 174, *175*
  individual Sussex pond puddings with lemon butter sauce 184, *185*
  Old English apple hat 182, *182*
  spotted Dick rides again 180, *181*
Steamers 20, *20*, 21
Sterilising jars 97
Stews see Casseroles and stews
Stuffed yellow peppers with pilau rice, currants and toasted pine nuts *191*, 193, *193*
Suet puddings 172
  individual Sussex pond puddings with lemon butter sauce 184, *185*
  old English apple hat 182, *182*
  spotted Dick rides again 180, *181*
Sugar 119
  jam-making 98
Sugar thermometers 20, *21*
Summer lunch or supper 220-33
Summer-fruit brûlée 60, *60-1*
Sussex pond puddings with lemon butter sauce 184, *185*
Sweet-and-sour red onion salad 158, *159*
Swordfish ceviche 124, *124*

Tahina paste
  hummus bi tahina 78, *78*
Tape measures 20
Tart tins 19
Tartare sauce 126
Tarts
  caramelised onion tartlets with goats' cheese and thyme *203*, 206
  gooseberry crème fraîche tart 226, *227*
  Lucy's tarte Tatin 32, *33*
  roasted red pepper and tomato tart 164, *165*
Teriyaki grilled marinated salmon with marinated cucumber and sesame salad 142, *142*
Thai crab salad with mango 140, *140*
Thai pork satays with Thai peanut sauce 208, *209*
Thermometers 20, *21*
Thousand Island dressing 125, *125*
Thyme

caramelised onion tartlets with goats' cheese and thyme *203*, 206
Timers 20
Tinned pulses 72
Tins 18-19, *19*
Tomatoes
  Bloody Mary soup with vodka tomato salsa 121, *121*
  Bloody Mary tomatoes 230, *230*
  braised beef goulash with smoked pimentón 24, *24*
  char-grilled squid with chilli jam 168, *169*
  Mexican chicken chilli with yellow tomato salsa 87, *87*
  pasta with pepper relish 141, *141*
  roasted red pepper and tomato tart 164, *165*
  smoky tomato chutney *107*, 108
  spiced lamb curry with chickpeas, green coconut sambal and tomato-and-red-onion pickle 90-1, *91*
  spiced lamb koftas braised in tomato sauce *191*, 192
  traditional lasagne al forno 215-16, *216-17*
Tongs *16*, 17, 20, *21*
Tovey, John 172
Traditional lasagne al forno 215-16, *216-17*
Traditional lemon meringue pie 28, *29*
Traditional Seville orange marmalade 100, *101*
Tropical fruit jellies 145, *145*
Trout
  Chinese steamed trout with ginger and spring onions 130, *130*
Turkey
  curried turkey salad with dried fruits *203*, 204
  turkey saltimbocca 132, *133*
Tuscan bean and pasta soup with rosemary 84, *85*

Vanilla bean ice cream with espresso 69, *69*
Veal
  coarse country pâté 154-5, *155*
Vegetables 119
  giardiniere pickles 110, *111*
  spiced mustard pickle (piccalilli) *107*, 109
Vegetarian shepherd's pie with goats' cheese mash 83, *83*
Venison
  grilled venison steaks with red onion, grape and raisin confit 143, *143*
Very sticky prune and date cake 26, *27*
Vinaigrette 125, *125*
  Anya potato salad with shallots and vinaigrette 224, *225*
  globe artichokes with shallot vinaigrette 163, *163*
Vodka
  Bloody Mary soup with vodka tomato salsa 121, *121*
  Bloody Mary tomatoes 230, *230*

Wafers, pistachio 197, *197*
Waist Watchers' dressings 125, *125*
Warm chocolate rum soufflés with chocolate sauce 178, *179*
Watercress
  baked whole salmon with sauce verte 222-3
  watercress soup 220, *221*
Waxed discs, for preserves 97
Weighing equipment 17, *17*
Whisks 16, *16*
  electric 38-9, *39*
Wild rice
  brown and wild rice salad with dried cranberries *203*, 207
Wine
  grilled venison steaks with red onion, grape and raisin confit 143, *143*
  spiced cranberry and claret jelly 104
  squidgy chocolate cakes with prunes in Marsala 148, *149*
  zabaglione 40, *40-1*
  zabaglione ice cream with biscotti 64, *64*
Wooden spoons 16, *16*

Yeast, in breadmakers 52-3
Yetman, Alison and Peter 168
Yoghurt 120
  blue-cheese dressing 125, *125*
  Greek orange and honey syrup cake with yoghurt and pistachios 198, *199*
  summer-fruit brûlée 60, *60-1*
Yorkshire puddings with rare beef and horseradish-and-mustard crème fraîche *203*, 205

Zabaglione 40, *40-1*
  zabaglione ice cream with biscotti 64, *64*
  zabaglione torta 218, *218-19*
Zesters *14*, 15